Being Human

Being Human
Philosophical Anthropology through Phenomenology

Robert E. Wood

The Catholic University of America Press
Washington, D.C.

Cataloging-in-Publication data available from the Library of Congress.

ISBN: 978-0-8132-3618-6

eISBN: 978-0-8132-3619-3

To Kenneth Schmitz, my teacher.

Contents

List of Tables

Acknowledgment

I would like to express my deepest gratitude to Christopher R. J. Richard, who has assisted me in editing my text over the past two years with much perseverance. His extensive work on my manuscript has been a great help to me.

Introduction

In the end modern man carries around with him an enormous load of these indigestible stones of knowledge, which then at every opportunity . . . rattle loudly inside his stomach. This rattling reveals modern man's most characteristic trait. And that is the strange contrast between an inward nature that lacks a corresponding exterior and an exterior nature that lacks a corresponding interior.

> Friedrich Nietzsche, *History in the Service and Disservice of Life*

How remote from their clumsy pride was that task which they considered insignificant and left in dust and musk—the task of description.

> Friedrich Nietzsche, *Beyond Good and Evil*

The present text was the fruit of many years teaching philosophical anthropology, conducting phenomenological workshops, and reading classic texts in the light of a reflective awareness of the field of experience. This text is intended to look to what is typically assumed but not examined in much of current philosophical literature.[1] Today what typically appear as philosophical are textual studies that draw upon wide-ranging scholarship to learn how past thinkers used to think; works that tend either to be "high-flying," operating at levels of abstraction far removed from experience and written in arcane style, and thus, for both reasons, difficult to assess (much of continental thought); minutely focused upon particular claims and the arguments that can be advanced for and against them (analytical thought); or deconstructing texts to show how they do not fully work (the followers of Jacques Derrida). Scholarly study, abstract constructions, refined arguments, and deconstructive strategies are each important in their own way, but they all take place within the structure of the field of experience, which is typically assumed without paying explicit atten-

---

1. For a presentation of the variety of contemporary views, see William Jaworski, *Philosophy of Mind: A Comprehensive Introduction* (Hoboken, N.J.: Wiley Blackwell, 2011).

tion to it. Especially in philosophy of mind, the overall field of experience has too often been ignored, usually in favor of some conjecture
as to how our ordinary categories would have to be changed when
neuro-physiology will be far enough advanced to explain all our
behavior.[2] My claim is that it is best to understand what it is that is
supposed to be explained before conjecturing about possible explanations.[3] But when one does that, one will have to come to terms with
what it means to seek explanation, what a *Who* is that seeks it, and
why it is sought.

* * *

As I said, for me phenomenological descriptions play in tandem
with the study of classic texts.[4] The texts that furnish the major background to this work are those of Plato, Aristotle, Kant, Hegel, Husserl,
Heidegger, and Lonergan.[5]

Most of the facets of *Plato's* approach are found in my work. He
said that the philosopher always has his eyes fixed on the Whole and
the whole character of each within the Whole.[6] In the *Republic*, he
introduces the Good, initially presented as the source of light and existence (*ousia* and *einai*) for intellect and the intelligible,[7] but later
described as "the principle of the Whole."[8] That shift indicates that the
Whole he is after is not simply the intelligible but includes everything

2. John Searle has chided the Anglo-American philosophy of mind community for
ignoring that which is the mind at work: human consciousness. Searle, *The Rediscovery of
the Mind* (Boston: MIT Press, 1992), 111–26.

3. See Robert Wood, "What Is Seeing? A Phenomenological-Introduction to Neuro-
Psychology," in *Being and the Cosmos* (Washington, D.C.: The Catholic University of America Press, 2018), 9–32.

4. As phenomenologist Robert Sokolowski admonishes us: take care to avoid the
danger of making the text the primary focus rather than the things it discloses. Sokolowski,
Eucharistic Presence: A Study in the Theology of Disclosure (Washington, D.C.: The Catholic
University of America Press, 1993), 141, 150.

5. For an explication of the context in which many of the references I make to classic
texts are located, see my *Placing Aesthetics: Reflections on the Reflections on the Philosophic
Tradition* (Athens: Ohio University Press, 1999); and *The Beautiful, the True, and the Good:
Studies in the History of Thought* (Washington, D.C.: The Catholic University of America
Press, 2015). Here I identify the overall conceptual framework of a dozen thinkers from
Plato to Heidegger within which aesthetic considerations are raised.

6. Plato, *Theaetetus* 173c.

7. Plato, *Republic* VI.506e.

8. Plato, *Republic* VI.511b.

that is. And this is linked to his claim that the philosopher focuses upon Being, a notion that includes everything and everything about everything.[9]

Jacob Klein speaks of Plato's thought as a fabric woven from two strands: the warp, the hard-twisted strand of *apodeixis*; and the woof, the soft-twisted strand of *paradeigma*.[10] *Apodeixis*, etymologically considered, is "showing (*deixis*) from the top down (*apo*)," found in geometric demonstration and in the hierarchies of forms, employing *bifurcatory diaresis*, which is found in the *Sophist* and the *Statesman*.[11] *Paradeigma*, etymologically considered, is "shown (*deigma*) alongside (*para*)," found in the use of images, diagrams, parables, allegories, and myths based upon a parallelism between what is immediately presented and the theme to which it is applied. In the *Republic* Socrates says, "See how I strain after images."[12]

What is also "shown alongside" are the characters in dialogue. Further, in the *Statesman*, he presents an anatomy of the city which includes the general and the louse-catcher as aspects of the Whole.[13] And in that dialogue, as well as in the *Sophist*, his hierarchies of forms include such ordinary operations as fishing, weaving, hunting, buying, selling, etc. The *Republic* provides an anatomy of three successive cities and the practices they involve. The first city includes farming, building, shoemaking, cloth production, toolmaking, and commerce: "the true and healthy city," dedicated to basic biological needs. There follows the luxurious city with pastry cooks, cosmetologists, complex musical instruments, and the like. And finally comes the analysis of the purged city, providing the first analysis of the eidetic features of poetry. Plato's concern for the Whole does not leave out ordinary types of objects. We will follow him in that regard.

My overall aim in this work is, developing from the all-encompassing character of the notion of Being, to become reflective about every facet of our experience. Our task is to pay careful attention to the field of experience, trying to follow Plato's advice to "carve along

9. Plato, *Sophist* 254a.

10. Jacob Klein, *Plato's Trilogy* (Chicago: University of Chicago Press, 1977), 165–66.

11. Plato, *Statesman* 258b–261c; *Sophist* 218a–232a.

12. Plato, *Statesman* 287a.

13. Plato, *Statesman* 287c.

the [eidetic] joints [of experience] and not hack through like a clumsy butcher."[14]

Here I will employ another method introduced by Allen Carlson for a deeper appreciation of the natural environment. It consists, among other things, in understanding the ecosystem and not simply beholding the beautiful surface in the aesthetic appreciation of the natural environment, but also adding a depth dimension by understanding the coming to be of the things in the environment. I will employ that in thinking about the built environment by becoming aware of the history of the coming to be of the artefacts that surround us every day but that we attend to (if we do) only in terms of their immediate presentation and function.[15] I want to gain an appreciative sense of the history of their coming to be. But that is true of everything we encounter: things in the natural environment and, most particularly, human beings. What is their substructure and the history of their coming to be? This involves not only the history of any person we encounter, but the history of the current situation as well as the coming to be of the human species. I attempt to make, in principle, *every type of thing, natural or manmade*, an object of reflection focused upon its deep structure and its history. This follows to its conclusion the intention of Being, which includes everything in its scope. That is why Plato does not spurn everyday objects. I want to push that a step further to learn to meditate on the history of the coming to be of the artefacts that surround us.

To return then to Plato, there is another, very central factor in his dialogues: *Eros* as the love of the mortal for the immortal, which is ultimately aimed at "Beauty Itself."[16] In the *Republic*, the Good is also introduced as "incomparable Beauty."[17] Further, Plato claims that philosophy has its roots in awe (*thaumazein*), the gift of the god

14. Plato, *Phaedrus* 265e.

15. See Allen Carlson's argument for a depth-esthetic that goes beyond the surface of nature to understand both the underlying structure and the evolutionary history of living things: Carlson, "Appreciation and the Natural Environment," in *The Aesthetics of Natural Environments*, ed. Allen Carlson and Arnold Berleant (Toronto: Broadview Press, 2004), 70–73. See my treatment of this in the chapter on Nature in my *Nature, Artforms, and the World around Us* (Cham, Switzerland: Palgrave-Macmillan, 2017), 13–15, 30–31.

16. Plato, *Symposium* 210a–211b.

17. Plato, *Republic* VI.509a.

Thaumas.[18] Awe is not the starting point that we leave behind but the soil that feeds and grounds the effort.[19] So in Plato's thought there is a simultaneous heightening of the argument and an elevation of profound feeling. Plato's thought is "holistic" both in relation to the objects considered and in terms of the subject engaged in the process.

Traditional philosophy largely ignores all but the arguments, since philosophy is, after all, about arguments! But arguments must ultimately appeal to what is given or implied in experience. And the point of Plato's philosophy is "dwelling" in relation to the Whole in the everyday and beyond. It attends not only to such more exalted forms as the five great kinds in the *Sophist*—Being, Sameness and Difference, Motion and Rest, along with the One and the Many—but also to the everyday objects we have listed.[20]

The present work explores all the approaches Plato uses and, above all, the Line of Knowledge: the first phenomenological inventory of the field of experience in the history of thought. Its major strata are visual presentations, the intelligible Forms they represent, and the Good as the principle of the Whole. I carry that over into a bipolar view of the field of experience: rooted in the organic and oriented, via the notion of Being,[21] toward the Whole, which grounds the apprehension of Forms.

Following the practice of dialogue in Plato's work, I place the dialogical aspect at the very beginning by addressing the relation between my written word and my readers, the basis of which I provide later. And I begin most immediately in attending to the page and the letters involved in their typical subsidiary function in reading. Throughout this work I am concerned (following Plato) with maximum concreteness and maximal abstract extension.

I also follow Plato's work in the employment of images. Parallel to Plato's Cave and as a basic orienting image, I introduce the image

---

18. Plato, *Theaetetus* 155d.

19. Heidegger, *What Is Philosophy?*, trans. J. Wilde and W. Kluback (Lanham: Rowan and Littlefield, 2003), 79–85, 185.

20. Plato, *Sophist* 254b–257a; Plato, *Parmenides* 137d–166d.

21. Throughout this work, I intend to use *being* for things that are and *Being* with the capital first letter for the notion as reference to the Whole of beings and for the Whole itself, for Heidegger's Being as the Mystery of revealing and concealing, and for God as Being Itself.

of multiple dimensions in considering human awareness as occupying three "inner" dimensions. Plato himself calls attention to the "depth dimension" left out by accepting the two-dimensional view of the psyche as symmetrical with the city that governs the *Republic* up to the introduction of the philosopher-king. It is only the philosopher-king who operates in the third depth dimension relating to the Totality beyond the polis.[22]

Also parallel to the Cave, I speak of *dashboard knowing*[23] to orient thinking about sensory awareness in animals and everyday knowing in humans. I speak of the sensory field as "a luminous bubble, opaque on the outside, blown by the nervous system." I speak of a network of a thousand invisible fibers that ties each thing, natural and manmade, to its environment and its temporal antecedents. I speak of the heart as generating a magnetic field of attractions, repulsions, and neutralities. The heart is directly related to Plato's notion of *Eros* as the center of humanness. I also speak of a *psychic hoopskirt* to characterize the relation of the visual horizon to one's own embodiment. And I use Kurt Vonnegut's image of reversing the firebombing of Dresden: the bombs sucking up the flames, the planes sucking up the bombs, running backward to their base and then back to where they were built, back to the work of the subcontractors supplying the parts, and back further still into their coming to be out of the raw materials extracted from the earth.[24] This

---

22. Plato employs the notion of a depth dimension in dealing with the inwardness of the soul. While introducing what will become the quadrivium, Socrates has passed from plane geometry to bodies in motion in astronomy, but then he backtracks. How can we study bodies in motion when we have left out what is essential to bodies: the depth dimension? Plato, *Republic* VII.527d. That, I claim, displays the structure of the dialogue where, having worked with the symmetry of the soul and the city, Socrates is at that point about to use what he has developed regarding the soul to measure regimes and character types when he is interrupted by the interlocutors who are interested in the community of wives and children. That—what I claim is a prurient interest—introduces at a low level the question of *Eros*, which propels the philosopher beyond the city. That is the depth dimension lacking up to the introduction of the philosopher-king. See my "Image, Structure, and Content: On a Passage in Plato's *Republic*," *The Review of Metaphysics* 40, no. 3 (March 1987): 495–514.

23. Owen Barfield uses this felicitous metaphor in his *Saving the Appearances: An Essay in Idolatry* (New York: Harcourt, Brace, and World, 1957), 28–35.

24. Vonnegut, *Slaughterhouse Five or The Children's Crusade: A Duty-Dance with Death* (New York: Dial Press, 1969), 93–95. This most impressive scene, easily replicated through the reversal of frames in the movie version of the book, was disappointingly absent from the movie.

image can be applied to everything natural and manmade to allow one to appreciate what is hidden from ordinary attention.

* * *

In relation to the heart, I work with *Heidegger's* basic distinction between two modes of thinking.[25] Traditional thinking is what he calls *das rechnende Denken*, translated as "representative-calculative thinking." It re-presents things in their absence and arranges them in order. It is found in everyday problem solving, but in the most sophisticated way in the operation of those with special gifts: mathematicians, scientists, engineers, philosophers, and systematic theologians.

Heidegger contrasts this with what he calls *das besinnliche Nachdenken*, translated as "meditative thinking." Literally translated, it is "meditative mediation." *Nachdenken*, etymologically, "thinking (*Denken*) after (*nach*)," parallels Gabriel Marcel's "second reflection" or reflection after first, abstractive, reflection. Second reflection brings the abstractions back to the lived world to deepen one's sense of participation, of heightened presence. Both thinkers here speak of "the ontological weight" of things.[26]

Heidegger's basic claim is that meditative thinking belongs to human beings as such. Human individuals are called to meditate, for example, on the beauty of the things around them, on their own death as a personal presence, on the meaning of life, on the peculiar way they are individually called, on their way of life and those who originated and communicated it, on the presence of the divine, etc. More than simply rational animals, human beings are meditative beings.

The overwhelming bypassing of meditative thinking because of the overwhelming predominance of representative-calculative thinking, especially in scientific technology and economics, has dried up the element in which humans live. Hence the widespread sense of

---

25. Martin Heidegger, "Memorial Address," in *Discourse on Thinking*, trans. J. Anderson and E. Freund (New York: Harper, 1966), 46. See also my "The Heart in Heidegger's Thought," *Continental Philosophy Review* 48, no. 4 (2015): 445–62.

26. Heidegger, *Introduction to Metaphysics*, trans. G. Fried and R. Polt (New Haven: Yale University Press, 2000), 12; Marcel, "The Ontological Mystery," in *The Philosophy of Existentialism*, trans. M. Harari (New York: Citadel, 1961), 9–46.

alienation and nihilism.[27] Heidegger lays this at the feet of traditional metaphysics aimed at mastery of what-is: it fails to consider its own ground, the soil in which the Tree of Knowledge is planted.[28] That distinction is central to what I am after.

Teilhard de Chardin, in the Foreword "Seeing" to his *Phenomenon of Man*, speaks of developing "new senses" regarding what science has uncovered: a sense of the vastness of space and time, deep inner complexity, and organic interrelation.[29] The *senses* he is talking about are what is involved in the distinction between having cognitive certitude that we are to die, but, as a recently deceased friend of mine said, "we don't *believe* it."[30] Or what Martin Buber meant when he spoke of "realization" over against "orientation," that is, knowing our way around or being experienced.[31]

I evoke meditative thinking early in thinking about the writer and the reader as arising from fertilized ova: not only does one add information, one learns to gain an enhanced and appreciative sense of one's own development. Meditative thinking appears again when I deal with phenomenally empty space carved out of completely filled real space beyond our visual apparatus. Meditation on that simple fact makes the ordinary matter-of-fact seem (as it really is) strange. Such thinking raises with existential bite the question of our own existence. A fortiori, it is evoked when I come to the notion of Being as the mystery out of which everything emerges.

Both facets are involved when I deal with the hidden pastness of ordinary artifacts to gain a meditative sense of what it took to arrive

27. Heidegger, "Letter on Humanism," in *Pathmarks*, trans. William McNeil (Cambridge: Cambridge University Press, 1998), 257–58.

28. Heidegger, "Introduction to 'What is Metaphysics?' (1949)," in *Pathmarks*, trans. William McNeil (Cambridge: Cambridge University Press, 1998), 277–90.

29. Pierre Teilhard de Chardin, Foreword, "Seeing," in *The Phenomenon of Man*, trans. B. Wall (New York: Harper, 1959), 33–34.

30. This is a significant sense of belief that does not involve simply accepting creed, code, and cult, but, as Paul Tillich would have it, "being gripped by Ultimate Concern." Tillich, *The Courage to Be* (New Haven: Yale University Press, 1952), 47, 82. This goes back to Martin Luther: "Faith is permitting ourselves to be seized by the things we cannot see." Heidegger quotes this in "Phenomenology and Theology," in *The Piety of Thinking*, trans. J. Hart and J. Maraldo (Bloomington: Indiana University Press, 1976), 10.

31. Martin Buber, *Daniel: Dialogues on Realization*, trans. M. Friedman (New York: McGraw-Hill, 1969), 26. See also my *Martin Buber's Ontology* (Evanston, Ill.: Northwestern University Press, 1969), 16–19.

at these present objects. As we said, this is following out the all-inclusiveness of the notion of Being. I extend meditation to the everyday world in tracing something of the development of book technology over centuries. I extend it to the built environment by applying the Vonnegut image in principle to each item in the built environment that conceals the vast history of its coming to be and the coming to be of the know-how that made it possible. In this way it presents itself as the object of an appreciative, meditative awareness. So I go beyond phenomenological description to trace the historical development of some of the items that surround us in our everyday dealings.[32] The otherwise tedious descriptions come to life as part of developing a meditative (i.e., appreciative) awareness.

We could do the same with a scientific grasp of the complex underpinning of the immediately seen organism and its evolutionary history. There is thus both ontological and historical depth to what is built as well as to the natural environment at whose surface we live. I make aspects of that explicit by way of the phenomenology of the book.

* * *

The *bipolar view* of human existence, grounded in the sensory and referred, via the notion of Being, to the Whole is also indebted to Hegel. I follow his procedure especially in two places: his *Phenomenology of Spirit* begins most immediately with Here, Now, Red.[33] He then proceeds to fill in the increasingly fuller context within which that is given, beginning with perception of functional wholes presented through the sensory features they display in a synesthetic way. I begin with the immediate context of "I as writer and You as reader," then go on to the seemingly unmediated presence of sensory fields involved in the page you are reading, and gradually work to uncover the grounds of being an *I* and, at the end, a cosmology presupposed for rational existence and flourishing—precisely Hegel's project.

---

32. Again, following out the notion of Being, I develop the regional ontology for the realm of aesthetics and the subfields within which the various artforms operate in my *Nature, Artforms, and the World*, 1–10.

33. Hegel, *Phenomenology of Spirit*, trans. A. Miller (Oxford: Oxford University Press, 1981), §90–91, p. 58ff.

In his *Science of Logic* Hegel begins with the empty notion of being and traces the route of its gradual filling. He ends both works with the milieu of the Absolute. In "Taking the Universal Point of View," I begin with the notion of Being and work out the eidetic features involved in moving from that mode of givenness. So I proceed in different places from the bipolar character of human experience, in working through the phenomenology of the book, examining first the sensory pole of human experience in its tension with the opposite pole in the notion of Being in the chapter on the universal point of view.[34]

* * *

I follow *Husserl*, the father of the phenomenological movement, in employing the phenomenological method, focused centrally on the phenomenon of *intentionality*: all awareness is *of* or *about* something, some focal matter, while implicitly being present to itself. When I am aware of anything, I am simultaneously but non-focally aware that I am aware.[35]

At its inception, phenomenology was viewed as getting back "to the things themselves," putting into brackets whatever theoretical claims we might make about things and attending directly to what is given in experience in order to illuminate the eidetic features, the essential characteristics of all the types and aspects of beings presented in experience as well as the corresponding types of mental acts that revealed the types.[36] Husserl develops *regional ontologies*: the laying out of the basic eidetic framework for each kind of human operation and its objects. The aim is to make explicit and systematic what—to employ Bertrand Russell's helpful distinction—we know by acquaintance but not by description.[37] In fact, the descriptions offered, even by philosophers and scientists, often do not match what is actually

---

34. See below, pt. III, chap. 9 of this book. See also my *Hegel's Introduction to the System*, trans. Robert E. Wood (Toronto: University of Toronto Press, 2014).

35. See my approach to Husserl through the Line of Knowledge in *The Beautiful, the True, and the Good*, 324–35.

36. Edmund Husserl, *Ideas for a Pure Phenomenology and Phenomenological Philosophy, First Book, General Introduction to Phenomenological Philosophy*, trans. D. Dahlstrom (Indianapolis: Hackett, 2014), 86–87.

37. Russell, *Mysticism and Logic* (Totowa, N.J.: Barnes and Noble Books, 1951), 152–67.

given in experience. Consider, for example, the widespread claim that what we see are images in the visual cortex.[38]

While Husserl began with mathematics and logic, he was eventually led back to the Lifeworld out of which all theory develops and in which it remains rooted.[39] Here we find what is "always already there" before, during, and after our theoretical high-wire acts. Here we return to earth and are thus enabled to link up continually within our own lived life what we are proximately concerned with in texts and arguments.

It is important to call attention to Husserl's distinction between external and internal horizons. Literally, the horizon is a visual factor, defined as the limit of the field of vision. We carry it as a kind of "psychic hoopskirt" that recedes as we move toward it. The "internal horizon" of things presented in immediate experience is likewise something that recedes as we approach it with experiential and inferential content. The interior horizons have a filling that never seems to reach the final word on anything in its existential fullness.[40]

* * *

Finally, there is Bernard Lonergan, two of whose central notions I adopt. First is his notion of Being as a priori reference to everything and to everything about everything. Then there is his insistence that everything is subject to revision except the conditions for the possibility of revision, which lie in the structure of the field of experience and its objective correlates.[41] I focus more on the structure of the field of experience as involving a sensory pole and a pole of reference, via the notion of Being, to the whole of what-is. That notion founds both intellectual apprehension and freedom to choose.

A basic issue in this work is how Lonergan's notion of Being and Heidegger's notion of Being can coexist. Lonergan's treatment is intel-

---

38. For a sustained treatment of that, see my "On Seeing: A Phenomenological Approach to Neuro-Psychology," in *Being and the Cosmos*, 9–32.

39. Husserl, *Crisis in European Philosophy and Transcendental Phenomenology*, trans. D. Carr (Evanston, Ill.: Northwestern University Press, 1970), 50–52, 139–40.

40. Husserl, *Crisis*, 162.

41. Lonergan, *Insight: A Study of Human Understanding* (London: Longmans Green, 1957): Being, 348–79; Revision, 36–39.

lectualist while Heidegger's concerns the heart.[42] As I indicated above, Being for Heidegger is the ground of the intellectualist tradition. It is neither the anticipation of the Fullness of Being beyond beings (*onto-theo-logy*, which Heidegger categorically rejects) nor some changeless principle or set of principles. It is a relation of humanness to the Whole, which acts upon human beings differently in different epochs. Its manifestations are always finite and temporal. Being remains, in principle, the *Lethe*, or hidden Mystery. Furthermore, there is no Ground of Being, no Cause: the Mystery is an *Ab-grund*, an abyss, which has no Ground.

Lonergan clearly stands on the eternality and infinity of God as Fullness of Being and as Cause of finite being. But he also maintains the finitude and temporality of our views of the Whole. On that I stand with Lonergan. Like Hegel, he has a place for "passion and inwardness." Heidegger's meditative thinking can develop within that context.

* * *

Approaches through the interrelation of abstract arguments and the study of great texts have their enduring ground in the things made explicit in phenomenological description. My motto is, "To the things themselves through the texts themselves," with the latter as the chief vehicle of philosophic development. That should become further evident, first in the discussion with different thinkers in the text and then through the footnotes, which are largely there to acknowledge a source to which I was indebted for a given insight. That is indeed eclectic, but I hope what I produce has its own coherence. And my selection is not without awareness of the overall conceptual framework within which each of the thinkers operates.[43]

42. Heidegger, *What Is Called Thinking?*, trans. F. Wieck and J. Glenn Grey (New York: Harper, 1968), 138–45.

43. See the exposition of the overall conceptual frame in Parmenides, Plato and Plotinus, Aristotle and Aquinas, Descartes and Spinoza, Leibniz, Kant and Hegel, Whitehead, and Heidegger in my *A Path into Metaphysics: Phenomenological, Hermeneutic, and Dialogical Studies* (Albany: State University of New York Press, 1991). See also Plato, Aristotle, Plotinus and the Latin Middle Ages, Kant, Hegel, Schopenhauer, Nietzsche, Dewey, Heidegger, and my *Placing Aesthetics*. I develop some themes in the history of Western thought in individual thinkers and sets of individuals in my *The Beautiful, the True, and the Good*.

While I rely primarily upon phenomenological description, I venture into an explanatory mode when the occasions arise. Phenomenology provides the enduring point of departure in the structure of the field of experience for the kinds of questions that emerge in the history of thought. In the process, I claim to have shed light on several problems in the history of thought, including the problems of universals, of natural kinds, of the basis for animal awareness of what is other, and of the single ground of the distinctively human characteristics.

* * *

When I heard Hans-Georg Gadamer say that one of the first seminars in the phenomenological movement was Adolf Reinach's on the phenomenology of the mailbox, I thought "How trivial!" When I myself decided to do a seminar in descriptive phenomenology, I realized that what emerged from developing such a focus was not trivial. It was a matter of making explicit what John Searle has called the huge, invisible first- and second-person ontology or what Hegel called Objective Spirit: the endurance of practices and institutions that support them beyond the lifetime of the subjective spirits who produced them.[44]

Science focuses, grammatically, on third-person objects, explaining everything in terms of impersonal processes. Searle's point is that such explanations depend upon the first person singular, the *I* of the scientist, speaking to the second person, the singular and plural You of her or his audience or readers. Those relations involve a vast complex of interrelations, resting upon the use of language.[45]

To begin with, there are the eidetic features of the various sensory fields and their togetherness learned by one's psycho-neural system, by which we typically ignore what is immediately given (perspectival shrinkage) because of past learning. This is not exactly a trivial insight. There is further the basic distinction between *techne* and *phusis* assumed but not explored in ordinary experience. Then there is mediation by systems: the production and distribution systems, the postal system, and, most basically, the linguistic system, as well as the differing struc-

---

44. John Searle, *Mind, Language and Society: Philosophy in the Real World* (New York: Basic Books, 1998), 42–43; G. W. F. Hegel, *Hegel's Philosophy of Mind*, trans. W. Wallace and A. Miller (Oxford: Clarendon Press, 1973), 241–92.
    45. Searle, *Mind, Language and Society,* 135–61.

tures involved in each of them. There is the presence and absence of writer and addressee. An orderly description of what is involved will occasion the refocusing of the origin of insights that are the basis for many basic positions in the tradition, even, as I said, occasionally affording new insights that will allow us to develop the tradition.[46] Beginning with the phenomenology of the book displays similar insights.

If readers will patiently follow these seemingly tedious eidetic and historical descriptions, then they will find many ways of moving into broader insights, both replicating some thinker and perhaps adding to the basis for the solution of many of the problems that arise from not carrying out the careful description we practice here. As I said, the tedium should be relieved if the objects are made the object of meditative thinking, or thinking as thanking, as appreciative.

There is another aspect toward what I am attempting, which is expressed in Descartes' eleventh rule for the direction of the mind:

> If, after we have recognized intuitively a number of simple truths, we wish to draw any inference from them, it is useful to run them over in a continuous and uninterrupted act of thought, to reflect upon their relations to one another, and to grasp together distinctly a number of these propositions so far as is possible at the same time. For this is a way of making our knowledge much more certain, and of greatly increasing the power of the mind.[47]

On the one hand, I have attempted to lay out the network of interconnections involved in the existence of a book. On the other hand, I recommend the attempt to go beyond the necessary linearity of my exposition and to hold these interconnections together as far as possible, to gain a contemplative sense of the "huge invisible ontology" that supports our lives.

---

46. See my "Phenomenology of the Mailbox," in *Ratio et Fides: A Preliminary Introduction to Philosophy for Theology* (Eugene, Ore.: Wipf and Stock, 2018), 15–37.

47. Descartes, *Rules for the Direction of the Mind*, in *Philosophical Works of Descartes*, vol. I, trans. E. Haldane and G. Ross (New York: Dover, 1931), 33. I think this is not far from Aquinas' distinction between *ratio* or the discursive movement of the mind and *intellectus* or the resting on the mind in the contemplation of the truth involved. *Summa theologiae*, trans. Laurence Shapcote, OP, ed. John Mortensen and Enrique Alarcón (Lander, Wyo.: The Aquinas Institute for the Study of Sacred Doctrine, 2012), II-II, q. 45, a. 5, ad 3.

Overall, this indeed is an eccentric way of "doing philosophy," but it anchors thought solidly in the presence of things and persons around us and follows the paths of several key thinkers, beginning especially with Plato and, as we will see, Aristotle,[48] but also following Hegel, Husserl, Heidegger, and Lonergan. Underlying all of this is Martin Buber on whom I wrote my first book. The current work is *existential* in the deepest sense.[49]

* * *

I will boldly suggest a seven-dimensional view of human experience, metaphorically thinking of the levels of consciousness as an inward turning of the four-dimensional, externally observable space-time world to the scene of its manifestation in the three "internal" dimensions of sensing, intellectual apprehension, and openness to Totality.[50]

The metaphor of dimensions is helpful first of all because it gives us a model of essential distinctness and inseparable unification. It helps us to conceive of inner dimensions without having to think of a separate mind or soul. It also reminds us to shift to a type of description that is radically different when talking about levels of awareness involving differing relations to space and time than when talking about sensorily encountered objects and imaginatively constructed models based on such objects. The image was initially developed to make clearer and more plausible Aristotle's psycho-physical holism against the perennial temptation to turn distinctions into separations.

---

48. I was surprised when I read Heidegger's claim that phenomenology is a return to Plato and Aristotle. But as I reflected upon their procedure, I realized how true that is. Hence one can see both of them referenced in my dealing with the eidetic features of experience. Heidegger, *Prolegomena to the History of the Concept of Time*, trans. T. Kisiel (Bloomington: Indiana University Press, 1992), 136. See also my "Phenomenology and the Perennial Task of Philosophy: A Study of Plato and Aristotle," in *The Beautiful, the True, and the Good*, 42–61.

49. See Wood, *Martin Buber's Ontology*, 7–8, 12–13, 17. My thought is beholden to Buber's basic distinction between *I-Thou* and *I-It* relations, which cuts across the distinction between relation to persons and relations to things. A "Thou" is a living presence—human, natural, or artefactual—that steps out of the ordinary and addresses us. Buber, *I and Thou*, trans. W. Kaufmann (New York: Charles Scribner's Sons, 1970), 53–57.

50. I have used the metaphor of dimensions derived from Edwin Abbott's *Flatland: A Romance of Many Dimensions*, which first appeared in 1884. It is available in a Dover edition (New York, 1992), 6, 14–15, 56–59. See my *Path into Metaphysics*, 31–33.

* * *

This book has three parts. The first and major part explores the structures involved in human existence; the second deals with applications to inter-human relations; and the third deals with applications to ontological extensions, exploring what is co-given with the notion of Being and how one might sketch the main lines of a cosmological view of the place of humanness in the whole scheme of things.

PART I. THE STRUCTURE OF EXPERIENCE

Chapter 1, the Prologue, tells the story of *Flatland*, which will orient our considerations in chapter 2, which gives the skeleton: the seven-dimensional framework of all human operations whose depth dimension is reference to Totality. As I said, it is a bipolar view: the sensory pole playing in tandem with the notion of Being that directs us toward the Totality as the object of an ongoing quest. Its immediate focus is upon the concrete act, Here-and-Now, of reading these pages, ferreting out the "intentional strands" involved in such activity. We begin with the eidetic features involved in looking at and handling the book, the synesthesia supposed in immediate recognition, the act of reading, the notion of Being as ground and the seven-dimensional view of human existence involved in this activity of reading and reflective explication.

Chapter 3 hones in upon the notion of time as it is lived through in individual lives, presents itself as a peculiar object, surrounds the individual in history, and is measured by clocks and calendars. Clocks and calendars allow us both to coordinate our contemporary actions and to locate past events in human history and in the history of the cosmos.

Chapter 4 attends to the deep subjectivity that lives within the skeletal structure examined in the first chapter. We explore the life of feeling anchored in the heart as the center of psycho-physical wholeness.

Chapter 5 explores institutional mediation, which progressively uncovers fields for the tapping of potentialities otherwise lying fallow in the human gene pool. It focuses upon that mediation by following up on the phenomenology of the book; focusing upon the distinction between *techne* and *physis*, or art and nature; the production and distribution process involving institutional mediation; the literary tradition; reading; and the grounding of writing in speech and thus in language as basic institution. We will conclude with a treatment of the nature of literature in relation to oral tradition. Language as primary institution, as it allows the interrelation of contemporaries, simultaneously allows the accumulated results of human understanding, choice, and action to be passed on to successive generations.

PART II. MORAL-POLITICAL EXTENSIONS

Basic to human existence and underscored in modern political forms is the polyvalent notion of freedom, which we will explore in chapter 6, while chapter 7 will zero in on sketches of moral and political extensions. Here I appeal to the ancient virtue tradition and the medieval natural moral law tradition, attempting to show how the Ten Commandments are, for the most part, secondary precepts of the natural moral law. I also treat Kant's contribution as an extension rather than a cancelling of the tradition we have examined. I conclude with an examination of the notion of happiness.

PART III. BEING AND HUMAN EXISTENCE

Once again I note that throughout this work, we have rested upon a bipolar view of human existence: the obvious organically based pole of sensation and desire and the not-so-obvious pole of reference to Being. Chapter 8 shows how everything distinctively human follows from the operation of that notion. As in the chapter on freedom, we move here from description to explanation, showing the ground of all the distinctive human properties. The *philosophic* animal lives in the light of Being, which founds everything distinctively human: we are ontological, by nature emptily directed toward the Totality, and therefore world-constructing, historical, rational, individually self-disposing, linguistic, political, technological, scientific, aesthetic, religious, and philosophic animals. The togetherness of these factors constitutes the various worlds in which we dwell, but it also sets the framework for entering into dialogue between individuals and between cultural worlds.

Chapter 9 looks, at the highest level of abstraction, to what is conceptually co-given with the notion of Being. As we previously noted, if our first chapter parallels Hegel's *Phenomenology of Spirit* by beginning with the sensory,[51] this chapter parallels his *Science of Logic* by beginning from the opposite pole in the abstract notion of Being.[52] Obviously, the parallel needs to underscore the immense sophistication and penetration of Hegel's work compared to my own modest attempts. But I hope that mine will, among other things, make approaching Hegel easier.[53]

Finally, chapter 10 is an opening to a broader view by situating human existence within the development of nature and history. It sketches out a view of history within a developing cosmos drawn upward by commitment to the transcendentals: truth, goodness, and beauty, but also unity and difference, and especially *creative empowerment*.

* * *

With the field of experience as the permanent point of departure, and with the previous separate publication of portions of this work, there is significant overlap in the chapters. I have decided to let much of that stand because the reader's apprehension of what is involved will be reinforced by returning again and again to the starting point in the field of experience.

The first three essays are largely original to this work, though parts of two of them have appeared elsewhere: the "Prologue" and "The Structure of Humanness" are developments from my *A Path into Metaphysics*;[54] the "Phenomenology of the Book" contains some material from my "Phenomenology of the Mailbox," which appeared in *Philosophy Today*,[55] in which the chapter on "Aspects of Freedom" first appeared;[56] "Being Human and the Question of Being" was published in *The Modern Schoolman*,[57] while "Taking the Universal Viewpoint"[58] and "Potentiality, Creativity, and Relationality" appeared in *The Review of Metaphysics*.[59]

---

51. Hegel, *Phenomenology of Spirit*, §90–91, p. 58ff.
52. *Hegel's Science of Logic*, trans. A. Miller (New York: Humanities Press, 1976), 67ff.
53. See my preface in *Introduction to the System*, 3–6, 9–10.
54. *Path into Metaphysics*, 29–60.
55. *Philosophy Today* 47, no. 2 (Summer 2003): 147–59.
56. *Philosophy Today* 35, no. 1 (Spring 1991): 106–15.
57. *The Modern Schoolman* 87, no. 1 (November 2009): 53–66.
58. *The Review of Metaphysics* 50, no. 4 (June 1997): 769–81.
59. *The Review of Metaphysics* 59, no. 2 (December 2005): 379–401.

Part I

The Structure of Experience

Chapter 1

Prologue
A Parable about Awareness[1]

n his *Crisis in European Philosophy and Transcendental Phenomenology* Husserl spoke of Helmholtz's image of "plane-beings" who have no sense of depth; he applied it to everyday life and even the life of scientists.[2] Husserl referred to the image but did not develop it. Edwin Abbott developed that into a story. Abbott was a late nineteenth-century geometer and Christian apologist who developed a multidimensional view to aid in understanding post-Resurrection narrative about the sudden appearance and disappearance of the One who died. In the present work, apart from the apologetic attempt, we take away with us the notion of multidimensionality and apply it to the field of human experience.

* * *

A long time ago in a land far removed from our own, there lived a geometer named Dr. A. Square. The land he inhabited was quite different than our own, for its inhabitants knew what *back and forth* and *around* meant but had no idea of what we would call *over* or *under* or *above* and *below*. I say they had no *idea*, but that means they could not *picture* to themselves the objects of such terms.

The land was called Flatland, for it was like the surface of a picture, only no one in Flatland could see it as such. Embedded as the inhabitants were in the surface of that land, what each observed of anything else was a line that moved when the object moved and, depending upon the kind of shape it had, changed the size of its appearance when it moved in different ways relative to the viewer. Thus, a circle appeared as a line of constant size if one viewed it from any position

---

1. Much of the material in chapters 1 and 2 of the present work is based on pages 29–59 of my *Path into Metaphysics*.

2. Husserl, *Crisis*, 119, 123.

at the same distance. A scalene triangle would appear to grow and diminish as it pivoted before a viewer.

The people who inhabited this land were ranked according to their form. The lowest of all were the women who were simple, one-dimensional lines. If they were stationary and faced you end for end, their appearance would shrink to a point. That was a dangerous situation, for one could easily fail to see one of them and thus get stuck. Consequently, there was a law in Flatland that women had to wiggle to and fro in public. Triangles were higher up because they were more "many-sided," and better still were rectangles, then pentagons, octagons, on to chiliagons, until one came to the circle, the most well-rounded and thus the best of the inhabitants of this strange land. Most men were triangles of greater or lesser breadth and balance in their sides. Dr. A. Square was a cut above them and was suited for the intellectual work of geometry, but not for the higher tasks of the more many-sided types, and especially not for the well-roundedness of philosopher-king types.

Recently Dr. Square had had a strange experience, a kind of alien encounter. He was sliding along from the market to his home when he almost got stuck on a motionless point. "Madam," said he, "you are breaking the law! You are not wiggling in public." A. Square was surprised when a booming male voice responded: "I beg your pardon! I am the King of Lineland!" A. Square stepped to the side and noticed that there was a whole string of dots and dashes of various sizes, all in a row. The King said something to the dashes on either side of himself, and they in turn spoke to the dash or dot next to him or her, and so on down the line. In this way messages came to and from the King, with various degrees of dilution in proportion to the distance from the King.

Dr. Square figured out what was happening and proudly informed the King that he was encountering an inhabitant of a second dimension. The King found the situation rather strange, since he could not see A. Square, and the latter's voice, being propagated perpendicular to the entire plane, pervaded Lineland, even seeming to come from within.

A. Square tried to convince the King of the second dimension by passing through the Line between the king and one of his flanking dashes who gave way before the pressure of Dr. Square's entrance. But all that the King and the dash could see was a point suddenly appearing when A. Square touched the line, persisting for as long as it took him to pass through it, and disappearing after he passed through. Lineland was in a state of confusion for quite some time, with stories and queries passing back and forth to the farthest region of the Kingdom. These were strange happenings—sudden appearances and sudden disappearances—that were reported, but no one could believe A. Square's explanation that a second dimension existed, because such a thing was strictly unimaginable!

One day Dr. Square was teaching introductory geometry to his grandson. He began thus: you start with a point and move it in a single direction to generate a line. Then move the line perpendicular to itself and you generate a plane. Thus, geometry has three basic parameters: point, line, and plane. But the grandson was perplexed: what would happen if you moved the plane perpendicular to itself? Dr. Square laughed at the naiveté of the child and ruled that to be a nonsense question.

But suddenly he heard a voice that both came from within himself and pervaded the environment. The voice asserted quite insistently: "It is not a nonsense question, for there is a third dimension!" A. Square was puzzled both at the inner character of the voice and at what the voice proclaimed. After a somewhat lengthy interchange, the owner of the voice, who happened to be a sphere, decided to show himself by passing through the plane. All Dr. Square observed was a point that suddenly appeared, grew into a line, increased until it reached the diameter, decreased progressively, and then disappeared.

Perplexed, Dr. Square continued his discussion with the strange voice. Then it dawned on him: in his recent encounter with the King of Lineland, the King was in a condition directly analogous to A. Square himself. The King encountered a two-dimensional inhabitant whose behavior he could not fathom because the King's imagination was built up from his unidimensional perceptual experience. A. Square thought of his grandson's question: if there were a third dimension, then he and his fellow Flatlandians could not imagine it because their imaginations were tied to their two-dimensional perceptual equipment.

Then another insight hit him, and he relayed it directly to his three-dimensional interlocutor in the form of a question: Might there be a fourth dimension? Of course, the inhabitants of the world that we—you and I, dear reader—are used to are bound in our imaginations to the three-dimensional objects of our own perceptual experience, construct whatever worlds of fancy we might. So Dr. Square's new and mysterious interlocutor immediately rejected the question as nonsense. But after some discussion with the geometer who related the story of his recent encounter with the King of Lineland, the visitor from the three-dimensional world recalled reports of strange visitations in an upper room with closed doors where suddenly a man appeared to a group of his friends and just as suddenly disappeared. Though he did not believe them, he had in mind the post-resurrection reports in the Gospels.

Here is what he was thinking. Let's say someone from a three-dimensional world was standing on the surface of Flatland and decided to step from where he was to a location several feet away. He lifts his feet one by one and takes two long steps. Our Flatland observer would see the two lines of his feet standing in the plane. Then one foot-line would disappear and suddenly appear several feet away, followed by the other foot disappearing and then reappearing without passing through the two-dimensional medium. The three-dimensional visitor was going *up*, *above* the plane, something a Flatlander could never even imagine. So in the post-resurrection narrative (and this was what Mr. Abbott had in mind when composing the work), Christ could have passed to a fourth physical dimension that sometimes joined our own world in the form of sudden apparitions and disappearances and inner voices. But of course, today—despite the fact that physics thinks in terms of multidimensional space, some unfolded (the four-dimensional space-time world of our experience), some "curled up"—such thinking seems absurd.[3] A. Square and his friend went on to conjecture as to the possibility of any number of further dimensions hidden from them by reason of the limitation of

---

3. See Stephen Hawking and Leonard Mlodinow, *The Grand Design* (New York: Bantam Books, 2010), 115–19, 140–42.

their perceptual equipment, but available to their judgment as conceptual but not imaginative possibilities.

In what follows I will apply the Flatland model to what, I would claim, are *seven* dimensions of human existence: the four-dimensional space-time of picturable bodily occupancy and the three non-picturable, "inward" dimensions of consciousness. The latter include sensing, the apprehension of universals, and reference to the Totality.

Chapter 2

The Structure of Experience
A Multidimensional View

Grant unto us men the skill, O God, in a little thing to descry those notions as be common to things both great and small.

Augustine, *Confessions* XI, 23

What is most obvious and universal in experience is most frequently overlooked, probably because it is too familiar to evoke special comment.

Errol Harris, *Nature, Mind and Modern Science*

Whoever is importunate with his eyes as a seeker of knowledge— how could he see more of things than their foregrounds?

Friedrich Nietzsche, *Thus Spoke Zarathustra*

THE BOOK

This exercise is an attempt to render experience explicit by systematically exploring all the eidetic features involved in the existence and functioning of the book. Though the starting point is obvious, the aim is to lay out the total framework of human experience systematically. In the process we will see how central questions have emerged and use the systematically arranged evidence to explore possible answers.

You in the present are reading in my absence the words I have generated in the past for you in your absence. Trivial perhaps; but the point is to make explicit and regular, as a matter of habit, reflection upon how one is engaged. As we proceed from the most external, sensory fields to the most internal, we will lay out the basis for being an *I*. The aim is to become comprehensively reflective about every eidetic facet of one's experience.

I am the specific individual who is generating this text, while *you* may be any individual interested in philosophy. Through successive acts of typing, I have spatially fixed on a page the temporal flow of my thoughts. Through your current reading, translating the static spatiality of the words on the page, you are making the flow of meaning present in your awareness. We will eventually show the foundation of being an *I* and will thereby establish the case for resisting the very strong temptation to reduce first- and second-person ontology to third-person ontology.[1]

My typing is a temporal process that eventuates in a static spatial inscription on the page. But that action is translating the fixed spatial inscription upon my brain of the meanings I draw upon while I write, as you are drawing upon meanings spatially inscribed in your brain in following what I have written and as what you read is also inscribed in it.[2]

Now, the neat rows of black figures on the white background are not what you are fixing your attention upon. Here the visually available is strictly subsidiary to your attending to the flow of thought.

Further, I am wearing my glasses as I read what I am writing. They are not like the words, directly present but strictly subsidiary; they do not normally appear at all. The same is true of the concepts you and I are employing, for which the words are placeholders. Concepts are like glasses: we typically understand *through* them and not by paying attention *to* them, as we will do later.

So immediately we have two significant insights: what is subsidiary but within awareness of the object to which we attend, and what is central to understanding but not at all focal in reading.[3] The medieval thinkers distinguished between *medium quod* and *medium quo*: that is, a medium *to which* we have to attend in its proper functioning but only subsidiarily (like the words on a page) and media *through*

---

1. John Searle, *The Mystery of Consciousness* (New York: New York Review Books, 1997), 212. See also Searle, *Rediscovery of Mind*, 95, 117, 157.

2. In *Of Grammatology* Jacques Derrida says that writing has priority over speech. What he seems to mean is that in speaking there is immediate presence to self and other which stands over against the possible mediated filling of such presence, whereas in writing there is a mediated double deferral of presence: over the system of differences that translates writing and over the deferral of full presence. Derrida, *Of Grammatology*, trans. G. Spivak (Baltimore: Johns Hopkins University Press, 1976), 6–94.

3. This is central to Michael Polayni's work. See *The Tacit Dimension* (Garden City: Doubleday, 1966), 7–13.

which we see or understand (like concepts and later, glasses).[4] What is now focal is what I am attempting to communicate; words and concepts are the means.

Reading involves touching the book by holding it in your hand and looking at the pages.[5] So let us focus upon seeing and touching. Touching especially is the humblest level of human experience and stands as the polar opposite to the grand notions that might attract students to philosophy: the meaning of life, what one should do or avoid, the existence and nature of God, the freedom and immortality of the soul, and so forth. As Nietzsche never tired of pointing out, the pursuit of these more ultimate questions has been all too often linked to contempt for the earth.[6] Focus upon tactility especially has the virtue of planting us securely upon the earth and grounding, literally and figuratively, these other more exalted pursuits. In what we do, we will be gathering various types of evidence. Everything I say should be readily verifiable in the field of any person's experience. I am making it explicit and systematic.

SEEING

But let us begin with *seeing*. As we proceed, check out what I have to say in the field of your own experience, and also check whether I have missed any essential feature of what is immediately evident.[7] Can there be any seeing that does not involve the factors I will make explicit?

You have in your hand a book (though it may be present on a screen available through manipulating the keys on your keyboard or sliding your finger across a screen) whose aim is to help reflect upon what is involved in touching, looking at, and thinking about the surrounding world in relation to your experience as a human being. Let's

4. St. Thomas Aquinas, *Quaestiones disputatae de veritate*, vol. 2, *Questions X–XX*, trans. James V. McGlynn (Chicago: Henry Regnery Company, 1953), 18.1 ad 1.

5. I am assuming for the moment a traditional book. There are obvious modifications to be made in the case of electronically available books.

6. Friedrich Nietzsche, *The Birth of Tragedy*, trans. W. Kaufmann (New York: Vintage, 1967), §5, 21; Nietzsche, *Genealogy of Morals*, trans. W. Kaufmann (New York: Vintage, 1969), §3.5, 154.

7. On the importance of providing a full inventory of the visual field in coming to terms with scientific discovery, ophthalmological practice, and reductionism, see my "On Seeing," in *Being and the Cosmos*, 1–32.

say the book was lying closed on your desk. The cover is blue, the pages white, containing neat rows of a limited set of black figures appearing in differing combinations. You recognize blue, white, and black as instances of a more generic notion—namely, *color*. Color is given as inhering in the extended surface of the book cover or located on the surface of the pages. In fact, color is not even imaginable without inhering in extension. But color is not identical with extension since extension is perceivable tactually in the dark and thus without color. The given color's extension is limited by the space the colored object occupies, and it stands in relation to other spatially limited objects in the visual field. Currently that field is not allowed its full extension because it is blocked by the walls of the room wherein the book sits upon the desk.

If one were in an open field, the horizon would extend to the limit of the field of vision, spread in a 180° arc with one's head as the fixed origin of the field. Rotating one's body would sequentially reveal a full circular horizon. But if one were to advance toward that horizon, it would continually recede. As we noted previously, we carry the horizon with us as a kind of psychic hoopskirt, although it is not purely psychic. As the limit of the field of vision, it is not there without one who sees; but that does not make it wholly subjective, since it is also not there without what is seen. It is, rather, part of a distinctive sort of relation, a relation of *manifestation* or appearance set up between a bodily situated perceiver and a physical object. Perceived space appears within a horizon and involves a separation between the seer and the object seen occupied by phenomenally empty space. Further, that things might appear, space must be suffused with light.

Further still, you know from previous experience that the book is rectangular; however, in viewing it from a given angle, it actually appears as larger on the side it presents to you than on the sides that recede from your viewing position. From a fixed position, one can at most see three sides of a book: the one presented frontally in its true dimension, the other two appearing as each rhomboidal. So one's viewing position results in perspectival shrinkage of the object. One sees this most clearly in the case of railroad tracks, which appear to converge toward the horizon even though they are known to be parallel. However, any given perspective is systematically related to all the other perspectives one might gain by moving in relation to the object, by the object's moving in relation to the viewer, or both. One might move farther from or closer to the object; one might move around it. The perspectives change, but they cohere in the thing seen. Our perceptual equipment discounts the distortions in order to serve our adjustment to the things themselves to such an extent that we rarely notice the perspectival shrinkage. It did not appear in painting until the fifteenth century.

Again, the book appears as a focal object surrounded by other objects that simultaneously appear non-focally, marginally, within the visual field. Those other objects, however, can in turn become focal as we attend to them one by one.

Color, extension, horizon, light, spatial separation of the seer from the seen, perspective, coherence of perspectives, and surrounding objects (focal as well as marginal) are the major features of the visual field. Following phenomenologist Edmund Husserl's employment of Plato's term for Forms (namely, *eidos*), we call these *eidetic features*.[8] It is important to ask yourself throughout whether these kinds of observations are merely matters of the writer's opinion that might easily be refuted by counterexamples or whether they are not in principle irrefutable because they are verified in every instance of visual perception, for they constitute the essential structure of the context of visual appearance. If, according to Karl Popper, scientific statements are in principle falsifiable, what we are examining are not scientific statements, but statements of experience upon which science itself rests, along with the ordinary experience of the scientist within whom it operates.[9] The scientist converses with those with whom he is working in other-than-scientific terms, for example: Can you fix this spectrograph? What are you doing for lunch, etc.? But both in his interrelation with his colleagues and in his experimental observations, the same structures of the field of experience obtain.

8. Husserl, *Ideas*, 16–24.

9. Karl Popper, *Conjectures and Refutations: The Growth of Scientific Knowledge*, vol. 2 (New York: Harper, 1963), 281–83, 291–92.

TOUCHING

Now let's turn to *touch*. You see the book and pick it up. It's a hard-back—heavier than the paperback version, but lighter than the Dallas phone directory. Its dust jacket is smooth. You take off the jacket: the cover is rougher than the jacket. You press your forefinger against the cover: it is harder than the cushion of the chair upon which you are sitting, but softer than the pen you have in hand to take notes. The fan has been blowing on the book: it has a slightly cool feel. Located next to the fireplace in winter, it would feel warmer. Or it's a hot, humid day and the air-conditioner has gone out. The slick cover of the paper-back book feels a bit sticky, slightly moist rather than dry as it would feel under conditions of low humidity. Heavy-light, smooth-rough, hard-soft, along with cool-hot, dry-moist: these are the eidetic features of the objects of touch.

All these aspects inhere in extension, the first three sets—hard and soft, smooth and rough, heavy and light—giving the combined experience of *resistance*. They are not absolute but relative. They are located on continua of qualities relative to one another and, indeed, relative also to the condition of the one who touches. That is their *fixed nature*. Their status as doubly relative is given to reflective thought as objectively true. In the case of heat or cold, one who comes into a room from a half-hour run on a summer day in Texas might find the room cool, while one who arrives from ten minutes in a meat locker would perceive the same room as warm. Nonetheless, each perceiver is not mistaken in the experience of cool and warm, respectively.[10] We get beyond the relativity of the experiences in an indirect way: by measuring the regular effect of heat or cold upon a calibrated column of mercury, which is independent of the heat or cold of our own tac-tual sensors. But that depends upon intellectual intervention in the sensory field: understanding the regularly observable causal relation between heat and cold, on the one hand, and a column of mercury, on the other, we calibrate that column to produce regular objective

10. Plato makes these observations in his *Theaetetus* (152b) against those who argued against the fixity of the Forms by reason of the changing character of experience and its being relative to a perceiving subject.

measurements of immediately perceived, experience-relative heat and cold. This independence of the state of the observer's body in the case of measurement and the appearance of measurable extension through both seeing and touching suggests that, whereas the sensory qualities may be relational, being activated by the presence of a perceiver, the extensive properties belong to "the thing itself." This is a direction indicated by Aristotle and followed out by modern physics within its own distinctively different assumptions.[11]

There is another crucial aspect of touch. Whereas the other senses have specific organs, the organ of touch is the whole surface of the body. When the reticular activating system in the brain stem is "on," feeling floods the organism, and the conscious being is in touch with its body as a functional whole. That is what allows the conscious being to touch, to feel the other, and to be touched. Feeling is the nonreflective self-presence of a conscious being which makes possible the manifestation of something *as other than* that conscious being. In animal life, seeing, hearing, and smelling culminate in apprehension of prey or mate or offspring. That is why all beings that are aware have at least the sense of touch, for the point of the senses is to reveal opportunities

---

11. In *On the Soul* 3.2.425b.27. Aristotle claims that the sensible thing when its sensibility is activated is cognitively identical with the sensory power when the sensible thing activates it. He calls the extensive properties of the things *common sensibles*, that is, factors available through several senses, while the factors peculiar to various senses are *proper sensibles*, which later in medieval times are called *formal objects*. At the beginnings of modern mathematical physics, Descartes distinguished primary and secondary qualities. *Meditations on First Philosophy,* in *Discourse on Method and Mediations on First Philosophy,* trans. Donald A. Cress (Indianapolis: Hackett, 1998), 59–103, VI, p. 75–76. The first, the features of extension and movement, belong to the things themselves. By reason of what is becoming known in the physics of light and the character of neuro-physiological structure, the second, the perceived sensory qualities, belong to the perceiver and occur within the brain which effects awareness "within." Locke and Hume made the same distinction. John Locke, *Essay Concerning Human Understanding* (Baltimore: Penguin, 1998), II, viii. This raised the problem of how we get outside of our cognitive inside. Later, Kant claimed that it was a scandal that we had not solved the problem. Immanuel Kant, preface (second edition) of *Critique of Pure Reason: Unified Edition,* trans. Werner S. Pluhar (Indianapolis: Hackett, 1996), B xl, p. 36–38. Heidegger claimed that the scandal is that anybody ever thought it was a problem: we always begin "outside," with the persons and things in our environment and within the public space of meaning through language. *Being and Time,* trans. J. Stambaugh (Albany: SUNY Press, 1996), II, I, 49, p. 229. The problem comes with following what I call *the optomorphic fallacy,* modeling all evidence on the character of visual objects.

or threats to organic flourishing.[12] Desire, pleasure, or pain are modulations, intensifications of feeling. We will explore this further in the chapter on Feeling and the Heart.

But consider seeing and touching as metaphors. Seeing is the dominant metaphor for talking about cognitive states: see how this cloth feels, how this CD sounds, how this food tastes, or how this perfume smells. We would not say, "Smell how this cloth feels" or "Hear how this perfume smells." Seeing as a metaphor gets extended to all cognitive states: "Do you see what I am getting at here?" However, consider that, whereas seeing involves a detachment, a distance, and absorption with the object, when we say that someone is touched by what happened, we are referring to a kind of holistic involvement, the co-implication of touching and what touches. Being touched is a movement of the heart, the core of ourselves open to transformation.

THE BOOK AGAIN

Returning to the book as our point of departure: it is a three-dimensional object generated at a certain time, having moved from the publisher to the distributor and on to you who are now moving your eyes over this page and turning pages as the text continues. The book's own spatiotemporal appearance depends upon your physiological-sensory system having retained and gathered various experiences from different senses in relation to this and similar objects. Such a display is *synesthetic*; it involves the togetherness (*sun-*) of all the fields of sensation (*aisthesis*): the feel, the look—even the sound, the smell, and (ugh!) the taste of the book—are given as grounded coherently in the object.[13] Aristotle called the synesthetic products *phantasmata*, a term linked to *phainomai*, or "I appear." What is immediately given is automatically mediated by our psychoneural system, which discounts the perspectives. Merleau-Ponty developed the idea further in focusing upon linkage to motor habits.[14]

The given visual or tactual perspective presents itself as continuous with past and future perspectives from different senses that gather

---

12. Aristotle makes this observation in his *On the Soul* 3.12.435a. That is why, after climbing up to *nous*, he ends with locomotion and tactility.

13. Aristotle, *On the Soul* 3.1.235a.26.

14. *The Structure of Behavior*, trans. A. Fisher (Boston: Beacon Press, 1942), 223–24.

around given things whose aspects we observe serially as we move around them and subject them to various sensorily observed tests. John Dewey points to the operation of such *synesthesia* within all the art-forms, each of which is centered upon a lead sense or senses but is closely linked to all the rest.[15] Of course, the book is different than many other objects, since it came into being by human skill and not by nature; but it makes its appearance within the field of the senses in the same general way as any other sensorily given object, natural or manmade.

Now, the book is not simply a spatiotemporal object that is available in a synesthetic way in the unified field of sensation; it is *something to be read*. The neat rows of differently arranged black patterns of a limited number of shapes appearing on a white field and continually repeated in differing combinations are objective correlates not only of a bodily-based sensibility but of a mind that can, by means of the shapes, apprehend the meaning developed and recorded in visual (i.e., written) form by another mind or by oneself at an earlier time than that of the present reading. Careful attention to the writing on these pages will allow one to notice that they are combinations of twenty-six figures (fifty-two if you include the capitals and sixty or so if you include punctuation).[16] This is parallel with a biological consideration of human behavior, attending only to the sensorily available (with or without instrumental magnification) and not the expressivity of the behavior. Such a view dominates attention today as human behavior is reduced to observable neural functions.

READING

Our primary intellectual relation to the book is as something to be read. And this leads to an immediate defocusing of attention from the sensory features, which sink into subsidiarity as we get absorbed in the movement of thought. The words are still present in the field of visual awareness as the necessary condition for reading the meanings they indicate

---

15. Dewey, *Art as Experience* (New York: Capricorn, 1934), 125–6, 237–44.
16. Paul Weiss, the founder of the Metaphysical Society of America and *The Review of Metaphysics*, said that his first philosophical experience was when he was introduced to the alphabet at age 6. "You mean you can write about *anything at all* just by using these twenty-six letters! That's astonishing!" (I can still hear his emphatic delivery.)

and are part of the object appearing, within the focus that is the page of a book, from out of the visual surround which is present only subsidiarily. As we noted earlier, the words are something like glasses, which are instrumental to focusing what is seen but which are usually *seen through* rather than *looked at*. The printed words slip to the status of being instrumental to the apprehension of the meanings they instantiate. But unlike glasses, which do not appear when we are seeing through them, the written word must appear as it is rendered subsidiary in reading. We have noted that concepts are more like glasses than like a page in a book, though both are subsidiary in ordinary experience.[17]

The development of meaning through writing as well as its apprehension through reading rest upon reader and writer having been introduced into a linguistic tradition of speaking and writing that is different than that of other ethnic communities. Language brings each of us out of our private world into a public world of meaning. Speaking and writing bind individuals together synchronically and diachronically, contemporaneously as well as across generations, and, at the same time, they separate those individuals and generations from those belonging to other ethnically generated linguistic traditions.[18]

But let's say that someone took it upon herself to translate this book into German or Japanese or Swahili. One could assume that what we have said thus far could be successfully communicated across these different linguistic traditions that belong to different language groups, the German being directly related by genesis to the English of this text. And the reason for this translatability is that the eidetic constants of the visual and tactual fields and the minimum eidetic constants of regular correlation between visual, audile, and meaning patterns belong to humans as such. Germans, Japanese, and Africans, as well as English-speaking peoples, experience the same eidetic features in their visual and tactual fields: color, extension, horizon, light, perspective, coherence of perspectives, focus, and fringe in the visual field; and

---

17. See Michael Polanyi on the central concept of subsidiarity in our awareness. *The Study of Man* (Chicago: University of Chicago Press, 1959), 11–27. For an extended treatment, see *Personal Knowledge: Towards a Post-Critical Philosophy* (New York: Harper, 1964), 88, 92, 115.

18. When I listen to a group of people speaking a foreign language, I have the image of a circle into which I am not allowed to enter. It is a strong experience of otherness.

hard and soft, heavy and light, rough and smooth, cold and hot, dry and moist—all linked to extension and resistance—in the tactual field. Having that kind of visual and tactual experience is a necessary condition for reading this text and thus for its translation, as it is the necessary condition for carrying on everyday routines.

EIDETIC FEATURES

Let's press further into the conditions for the possibility of being able to give a trans-cultural eidetic account at these most rudimentary levels of human experience. Visual and tactual experience, and indeed all sensory experience, yields *individual* aspects of *individual* things in the environment of one's own bodily location. The eidetic features are not individual but universal; that is, they are known to apply wherever in space and whenever in time the conditions for their individual instantiation are met.[19] The Wherever and Whenever are given as encompassing the Here-and-Now of any given sensory experience. Distinctively human experience involves locating any here-and-now within the encompassing whole of Space and Time indeterminately exceeding whatever experiential or inferential filling we give to them.[20] We are not only located at a particular place in Space and Time, but we encompass these forms in thought and are thus able to view things *sub specie aeternitatis*, or under the aspect of eternity.[21]

The eidetic features arise from a sorting process in the accumulation of experiences. We learn to recognize, for example, that blue is not restricted to a given instance and is independent of what might accompany it, such as size or shape or distance or motion or rest or roughness or smoothness, etc. We also recognize that it appears in individuals within a range of hues and is affected by its appearance

19. See Aristotle: the senses give us the individual, the intellect, and the universal. *On the Soul* 3.4.417b.24.

20. In *Critique of Pure Reason*, Kant rightly viewed space and time as a priori forms of sensibility. I consider them the conditions for the possibility of apprehending universals, which apply "always and everywhere" their instances are found (A23/B37, p. 76ff).

21. John Locke, the father of sensate empiricism, remarked that if anything exists, eternity does. *Essay Concerning Human Understanding*, X, viii. Reflection upon the *conditions for* the possibility of that recognition would have shown the extreme limitation of his or any sensory empiricism. That seems an evident insight: How is that possible? How must we be in order that we have immediate access to that?

relative to other colors. At a higher level of abstraction, we learn to recognize that the notion *color* is not restricted to a given color but applies to all—blue, green, red, yellow, black, white and their combinations. Color is the generic correlate to the power of seeing. Unlike the concepts of its species (blue, red, yellow, etc.), there is no specific image associated with the notion of color.[22] Further, we learn to distinguish chromatic colors from (oxymoronically expressed) *achromatic* colors, where the latter—black, white, and their various gray combinations—are clearly distinguishable from the former. (It is the former color-type that color blind people cannot see.) We further learn to recognize primary colors by seeing how they combine to produce, and thus are ingredients in, other colors that are their respective complements: yellow and blue combining to produce green; red and yellow to produce orange; blue and red to produce purple; red, yellow, and blue, in certain proportions, to produce brown; and on and on to the myriad possible combinations used by painters.

The ability to abstract the eidetic constants is rooted, as we said, in our being referred in the first place to Space and Time as encompassing wholes. But that, in turn, is linked to the fact that any assertion one might make about a thing is a way of articulating the way in which the object of the assertion *is*. The notion of Being is articulated in each case in such a way as to anticipate all that a given thing *is*. We name *tree* the natural object from which the paper of this book has been made. Not only does that naming involve the subsumption of a given individual under the type, but it names the wholeness of what both the type and each given instance of it *is*. That wholeness in the case of the type *tree* is what the future of botanical inquiry will discover, much of which has already been disclosed, much more of which still remains to be disclosed.[23] Normally, in the case of the individual, the only

---

22. This gets us around Hume's view that a higher genus *involves* a washed-out image. *An Enquiry Concerning Human Understanding*, ed. E. Steinberg (Indianapolis: Hackett, 1977), §II, pp. 9–13. There is no image at all (except the images, essential to all thinking, involved in language) in the concept of awareness and the notion of Being that applies both to the sensorily given and to the imageless field of awareness.

23. See Husserl's empty and filled intentions in *Ideas*, 96, 121–24. See also Investigation 6 in his *Logical Investigations*, trans. J. N. Findlay, vol. 2 (Oxford: Routledge and Kegan, 1970), 220–22, 233–34.

aspects of the variations on that wholeness that are disclosed are those indicated by the external, sensorily presented face of the observed instance. In Owen Barfield's expression, our ordinary knowledge is "dashboard knowledge": knowing what to push, pull, and turn on the sensory surface to get the desired output, with little or no knowledge of what lies "under the hood" of that surface.

HIERARCHY OF TYPES

In explaining anything at all, we proceed in terms of showing its identity with and difference from others of its type. And in explaining the type, we proceed in the same manner, showing sameness and difference within a hierarchy of types, culminating, on the one hand, in the notions of *Thing* and *Properties*, and, on the other, in the notions of Sameness and Difference, Change and Fixity, all of which articulate the whole of the things that *are*. As Plato maintained, the fundamental eidetic features that run through all human experience are Being, articulated in Motion; and Rest, with all three concepts exhibiting Sameness and Difference, and with the latter pair of concepts participating in each other: Sameness is different from Difference, and Difference is the Same as itself.[24] Being is different from Motion or Rest, or else if it were the same as one of them, the other could not participate in it. And as Aristotle noted, Being is articulated into the changing things and the changeless types they instantiate; and the types are arranged in hierarchies of genera and species, exhibiting species-sameness among different individuals and generic sameness among different species, with each type differing from the others.[25]

Thus, in the case of our book, we identify *blue* or *heavy* as subtypes of *color* or *tactual quality* respectively, both of which, in turn, are specifications of *sensory quality*, which is a *property* (along with, perhaps, *intelligently* or *beautifully written*) of the *thing* we call a book. Blue, color, sensory feature, Property, and Thing are the progressively broader meanings implied in our identification of the book as blue.

---

24. Plato, *Sophist* 254d.
25. Aristotle, *Categories* 2a 13–3b 24.

The book came into being, is moved from place to place, and will eventually—alas!—disintegrate, whereas the notions of change, place, time, and disintegration, as well as the notion of book, remain fixed in their natures (although the book, unlike change, place, time, and disintegration, while also instantiating these features, came into being through human invention). And, of course, the visual patterns we use to represent the meanings themselves came into being at a certain point in the development of the English language into literacy and are fixed by convention, though they have themselves undergone modifications through time.

THE NOTION OF BEING

Let us have another go at the *notion of Being*. According to Aquinas and in truth, being is that which first arises in the mind when a developing person becomes able to reason, that is, to think of and apply principles.[26] When one reflects upon the notion of Being, one realizes that it has unrestricted generality: the notion of Being applies to absolutely everything and to everything about everything.[27] The claim that there is something "beyond Being" is nonsense since, if it *is*, then it is an instance of Being, understood as "what is the case."[28] The notion applies to what we know and to what we are only able to think as possible—an odd notion, since we only *know* what we encounter sensorily, what we can choose to infer from that, and from reflection upon our minds as encountering and inferring and choosing. The notion of Being is present from the first dim awakening to rationality as an empty reference: we are, as Heidegger rightly says, the *Question* of Being as the question about the Totality.[29] "What's it *all* about?" is a

26. *Summa theologiae*, I, q. 5. a. 3. For a sketch of the varying positions on the notion of Being in the history of the West, see my "First Things First: On the Primacy of the Notion of Being," *The Review of Metaphysics* 67, no. 4 (June 2014): 719–41.

27. See the chapter, "The Notion of Being," in Lonergan's *Insight*, 348–78. The claim to something "beyond being" presupposes a particular concept of being, beyond which there is something else in being.

28. To translate "beyond being" Plato's talk of the Good as *epekeina tes ousias*, makes little sense in Plato and in fact, Plato also described the Good as *to tou ontos phanotation*, "the most manifest *of being.*" *Republic* VI.518c.

29. Heidegger, Intro., I, 1, p. 3 and Intro., I, 4, p. 12. Human reality is not only concerned with its own being, but it has an understanding of the being of all beings unlike

question that tends to arise when what we cherish becomes impossible to obtain.

As the first notion to arise in the mind, the notion of Being, having unrestricted generality, orients us emptily toward the Whole. It also provides the unrestricted quality of the principle of noncontradiction, which we will shortly explore. Further, as Aristotle noted, Being cannot be a genus because it includes everything from which we abstracted to arrive at it.[30]

Nonetheless, there *is* a generic concept of Being: the *univocal* concept of Being-outside-of-nothing only as a minimum ground floor. The full being of each thing having existence is determined by the kind of being it is and by the way it instantiates its kind. This involves an *analogical* notion of Being referring to the plenitude of each being. Each being is a relation of essence and existence found in two great types: finite, where the type limits the level of existence; and Infinite, Whose essence is to be.[31] The kinds of being stand in a hierarchy determined in its finite types by how form is related to the matter it organizes, rising progressively above it as we move from life, to animal awareness, and on to the human mind.[32] Through experience and inference we discover and construct the articulations that fill in the initially empty space of meaning—a process that takes millennia and continues to develop through controlled experimentation.

By questioning we see that Being is not restricted to being finite, because we can continue to ask what might lie beyond any putative limit. The limitation of beings is a negation of the plenitude that would terminate our questioning. Further, in knowing an essence, Being takes on a universal mode as distinct from the individual mode it has in real existence. That means that essence is indifferent from being

---

itself. *BT,* Intro. II, 5, 13. The fundamental question, "Why is there being and not rather nothing?" covers every being.

30. Aristotle, *Metaphysics* III.iii.908a.

31. Aquinas, *On Being and Essence*, trans. A. Maurer (Toronto: The Pontificate Institute of Medieval Studies, 1968), 60.

32. As we noted earlier, in the general structure of *On the Soul,* Aristotle moves from general consideration of soul to the particulars of life, sensibility, and intellection, and from the height of the argument back to the sphere of locomotion, ending in touch: for the point of existence is to deal handily with things (e.g., writing down one's thoughts or lending a hand).

either in an individual or in a universal mode. That it exists in either mode involves something other than essence. That could not be a finite being because its essence is distinct from its mode of being. The only adequate explanation for the factual existence of essence in these two modes is a Being Whose Essence is To-Be. Limited beings can be because there is an Unlimited Ground: the Fullness of Being. Finite things as enduring relations to the Infinite Creative Source are thus linked to an abyss of Mystery.[33]

All of this is in the mode of universal abstraction. Heidegger's ground of metaphysics has to do with the heart: that whereby we are gripped by the concrete existence of beings and opened to an overarching sense of Being as a relation of the hidden Whole to us.[34] Being, so understood, is not a being, not even an Infinite Being. It is neither exclusively in the human being nor in that to which we attend; it is the basis for the manifestness of things to us. It is the essentially hidden, all-encompassing, the *Lethe* from which *a-letheia*, the unhiddenness, opens up a way of thinking.

* * *

Let us now turn to the *principle of noncontradiction*, which has the unrestricted universality of the notion of Being that it articulates. As Aristotle formulated it, *a being cannot both have and not have the same property at the same time and in the same respect.*[35] The instance of being from which we took our starting point, the book you are

33. See Aquinas, *Commentary on Dionysius's Divine Names* I.3.83–4, trans. Brian Davies, in his *Aquinas* (New York: Continuum, 2002), 54: "The most perfect [state] to which we can attain in this life in our knowledge of God is that he transcends all that can be conceived by us, and that the naming of God through remotion is most proper . . . The primary mode of naming God is through the negation of all things, since he is beyond all, and whatever is signified by any name whatsoever is less than that which God is." This parallels the basic moves made by Hegel, who begins with empty Being and points out that we can always question beyond any putative limit and that such a process can end only in an absolutely Infinite Being as "the Being of beings." He claims, with Parmenides, that the existence of nonbeing is a contradiction, but that multiple contradictions exist and call for their resolution in the infinite Ground. Needless to say, that requires much clarification and is subject to much dispute. See Hegel, *Hegel's Science of Logic*, 106.

34. Heidegger, "On the Essence of Truth," in *Basic Writings*, ed. and trans. D. Krell (New York: Harper and Row, 1977), 132ff. See my "The Heart in Heidegger's Thought," 445–62.

35. Aristotle, *Metaphysics* IV.iii.1005b.

reading, can be both blue and also not-blue—for example, black and white: blue on the book's cover, black and white alternating on each of its pages; but it cannot be both blue and black and white at the same time and in the same respect. Soaked in a vat of a certain type of blue dye, it could be all blue. But then it would cease to be the book that it is: it would be an empty book with blue pages. Further, it cannot be a book and not a book, though the components from which it is made can be, have been, and will be without being a book; and one day this book will be no longer, just as in days past it was not yet. Certain of its chemical components, modified, will continue, even when the book does not. Again, the logical hierarchy of types—color, sense-quality, property—each have their own identity; they are what they are and are not the other types that are at their respective logical levels: color is not sound or tactual feature, sense-quality is not intellectual content or behavioral property, and property is not the thing that has the property. And yet, color is a sense-quality, and any sense-quality is a property, and any property belongs to a thing. The principles of noncontradiction and identity involved here govern all rational discourse and are given, like the notion of Being they articulate, as having absolutely unrestricted universality. That's actually quite startling: we who have extremely restricted experience are aware of the absolutely unrestricted! How is that possible?

Though the principle of noncontradiction is always operative, we come to awareness of it only through developed experience. In order to formulate the principle, we need the sensory appearance of things and the operation of language that we have already analyzed, its flow through speech, and its fixity in meaning. But several other factors are involved. Recognizing *a being* implies its being *one* of *many*. Further, we identify a being by its endurance over time in displaying the sensory features as immediately given properties, which our sensory system produces as *phantasms*: modes of holistic and multifaceted appearance linked to our motor-habits. *Can* plays in relation to *is* as *possibility*; and *not* involves a negation that here becomes *impossibility*. *Property* involves an aspect of a being that itself may be observed in different respects at a given time and that may appear in a different respect at the same time or at a different time, but only as a dependent aspect of the thing whose property it is. *Time* involves being simultaneous with, prior to, or after. *And* as well as *both* involve joining several items. And each of the terms involves *sameness* in the empirical differences from which they abstract and a *difference* from both the empirical instances and other terms compatible with a generic sameness. *Being, Becoming and Fixity, Sameness and Difference* (Plato's Five Kinds), *Unity and Multiplicity, Possibility and Impossibility, Negation and Affirmation, Thing and Property, Joining and Separating, Past-Present-Future, Appearance and Reality, Part and Whole,* and *Awareness* in all the aspects operative within it—these various concepts are involved in recognizing and being able to formulate the principle of noncontradiction.

Aristotle first made explicit not only the principle but also the recognitions involved in formulating it. They remain the basis for all rational thought and the languages used to express it. Even Kant, with his restriction of knowing to the phenomenal order or order of appearance, nonetheless claimed at least the *thinkability* of the noumenal, or the thing-in-itself, with the understanding that whatever is thought about must be noncontradictory both in itself and with everything knowable in the phenomenal order.[36]

Being names the wholeness of the individual as instantiating the wholeness of its type, both of which—individual as well as typical wholeness—are included in the wholeness of whatever is. The notion of Being indicates that being human is referred to the encompassing Whole of what is, on account of which we have come to live out of some answer to the basic question: What's it *all* about? Or: How do we fit in *the whole scheme of things*? That is involved in the origin of religion; it is the basis for speculative philosophy; it is the basis for scientific inquiry; it is the basis for human language as such.

To repeat: the principles of noncontradiction and identity involved here govern all rational discourse, and like the notion of Being they articulate, they are given as having absolutely unrestricted universality. How is that possible? Let's leave that as a question for further exploration.[37]

---

36. Kant, *Critique of Pure Reason*, B188/A151–B191/A152, p. 220–23.
37. This is linked to another startling fact that Aquinas notes: any contingent event—one that need not exist but factually does—is such that, after the fact, it remains true *ever*

SENSORY INWARDNESS

Come back to seeing and touching the book. The former requires eye-balls, the latter hands, both located in a definite here-and-now, though capable of being in successively different Here's-and-Now's. Seeing and touching proceed respectively from the point of view or the physical state of one's organism; yet what they display is not just some state of one's organism but are instead the features of what lies *outside* that organism. From the standpoint of seeing and touching, an observing organism is spatially circumscribed, yet seeing and touching are not spatially circumscribed—or at least not in the same way. They involve a different way of being in space, a transcendence of observable organic circumscription, a manifestation of what lies outside—in the case of a given act of seeing, of whatever appears within the horizon set up by the location of one's own organism. All animals—including us—live *outside* their organic insides. As Dewey put it, they live "outside their skins," cognitively "out there," *with* what appears in its environment.[38] Seeing is not just inside one's head. It is clearly and astonishingly *with* what is seen outside the organism in the peculiar mode of being-with that we call *manifestation* or *appearance.*

I underscore "*astonishingly*" here as well as "*outside* the organism" because an empirical description of the process traces the route of light transmission, absorption by and reflection from bodily surfaces, refraction through the lenses inside the eyeballs, projection of images on the rods and cones of the retina, and electrical stimulation of the optic nerve, which carries the stimulus via a series of electro-chemical switches to the visual cortex in the back of the brain. All this "naturally" leads one to conclude that what I see are images in the back of my brain produced by the process just described.[39] It is just that claim

---

after, through and beyond the time that it existed. Aquinas, *Quaestiones*, I, 6 ad 4. See also *De interpretatione* I.12n5; *Summa theologiae*, I, q. 22, a. 4, ad 1–3. What is startling is that we can recognize this. How must we then be structured? Or, in Kantian terms, what are the conditions of possibility in us of this recognition?

38. John Dewey, *Experience and Nature* (London: Allen and Unwin, 1929), 282–86, 333–40.

39. For this position, see Francis Crick, *The Astonishing Hypothesis: The Scientific Search for the Soul* (New York: Charles Scribner's Sons, 1994), 167, 219, 222. See my refutation in "What Is Seeing? A Phenomenological Approach to Neuro-Psychology," 10.

which exceeds scientific evidence and becomes a philosophic claim that is self-refuting.

If it is the case that what I see are images inside my brain, then I could not exhibit the visual evidence for the above description of events outside my organic inside. Vision itself is not part of visual evidence. I call *natural* the conclusion that what we see are images in the brain, because it spontaneously follows from taking empirical objectivity as the exclusive index of reality—an instance of what I call the *optomorphic fallacy*, that is, considering all things in terms of how they appear to our optical equipment. This is a subspecies of the more general *empiriomorphic fallacy* (viewing all things in terms of sensory objectivity) to which I will return later.[40]

With the physical-physiological description of what is involved in seeing, *nothing has been revealed about seeing itself*, though much has been discovered about its necessary preconditions, which allow ophthalmologists to fix problems with visual functioning. One is tempted—and all too often one gives in to the temptation—to understand seeing as focused upon that supposed image in the back of the brain. But what we want to know is what it is it to see focally. The physical-physiological account, fascinating—indeed, astonishing!—and helpful as it is in many ways, only puts off the question. Seeing the image in the back of the brain would still involve the differentiation of seeing from the seen. Seeing transcends the seeable apparatus that makes seeing itself possible. Seeing furnishes the framework within which the seeable can appear; but seeing cannot appear within that framework because, though seeing is *spatially* confined by its relation to the horizon, it is not (as is what is seen) an organically circumscribed object inside the head.

So seeing involves a different way of being in space than that of a seeable body, "inhabiting" as it does the perceptual space *outside* its own seeable boundaries within the horizon of the field of vision. Once again, seeing is "with" the seeable objects in a *sui generis* way of being-with, namely, in the mode of the objects' *appearing*, of their *manifes-*

---

40. Democritus had a less refined version of the above: seeing for him was having an image in his head. Aristotle noted that Democritus would then have to explain why mirrors do not see. *On Sense and Sensible Objects* 6.445b10.

tation to a seeing organism. One is engaged with them "out there": outside one's own organic inside, outside the brain and the visual apparatus. Through the existence of seeing animals, things not only *are*, but are *manifest*; they *appear*.

Again, a given act of seeing occurs from a point of view and is supplemented by moving the object or by moving around it, by touching it, and by other avenues of sensory experience. As we noted before, past experiences are automatically retained and synthesized, so that we recognize the sameness of the object in and through the differentness of the aspects experienced within the field of a given sense and in correlation with experiences from other senses. Our point here is that seeing is also not confined to the present moment, but that in it the past it enters through re-cognition into the constitution of present experience. Further, that the sameness of an object, given as one through the variations of differing perspectives within differing sensory fields, can be so given involves the temporal endurance of a retentive center of awareness in correlation with the temporal endurance of the objects upon which it focuses. The seer must endure through time, as must the seen, each continuing in some real sense as the same through the different variation of their aspects.

Again, in the early stages of human development—which parallel animal development—what is seen, touched, heard, and smelt function in relation to taste as serving the organism's needs for food and drink. The sensory features evoke appetite, which anticipates its future satisfaction. In the adolescent stage of development, the emergence of sexual desire for the most part follows the sensory presentation of members of the opposite sex. Operating in function of organically based desire, the sensory field involves the anticipation of the future of organic satisfaction in terms of nutrition and sex, which serve the survival needs of the individual in the first case and of the species in the second. Sensing thus occurs and takes on its present tonality in function of the anticipation of future satisfaction.

How things appear in the sensory field, then, involves a way of being in space and time for the activity of sensing that exceeds simply observable location and spatial circumscription of the observing organism and that exceeds the immediate co-presence of the sensed and the sensing. Focused upon objects given as outside one's own spatially circumscribed organism, the system that underpins awareness gathers up the past through learning to recognize and act; and it anticipates the future satisfaction of organic need. Awareness thus exhibits a triple "ecstasy": it stands out of its own physical circumscription in being present to objects outside in its environment, it stands out of its own present by gathering the past through having learnt to identify and deal with types of things, and it stands out of its own past and present by anticipating future satisfaction. Futurity thus takes priority in sensory observation.[41]

In phenomenological terms, the reference of awareness beyond itself to its objects, past, present, and future, is called the *intentionality* of consciousness. The term has a narrower and a wider usage. In ordinary usage it is associated with what we do deliberately, as in "I didn't do that *intentionally*." But in phenomenology, it has a wider, more generic usage. Deliberate intentionality is rafted upon a more basic *spontaneously functioning intentionality*.[42] Things in the environment must make their original appearance in my wakeful life before I can take up a deliberate relation to them. "As I open my eyes, I might see you coming at a distance." (This "mere seeing" is an example of this *spontaneously functioning intentionality*). "Realizing that I owe you some long overdue money, I *intentionally* try to avoid you." (This is the *deliberate sense of intentionality* that builds on the first). Opening my eyes provides me with an operative field that forces itself upon my attention; seeing spontaneously intends the object. Within that spontaneously given operative field, I am able to make my own deliberate choices regarding my relation to the objects presented.

PHENOMENALLY EMPTY SPACE

Return now to your seeing and touching the book in relation to the discoveries of physics. As you turn the pages, they appear quite smooth. As you read, they appear as separated from your eyeballs by empty space and the book itself appears as a solid and placid object. But con-

---

41. See Heidegger, *BT*, II, III, 65, 329ff, though his focus is upon distinctively human spatiotemporal "ecstasy."
42. Edmund Husserl, *Crisis*, 233–37.

sider a microbe crawling over the surface of the page: to it the surface is craggy. Consider what physics tells us about the character of the underlying components: they are not so much things as processes, pulsating centers of energy irradiating their light spectra. Further, when rays of light penetrate the room, you discover the "empty" space to be full of dust particles. When you consider the sound of the air conditioner, you realize that sound invisibly occupies the apparently empty space between your eyeball and the book. Then, from what you learned by trusting the reports found in physics texts, you realize that between your eyeballs and the book, there are air molecules, photons, radio and television waves, and all the other irradiations of the electro-magnetic spectrum uncovered instrumentally by physics—all of which do not appear directly within the field in which the book appears to you. All of this appears through understanding certain regularities within the field of appearance that have grounded the construction of instruments. By reading the screens on the surfaces of such instruments, we come to know something of what underlies our immediate field of awareness. We witness a recording of the impact of the otherwise unseeable within the field of unaided observation.

We therefore understand that seeing and touching operate within fixed thresholds that filter out much more than they admit. Seeing is only possible if we cannot see all. If we could see the air molecules, then we could not see our food or mate or approaching enemy; if we could feel all that impacts our skin, then we would go mad. The senses carve out a limited field of manifestation, in the first place to serve biological need. As Nietzsche said, the senses lie: they give the illusion of the smoothness, placidity, and solidity of objects separated from our eyeballs by empty space; but such a "lie" is necessary for the ends of life.[43] Though a kind of illusion occurs, what is presented is not pseudo-food, pseudo-mate, pseudo-offspring, and pseudo-enemy, but *real* food and mate and offspring and enemy.[44] The mode of presenta-

43. Nietzsche, "On Truth and Lies in an Extra-Moral Sense," in *Portable Nietzsche*, trans. W. Kaufmann (New York: Viking, 1954), 42–47. See my commentary on this in *Existentia* 25, fasc. 3–4 (2015): 201–13.

44. I think Kant should be read this way: things appear for us, in terms of the structure of our experience and especially in terms of appetite, as real "things in themselves," although the inner reality is hidden from us. *Critique of Pure Reason*, A46/B63, p. 96–97.

tion is regular and is linked causally to the regularities of the things apprehended so that one can rely upon it to reach one's organic ends and to move beyond organic need to explore scientifically what "underlies" or "stands behind" sensory appearance.[45] Meditation on the phenomenal character of perceived space combined with what is known scientifically about all that fills this space could again lead to the *realization* of the strangeness of everyday givenness.

GENERIC FEATURES OF SENSORY OBJECTS

Not only seeing and touching, but every act of sensing presents to us objects that are: (1) individual; (2) actual; (3) immediately present here-and-now; (4) circumscribed by their solid boundaries, especially in the case of the living; and (5) set in immediately verifiable causal relations with their antecedents and consequents. In examining these features, we contrast each of them with the status of the mind that views them, and we can also consider their relation to the powers that underlie sensory surface. I have already shown how animal awareness involves being, not physically, but in living awareness, outside of its sensorily observable outside and outside the immediate present, through having learnt from experience and anticipating future satisfaction and thus having every "immediate now" mediated. I have chosen first to attend abstractly to the sensory features I have isolated, disregarding their characteristic of always having entered into awareness as announcements of holistically functioning things.[46]

We might note that the previous sentences consist of universal terms, describing what I take to be essential features of *all instances* of what is given in sensation in its various forms. There is a double reflective move involved here: a comprehensive reflection upon the general features of what is given in sensation (which we have pursued above) and a reflection upon what is involved in that reflection, namely, universal terms. I have already called attention to the alternation of personal presence and absence as well as the alternation of

45. Descartes, *Meditations*, VI, p. 75–80.
46. Here we are following Hegel; in his survey of the field of experience, he begins with sensation, moves to perception, and on to intellection. *Introduction to the System*, 44ff.

spatial fixity and the temporal flow of thought in generating and in reading the text. I have suggested sets of reflective moves and will further suggest a set that will position all of this within the most encompassing framework. Let this strategy be part of the mental horizon that you, the reader, take with you throughout this text—reflecting upon immediate awareness and then reflecting in ever more comprehensive ways upon that reflection.[47]

Sensory objects are all *individual*. One cannot even imagine a sensory object that is not so. This is an indubitable *eidos*, and thus a *universal* truth about this realm. Sensory objects are also all *actual*. This contrasts with what is potential. What we cannot visually see or in any way sensorily apprehend is the *potentiality* or the *power behind*, so to speak, or *beneath* the manifest surface: that of the sensed as well as of the sensing. And what is peculiar about the native power of any entity is that each individual power (for example, my own power of seeing) is not simply individual like all sensorily observable objects but is a *universal* orientation that requires not simply individuals, but individuals of a corresponding *natural kind* of object in the environment.[48] Seeing as a power is oriented toward *all* individual features of the kind that we call colored. And the capacity to be seen is oriented toward *all* organisms that can see. Now kinds are universal: a kind is found in *all* individual instances; but sensory objects are all individual.

In "The Imaginary Invalid" in 1673, Moliere made fun of the claim that the reason opium puts one to sleep is that it has "dormitive power." That does not at all explain what there is about opium in particular that has this power. However, the notion of power here is important at a more general level where we note that a power in any given individual is not simply individual but has a universal orientation. The notion of power thus undercuts the split between individual and universal that we tend to assign to things, on the one hand, and to intellectual recognition, on the other. In a given power, the distinction is *aufgehoben*, or "synthesized."

---

47. I would claim that in this we are simply following the directions Plato gives in his Line of Knowledge in *Republic* VI. See my "Image, Structure, and Content," 495–514.

48. This clearly grounds the existence of natural kinds, despite all attempts to deny them.

We have the capacity to move beyond individuals and recognize the universality of the orientation of powers and the universality of object-types as such. That is why we can have science, and, indeed, why we can have language where the sound or visual shape of a word is a sensorily available stand-in for the intellectual apprehension of the type in a concept. As we noted, concepts function like glasses: we normally and unreflectively look *through* them and not *at* them; but we are now attending reflectively *to* them.

This gives a way of taking up Plato's idea that the definition of Being is the capacity of acting and being acted upon.[49] To be at all involves a set of capacities related to whatever surrounds it in the system it inhabits. An isolated atom is imaginable, but it cannot exist; things come in systems. Science puts them to the test to find out what their capacities are for acting and being acted upon.

What is true of native powers is also true of acquired skills. A skill is a capacity to deal with *all* the individuals of the kind correlative to the skill. If I become a skilled carpenter, then I can deal with all individual instances requiring the work of a carpenter that are correlative with the level of skill I acquire. An ophthalmologist is one who has mastered the skill of curing problems with the eyes *as such*, that is, not just the eyes of the patient with whom she is dealing in any given instance, but of any and every individual who comes to the doctor with eye problems. The universality involved on the part of the skilled physician and on the part of the patients she cures is not something one can see, but clearly something one can and does come to know—even though one might say, metaphorically speaking, "I *see* what the problem is."

Though sensing is the kind of experience that involves sensing beings living, as Dewey put it, "outside their skin," focused upon things that appear in the environment, the claim of scientific empiricism is that sensing occurs inside the brain.

INSIDE AND OUTSIDE: APPEARANCE AND BEING

Returning to our observations on the functioning of the notion of Being, we see the basis for a distinction between the organ-dependent

49. Plato, *Sophist* 348c.

appearance and the *being* or the full reality of what is there to be sensorily apprehended. Whereas animals are monopolar, living outside in their environment and directed by their appetites in relation to what appears in that environment, human beings are bipolar, like a magnet, with the sensory pole appearing in tandem with the reference to Being as a whole. Animals live in the sensorily appearing world; but in the human case, the sensory surface expresses (to a reflective mind) the rising up to appearance and the sinking back into hiddenness of what appears in the sensory field. But to grasp that is to detach oneself from organic need in order to consider the truth of what is, including the eidetic constants involved in the mode of sensory presentation. Here the senses do not serve organic need but furnish the starting point for reflection that terminates in understanding universal truths both regarding appearance, such as we have been exercising, and regarding the underlying fullness that is partially revealed and enduringly concealed as science instrumentally presses further into the underlying structure of things.

In considering the findings of physics, chemistry, and biology, we should note the distinction between the presentation of the body as empirical object and that same body as lived through by a conscious subject. In the latter case, the sensory presentation mediates the *expressivity* of the body through gesture, through general comportment, and especially through linguistic expression. The physiologist and the ophthalmologist, though concretely focused upon the sensory object, nevertheless *abstract* from the concrete expressivity of the body as such and especially of the eyes. Even in the case of botany, the kinds of things investigated express their moving toward their adult stage in growth, their sustenance of that stage in nutrition, and their moving toward reproduction in developing from their seed.

And, as we already noted, insofar as seeing and touching are functions that serve organic needs, they are focused not simply upon kinds of *aspects* (like color and heaviness revealed by seeing and touching respectively), but upon those kinds of *things* correlated with those needs—that is, upon those kinds of things that can nourish and those kinds that can satisfy sexual desire. The kinds of aspects are correlated with the sensory capacities, the kinds of things with the appetites that follow synesthetic presentation. If the sensing capacities are selective and to some extent distortive and are thus phenomenal, the appetites require the *realities* presented in this partial way through sensation. Furthermore, synesthetic presentation and the evocation of organic need are tied to the capacity for locomotion and move the animal in the direction of the desired object or away from the threatening object. The achievement of the end is realized through the apprehension of the object involved: eating food, mating with one's sexual partner, fighting with one's enemy, or taking care of one's offspring. Thus, as we have noted, all the senses culminate in tactual apprehension. This synthetic series displays the unity of animal being over the time of its various linked operations.

Sensing does not occur as the appearance of discrete features presented in a perspectival way to distinct senses in a purely theoretical manner. It occurs as focused pragmatically upon what appears in a "synesthetic" way as functioning wholes, objects of appetite. The display of such objects allows animal perceivers to adjust their behavior to reach their own organic goals. Recognizing the priority of this "lived" relation, our approach, nonetheless, abstractly isolate the various "intentional strands" from the experience in order to let our judgments be measured by what is given eidetically.[50]

INTELLECTION AND CHOICE

If sensing involves a different way of being in space and time than that of a physically circumscribed body, then mind or intellect involves a different way than that of a sensing being. Mind involves being in relation to *Space and Time as encompassing wholes* by reason of being directed beyond to the question of *Being as a whole*. Like

50. This integrates some otherwise disjunct observations of Aristotle in *On the Soul*: that touch is the basic sense (2.4.415a 4, 3.12.434b.24); that the specialized senses are rooted in a "common sense" that involves "awareness of awareness" (3.2.425b.12); and that Democritus, who held seeing to be identical with mirroring, had no explanation for why mirrors do not see, even though they hold an image. Aristotle's order of treatment in *On the Soul* moves from the general notion of *psyche* (2.1.412aff) through the hierarchy of capacities—from nutritive (2.4.415b.28aff), to sentient (2.4.416b.332ff), to rational (3.4.429a.10ff)—only to "descend" to locomotion (3.9.432a.15) and culminate in touch (3.12.434a.22ff). See my "On Touch: A Phenomenological Inquiry," *Southwestern Philosophy Review* 17, no. 1 (January 2000): 19–26.

the notion of Being, Space and Time are empty notions, but they contract Being to the domain within which we, as embodied beings, dwell. This directedness toward Being as a whole not only makes possible the ongoing filling in of the space of meaning between the plenitude of sensory evidence and the emptily intended Whole by eidetic inventory, inference, and construction—it also pries us loose from all the determinate modes of givenness, both of things and of ourselves, and condemns us to choose between the real possibilities for understanding and for action in our situation, insofar as we are aware of them. Mentally, through the operation of the notion of Being aimed at the fullness of what-is, we stand at a distance from every individual aspect and thing: that is the privilege and the curse of our native freedom. Because we have such freedom, we each stand before a unique set of possibilities from which we must choose. Choice involves a non-sensorily observable causal origin of action that enters into the visually observable seamless continuity of antecedents and consequents.

But choosing one set of possibilities kills others. There is thus always a measure of unfulfillment and unfulfillability about our situation this side of the grave. Contrary to what the U.S. Army claims, you cannot "Be all that you can be"; at best it should say, "Be the *most* you can be." You must choose what you will be and not be, as your situation presents it and as you understand it; and choosing one line of action precludes others.

Yet sensing observation alone yields, as Hume claimed, a seamless continuity between antecedent and consequent states, with no indication of the causal grounds expressed through that surface.[51] Such sensory empiricism abstracts from the *expressivity* of living forms. Every living thing expresses, through the way it grows, the end toward which it is headed: its fully functional, reproductive adult stage. Hume's sensory empiricism abstracts from the expressivity of animal behavior. The ophthalmologist abstracts from the expressivity of the eyes to focus solely upon the full sensory presence of the eyeballs— not to mention the expressivity involved in the use of language. Purely

---

51. Hume, *A Treatise of Human Nature*, vol. 1, bk. 1 (London: J. M. Dent and Sons, 1911), §6, pp. 242–45.

sensory empiricism has no access to the state of awareness from the depth of which free choice and freely chosen action arise.

Further, let me add that reference to Being, by giving us distance from our appetitive relation to things, allows for the possibility of things being present fully *as other-in-themselves* and not simply as other-for-my-needs. It allows one to seek and acknowledge the truth of things. It also allows one to act and even to sacrifice oneself for the sake of the other. This distance functions likewise in relation to the sensory appearance itself: we can experience it as beautiful, giving it, as Kant would have it, "disinterested" favoring, unconstrained by our appetites.

HUMAN BIPOLARITY

So as human beings we have by nature several tiers of structure: (1) the level investigated by physics and chemistry, which is subsumed under (2) the operation of a comprehensively functioning organism examined by physiology, which in the case of the animal, produces organs for (3) the emergence of the field of desirous sensation as one pole of the field of consciousness whose other pole is (4) empty reference to the encompassing totality. The latter grounds intellectual operations not only of eidetic inventory, but also of thinking of alternative ways of construing the character of the hidden totality out of which the immediate field of manifestation emerges. Reference to the totality also grounds choice among those possibilities of action determined by the scope of one's understanding of the given situation.

Ways of thinking and ways of acting become habitual and are passed on to the ones born of those who inculcate in their offspring their ways in the form of practices and the institutions that support the practices. Thus emerges a cultural field of meaning and action to fill the initially empty space of meaning situated between the plenitude of the sensory field and the naturally empty reference to the totality. Because of the limited mode of understanding involved in any cultural world, and because of the selection of certain lines of action among the many that are possible, correlate with limited understanding, such worlds are necessarily plural. But the founding structure of humanness as empty reference to the Whole grounds a dialogical imperative to measure any putative claims about the character of the Whole against the eidetic constants in the field of experience. This founding structure equally grounds the expansion of experience involved in the experience of different cultures and in the various modes of methodically controlled inquiry into different aspects of experience found in the sciences.

As I have said, while animals are monopolar, human beings are essentially and magnetically bipolar: animals are sensorily aware, caught in the extended and flowing Now, and governed by their appetites, while intellectual beings are referred to the Whole as eternally encompassing. As organisms, we are observable; we are objects of public encounter and scientific inspection. But observability is relative to the peculiarities of sensory observation that gives us directly neither the underlying powers of the organism nor the awareness that inhabits it, as I have taken some pains to show. Our basic relation to our own organism is a "lived" one. We each live in and through our bodies, "in touch" with them as functional wholes. The organism generates the sensory field as a synesthetic-orectic-kinesthetic whole: synthesizing, desiring, and moving in order to apprehend. Sensory features are automatically retained and put together (synthesized) with other sensory features. Their organic function is to manifest opportunities and threats to the appetites (the *orectic* or desirous feature) that move us (the kinesthetic feature) in the direction of the fulfillment of our appetites.

This is the most obvious, the "positive" focus of our awareness. But that stands in polar opposition to our reference to the Whole via the notion of Being as all-encompassing. That notion expresses the basic *eros* of distinctively human existence: emptiness aimed at plenitude, the mortal seeking the immortal, as Plato would have it.[52] This gives us fundamental distance from any aspect within the Whole—even the whole of our own lives—so that we can assess and choose among the possibilities afforded by our individual situations. We choose from among the possibilities as we understand them; the broader our understanding, the wider the range of choices. Understanding and choice become habitual; passed on to others, they form the traditions of understanding and practice that constitute a cultural world.

52. Plato, *Symposium* 208a.

ENCULTURATION AND THE HEART

Any given individual enters into a cultural world with a genetic stamp and a natural reference to totality. Enculturation narrows and focuses the more remote possibilities that such a nature has, establishing the proximate possibility of discovering and unlocking more complex proximate possibilities for action and thought. There was no proximate possibility of Neanderthals discovering their talent as pianists, because during their time there were no pianos, no piano repertoires, and no developed techniques for complex performance. Only a long history of instrumental technology and of the development of complex musical forms and performance techniques institutionalized in the conservatory allowed the possibilities lying fallow in the gene pool to be discovered, actualized, and perfected. The institutional matrix frees distinctively human possibilities for multiple forms of development.

Born with distinctive genetically based individual possibilities into a specific culture, yet set at an infinite distance from the determinate features of both biology and culture because of one's natural empty reference to the totality, one gradually makes one's own choices among the understood possibilities. Stamped by genes and culture, one produces one's own stamp upon that stamp by the sedimented history of one's choices: one forms one's own character (from the Greek *karakter* or "stamp"). This three-leveled structure (genetic, cultural, and personal-historical) provides at each wakeful moment and for each individual human the concrete Me, everything an individual objectively is. Any Me is fixed by its past; but such fixing provides the self with its real possibilities as the artist's material, the understanding and shaping of which is the responsibility of the conscious *I*, the cutting edge of the multidimensional psychophysical whole we call a human being. What am I going to do with Me?

Now, at the center of the Me is what a long tradition calls *the heart*.[53] Residue of the whole of one's past, the heart is the locus of the felt proclivity to behave in a determinate manner as correlated with significant presences, magnetic attractors that immediately solicit our attention. Each individual lives in and through her or his heart. The

---

53. We will explore this in more detail in chapter 4, pp. 83–106.

heart spontaneously defines what is of interest, on which one is inclined to spend time and effort. As its default mode, it moves automatically toward friends and particular projects. One is most deeply and fully present to the objects of the heart, while other things fall away in zones of progressive indifference or hostility.

Aristotle noted that there are two ways of understanding anger: from the standpoint of the *phusikos* (today's physiologist), it is the heating of blood around the heart; and from the standpoint of the *dialektikos* (philosopher), it is a response to perceived wrongs.[54] That distinction and the relation between the two aspects remains the perennial issue.

The linkage of living experience with the heart as a physiological organ involves emotional phenomena, ways in which we are moved simultaneously physically and psychologically. The consideration of the heart as a muscle that is observable within the visual field abstracts from its direct relation to emotional phenomena. It follows the abstractions that visual and tactual manipulation provide by their nature and that ground the scientific study of the heart as a muscular pump in the center of the chest. But the fundamental question here is whether the emotional experiences of *the heart* belong to a "mental" substance other than the "physical" or whether the observable heart muscle is an external expression relative to a seeing organism (the cardiologist) of what "from the inside" is an emotional state of an indissolubly psycho-physical whole.

The heart is the locus for our passions, which beyond those grounded immediately in our physiology, arise by reason of culture's provision of differing kinds of goods, not only physical possessions and things of beauty, but also sports, arts, sciences, businesses, and religious understandings and practices. To the biologically based desire for sex, culture adds exclusivist possession, which evokes feelings of tenderness and care as well as those of rage and jealousy.

Nonetheless, by reason of our founding but empty reference to the whole of Being, we are, at the highest level of our being, set at a distance from our own hearts and must assess their concrete direction. We are

---

54. Aristotle, *On the Soul* 1.1.403a.29.

guided in this by the deep dimension Plato identified as *Eros*, or the desire of the mortal for the immortal, appearing at the highest level in the underlying desire of our nature for the principle of the Whole. This underlying desire is generated by our "heart of hearts," alignment with which is the fundamental task of our nature. Because of the limitation of understanding (by individuals and cultures) of the Whole and the wholeness of each entity within the Whole, and by reason of the requirement of killing lines of real possibility for action by individuals and cultures making choices, there is a sense of in-principle incompletion built into the nature of humanness. Hence the structural grounds of what Augustine described as the essentially "restless heart."[55]

There is a peculiar dialectic, in the dispassionately passionate pursuit of the truth about our place in the Whole, between *What* we might affirm and *How* we are related to it. Søren Kierkegaard calls attention to this in his distinction between the objective thinker and the subjective thinker.[56] The focus on intellectual endeavor is upon the *What*, whatever is objectively true, independent of perceiving beings. The *How* is a matter of one's disposition. In considering death—even one's own death—one can take it objectively and on its basis purchase an insurance policy for one's family. But one's death can also become "a living presence." As a recently deceased friend of mine said, "We all know we are going to die; but we don't *believe* it." Belief here is not an assent to propositions; it is "being gripped by Ultimate Concern," as Tillich would have it.

Martin Heidegger distinguished "authentic," or subjectively appropriated existence, and "inauthentic," or not fully appropriated existence.[57] The second is the mode of the "They"—the anonymous "One" in which a person is largely a reflex of the culture or group to which she or he belongs and to which she or he is inclined to appeal

55. Augustine, *Confessions*, trans. W. Watts, vol. 1 (Cambridge, Mass.: Harvard University Press, 1974), I.i.I/2. We will explore further the notion of the heart and the life of feeling in our next chapter.

56. Kierkegaard, *Concluding Unscientific Postscript to Philosophical Fragments*, trans. A. Hannay (Cambridge: Cambridge University Press, 2009), 77–79, 136–38.

57. *BT*, II, IV, 69, 355. *Authentic* plays opposite *inauthentic*, which suggests phoniness and is not at all what Heidegger is after. That is why I suggest "appropriated" and "unappropriated" as better translations of *eigentlich* and *uneigentlich*.

for authorization. It is the situation of Kierkegaard's suspicious "Christendom," that is, of sociological Christianity where what it means to *become* a Christian is buried underneath the supposition that one, like all typical others in one's milieu, *is* a Christian. In fully appropriated existence, the What penetrates to the heart, and the individual person is more deeply present, more fully engaged. In Martin Buber's terms, one moves from Object to Presence and from apprehending to being-apprehended.[58]

The plurality of cultures clues us in to the fact that there is a peculiar surplus of mystery over any verifiable hold we have on things. Even our scientifically expanded "island of light" is rafted upon the encompassing darkness of the mystery of Being, which always exceeds our grasp, no matter how comprehensive.[59] Here the heart operates at its deepest level as native longing for the Plenitude permanently deferred this side of the grave. The "sense of mystery" is something we can deliberately cultivate through appropriate meditation. Such meditation is not aimed, as in René Descartes' *Meditations on First Philosophy*, at conceptual mastery reserved for a talented elite; it is aimed—in Heidegger's terms—at "letting things be," letting them take hold of us. Such meditation can deepen our sense of the coming to presence of their mysterious depth into which they sink back even as they rise up into our field of experience.[60]

Our founding reference to the Whole, always projected into a reserve of encompassing mystery, imposes upon us a dialogical imperative: a requirement of entering sympathetically into ways of understanding and behavior different than our own. That entry involves an understanding of the formation of traditions. Its aim is to expand our own hold on things and the range of possibilities for our own choices. It gives us different eyes with which to see. It shows us how to see the same differently and thus in an enriched fashion. I propose this as a central goal of liberal education. It involves freeing us from the limi-

---

58. Heidegger, *BT*, I, IV, 27, 118–22; Kierkegaard, *Concluding Unscientific Postscript*, 308–9, 313–14; Buber, *I and Thou*, 63–67, 113–15.

59. David Hume recommended expanding the island of light and forgetting about the surrounding darkness. He never asked how we apprehend the latter. *Enquiry Concerning Human Understanding*, I, 5–6.

60. Heidegger, "Memorial Address," 54–57.

tations of our own individual proclivities and our own upbringing. It teaches us both appreciation for the concrete possibilities afforded by a given tradition and critical assessment of the limitations involved therein. Indeed, that is the explicit aim of this book: to examine differing ways of looking at the human phenomena with a view toward understanding them in a fashion that is more enriched than that of our unreflective opinions.

Especially with regard to religious tradition, one needs the reflective step back afforded by philosophy and science. Though providing security and meaning, religion is often afflicted by the narrowness of intolerance, fanaticism, and superstition, all too often spilling over into destructive behavior in inquisitions, crusades, and jihads, which are "holy wars" that violate the integrity and freedom of the victims. As Martin Buber said, "Just as there is nothing that can hide from us the face of the other as morality can, so there is nothing that can hide from us the face of God as religion can."[61] What we especially need is an examination of the generation and transformation of a religious tradition to begin to understand the possibilities for its own enrichment and the limitation of its self-understanding in any given epoch. We see such a development especially in Augustine (who assimilated Neoplatonism), Aquinas (who assimilated Aristotle and Augustine), and Hegel (who assimilated the tradition as a whole).[62]

FLATLAND REVISITED

Armed with the observations we have made, let us return to the Flatland story in the Prologue. The physical-physiological account of visual and tactile sensation I briefly sketched limited its evidence to the particulars of individual actuality, seen and touched. It seemed to necessitate thinking of individual seers as inside the observable limits of their skins, of seeing as an event that takes place inside the skull at the back of the brain, of what-is as actual and contained within the present moment, and of all experience as determined by antecedent conditions. Pressed along the lines of the manipulative observation of

61. Buber, *Between Man and Man*, trans. R. G. Smith (Boston: Beacon, 1961), 18.
62. For a treatment of these assimilations, see my *Ratio et Fides*, 67–108, 130–50.

more and more mechanisms, it terminates in the vision of humanness as a highly complex mechanism that is different from other mechanisms only in degree and not in kind.

My contention is that this is a Flatlandian account and that its claimants are victims of an *optomorphic* or a more general *empiriomorphic fallacy*, thinking that the only thing that is evident is what can be seen and touched (correlatable with the heard, smelt, and tasted) or is modeled upon the actuality and individuality of so-called "empirical objects." That means that one thinks only in terms of how things appear as three-dimensional solids, having length, breadth, and depth, and moving in time as a fourth measurable parameter or a fourth *dimension*.

I would maintain that the kinds of evidence indicated entail our thinking in a way that cannot be reduced to such dimensions, and that we must think of ourselves as constituted not only by the ordinary four dimensions, but also by a further set of "dimensions" that stand to the sensorily appearing dimensions as inner to outer. Indeed, I would maintain that there are three progressively deeper "interior" dimensions related both to the observable body and to each other as inside to outside or as surface to depth, depending upon how each inner dimension is related to Space and Time.

I place the word "dimension" in quotation marks to indicate its metaphoric usage. Beyond Space and Time there are no other *measurable* parameters, so the metaphor "limps." But employing the metaphor indicates there are further features than what appears non-expressively in sensory experience and upon which natural science tends to focus. The further "dimensions" are "interior" because they cannot be found by exploring the sensorily available as such, no matter how far electron microscopes can penetrate into the deeper layers of the interior of the brain. The metaphor of "inner dimensions" indicates the difference of conscious life from the visually accessible. But the metaphor of dimensions suggests distinguishable difference together with inseparable conjunction. The human being is one psycho-physical whole; and the distinction and relation between inner and outer "dimensions" eliminates the position that distinction here involves separateness, as in Descartes' radical distinction between

Extension and Thought, which lies behind the modern scientific tradition.[63] Mindless matter is now thought to eliminate thought as significantly other than the brain or as an inexplicable functionless epi-
phenomenon.[64]

Reflecting upon the act of seeing, we maintain that it cannot be
properly considered as wholly inside the skin and in the back of the
brain of the seer. What are actually seen by the physicist examining the
physical basis for color and the physiologist inspecting the organic basis
for visual perception are things appearing precisely *outside* the organic
insides of the scientific observers. Furthermore, immediately given
colors usually function subsidiarily in relation to the recognition of
objects enduring through changes and exhibiting different sensible
qualities from different perspectives. Such recognition involves the
retention of past experiences. And, since, from the standpoint of biological existence, sensory presentation is tied to the evocation of desires
aiming at the survival and prospering of the individual organism and
the species of which it is a carrier, past retention is tied to future expec-
tation. As an animal perceives, it anticipates food and drink, mate and
offspring, as well as situations and things that are inimical to the
achievement of its immanent organic goals. So the perceptual field is a
dynamic synesthetic-orectic-kinesthetic whole, spontaneously putting
together sensory experiences within any given sense and from all the
senses, evoking desire and leading to experienced motion, culminating
in pleasure when the desired object is tactually apprehended and eaten
or mated with or cared for. The sensory components in such experience
in their togetherness display the opportunities for and threats to the
wellbeing of the organism in its environment.

Such a field exceeds the character of immediate sensory objects
and its own apparently self-contained organic ground by cognitive-
desirous "ec-stasy," or standing "out there," being-with what is outside
its own empirical boundaries. Further, such a field transcends the
immediate moment of spatial "ecstasy" by retaining the past and
anticipating the future. As a different mode of being in Space and
Time than empirical objects, the sensory field is the opening of a *fifth*

63. Descartes, *Meditations*, VI, 72–73, p. 78–80, 82–90.
64. See John Searle, *Mystery*.

dimension, a first "inward dimension." It is called "inward" because it is not directly accessible to outward sensory observation, no matter how expanded instrumentally. But the peculiar "inwardness" of awareness is not a matter of its being spatially inside the organism, even though it is grounded there, nor is it a matter of an interior apart from manifest things; its "inwardness" is a matter of the manifestation of "outwardness." "Inner" dimensions take one outside of one's observable insides. At the same time, sensing involves the felt self-presence of the sensing being as the basis for the manifestation of what is *other than* that being. Being "out there" and present to itself involves what Aristotle called an "immaterial" mode of being.[65] To think of it purely in terms of identifiable physical and physiological causal relations is to remain in philosophical Flatland.

But beyond that, the capacity to reflect and apprehend the essential distinction between sensory awareness and sensory objects and to apprehend the eidetic features on both sides of the subject-object relation involves a different, more comprehensive, and thus "deeper" mode of inwardness: a *sixth dimension.* At this level, what we have come to call *intellectual* awareness involves a further transformation of how we are in Space and Time. Eidetic apprehension involves abstracting from the Here-and-Now of our own sensory experiences as well as of the individual objects of that experience. It involves grasping features that are understood to hold *any* time and *any* place in which the kinds of individuals involved are existent. In this it follows the character of the underlying powers that sustain focus on sensorily given individuals. Such awareness is, in a way, *omni*-temporal and *omni*-spatial, not simply—as is the case with natural powers—by way of unconscious orientation, but by way of (usually non-focal) manifestation. And that relation to Space and Time as encompassing wholes grants us the distance from the current way in which we are present to things—gathering the past in function of how we project the future—so that we can deliberately go in search of the past and choose from among various possibilities as our future goals. So there is a *sixth dimension,* standing in relation to the fifth dimension that is

---

65. Aristotle, *On the Soul* 2.12.424b.

the sensory field as inner to outer. Our superficial inner life is our sensory life; our deeper life is our intellectual life.

The distance provided by the notion of Being grounds both intellection as the apprehension of concepts that apply any time and any place individual instances are found, and free choice as the ability to determine specific lines of conduct. When we see a human being, we observe, as in the case of any other observable entity, a seamless connection between antecedent and consequent states that gives rise to a Humean notion of causality.[66] What that does not show us, among many other things, is the source of the empirically observed body in action. In the case of a normally functioning human being, it conceals the free act that originates and sustains action.

But I would maintain that there is a further dimension, deeper than the capacity to grasp universals. It is, indeed, the deepest dimension, a *seventh dimension*: that of reference to the Whole of being. Beyond the limited horizons of our grasping, gathering, projecting, and pursuing, there is the Whole of what is and the wholeness of each thing we encounter as well as the wholeness of each of us who encounter them. That wholeness is always just partly revealed and even more greatly concealed, especially when we think we have things most firmly in hand. Our fundamental relation to it is a matter of *the heart*: that which constitutes the center that gathers up "the whole self" and not just the abstractive intellect and controlling will. At its deepest, the heart lives out a sense of the environing mystery of Being as the mystery of wholeness, both of the beings we meet as well as of ourselves who meet them, and of their pervasive ground as *the Whole*. The encompassing mystery can unexpectedly invade our ordinary awareness as an arresting Presence, like Plato's Beauty Itself, which appears suddenly (*exaiphnes*) as a lightning flash, or as personal address, like Buber's Eternal Thou. From then on it haunts our memory and beckons us to deeper reflectiveness and a more serious sense of responsibility.

So we have a multidimensional, indeed, *seven*-dimensional view of human existence: grounded in the extended (3-D) and moving (4-D) observable organic body, with an articulated physical inwardness,

66. David O'Connor, *Hume on Religion* (London and New York: Routledge, 2001), 65.

which grounds the first of the inner mental dimensions, the sensory field in function of biological need (5-D), yet rising above that to situate our existence in relation to space-time as a whole (6-D) and oriented in our wholeness beyond that to the mystery of the fullness of what is as the seventh and final dimension. Here we have not several things (an organically functioning body, a sensory field, an intellectual field, and a mode of final transcendence) nor simply two things (a mind and a body), but a single multidimensional entity, rooted in the earth and stretched toward the Whole. Mind is the deepest inwardness of this single entity. Intellectual and volitional capacities are employed by each *I* that is the cutting edge of the seven-dimensional totality we call a human being, whose mode of being present is gathered in the heart.

We have shown in various ways how the sensorily given object, sole evidence for a certain type of empiricism, is always (1) individual, (2) immediately given, (3) actual, (4) circumscribed within its own boundaries, and (5) in observable seamless connection between antecedent and consequent states and thus masks what it presupposes. Thus taken, it does not immediately reveal what it masks: (1) the universality of the power and types correlative to the powers; (2) the mediation of present by past experience so that we recognize what we encounter; (3) the possibilities of a given entity for acting and being acted upon; (4) the exceeding of visually given boundaries by animal awareness focused upon what is out-there in the environment, by gathering the past in function of the future of anticipated satisfaction, by human beings thinking against the background of space and time as encompassing wholes, and even more by the functioning of the notion of Being; and (5) the inner origin of observable action in free choice expressed through observation. It is expression that reveals what underlies sensory presentation to an outsider and reflection that reveals it to a human being.

PHILOSOPHIC QUESTIONING

What we have observed thus far provides us with a basis for approaching philosophical questions. The descriptions put in temporary abeyance are the questions that often draw students into philosophy: What should I do and avoid? What are my obligations to myself and to others? What is the best way to organize our lives collectively? Is there something in us that transcends matter? How is mind related to body? Is there a God? How and what can I know? Am I self-determining or predetermined? But putting into temporary abeyance such questions grants us the psychic distance that frees us from whatever psychological capital we have invested in particular answers and forces us to attend with care even to the humblest levels of experience.

Keeping in mind our descriptive observations and the seven-dimensional view that puts them together, we can see how such questions arise and can then approach, with something more than an antiquarian interest, the study of chosen classics that address the larger questions. I would maintain that the general structural features of the field of experience we have examined are always given and are implicitly and explicitly functioning in the accounts given by the classics. In fact, as I mentioned before, it was originally with some surprise that I read Heidegger's remark that phenomenology was a return to Plato and Aristotle, not to repeat their "opinions," but to practice examination of what grounded their endeavors.

Plato said that the task of philosophy was "to carve along the joints like a good butcher"—that is, to display the distinctions and relations already given in the field of experience, "with eyes fixed upon the Whole" of being and upon "the whole nature of each within the whole."[67] As I read and re-read Plato and Aristotle, I was astonished to find that Heidegger's startling remark was readily verifiable and that practicing careful eidetic description of how things appear in experience served to clarify many of the otherwise puzzling things these thinkers have to say. That can be extended to all the classics, since each of them operates out of attention to what is given in experience, selecting now this, now that aspect for emphasis and for point of departure in quest of their larger speculative claims. I hope this work will give aspiring thinkers the basis for a richer reading of the great textual tradition from which I have drawn for the present work.

---

67. Plato, *Phaedrus* 265d–266c.

Chapter 3

Human and Cosmological Time
Sketches

We have distinguished and related sensory and intellectual awareness with its ground in the notion of Being and called attention to the temporal extendedness of awareness, which involves immediate retentions and expectations as well as deliberate searching out of the past and projecting of the future. In this short chapter, though the method remains phenomenological, I want to relate those considerations first to a consideration that comes out of Plato and was developed in Augustine, not to repeat their opinions but to look at the things they indicate. This is a *philosophical* as distinct from an *historical* way of approaching classic texts. As a matter of fact, as I said from the beginning, very much of my text took its cues from observations gleaned from a lifetime of close study of classic texts from Plato to Heidegger.

In his *Republic* when dealing with the Line of Knowledge, Plato locates the distinction between the sensory and the intellectual levels of awareness within the overall distinction in experience between *genesis* or Becoming and *ousia* or Beingness: the former being the realm of individuals given in sensation, the latter the realm of the universals through which we understand individuals. Beingness is *the realm of Forms* and is divided into mathematical Forms and what we might call *meta-mathematical Forms*, or Forms that go beyond mathematics (among other things) by providing its frame in the *play of the fourfold*—the visible and the intelligible interplaying with vision and intellection—which makes mathematics, and indeed all eidetic apprehension, possible. Such is the framework for the whole of our experience. But when he introduced it in the Line of Knowledge in the *Republic*, Plato left the higher level of the Forms empty, gesturing to us to fill it in. The obvious filling would involve unpacking the universal or eidetic features of the fourfold itself.

I want to focus upon the link between the realm of Becoming and the realm of Forms by focusing upon what is central to Becoming: time as the fourth dimension of three-dimensional bodies. Plato says that, while the level of the Forms *is*, and is not subject to change, Becoming is "a mixture of being and nonbeing," of *is* and *is-not*.[1] This involves individuals coming into being, changing, and passing out of being in accordance with their respective Forms or the type of things they are. The realm of Becoming is the realm of time. Let us explore its eidetic features for ourselves, following the claim that Becoming is a "mixture of being and nonbeing," and thus continue to fill in the otherwise empty realm of the Forms—a project with which we have been engaged from the beginning of this text.

In thinking about time, we must distinguish and relate past, present, and future, then inquire into each of them in turn.[2] The past is what was and no longer is, except *now* as the past. The future is that which will be but currently is not, except *now* as that which is to come. It seems that the present alone, *now*, is that which *is*. The present is certainly what *is* in the emphatic sense: it is where things happen. The present is that in which both past and future *are* in their differing modes of being. But the present itself is a constant movement out of the past and into the future whereby the past is added to and the future as the realm of possibility is "subtracted from," as some possibilities are actualized while others lie fallow. Past and future have a certain "thickness," whereas the present, more carefully examined, seems to have no thickness.

What is the present, what is *now*? The time while I am composing this reflection? The second when I strike a given key? The few hundredths of a second that divide one downhill skier from another? The micro milliseconds of happenings at the subatomic level? But even the micro millisecond can be theoretically analyzed into past, present, and future during its occurrence. What we might call *the absolute temporal present* is "the flowing Now," like a geometric point, having no temporal thickness, always moving out of the no-longer into the not-yet, "digging into" the future possibilities, and "piling up" what occurs into

---

1. Plato, *Sophist* 237a, 256d.
2. Augustine did this analysis in *Confessions*, vol. 2, XI.xxviii.xxxvii/276.

the past. So we have two modes of not-being (past and future) separated by a moving divider (the present) that has no temporal thickness! Time is the unity of three modes of not-being—which is why Plato called it a "mixture of being and nonbeing." It was precisely such considerations that led Parmenides to claim that Being Itself cannot change, for, under penalty of contradiction, nonbeing cannot be.

The "piling up" of the past, its ongoing accumulation of what happens in the flowing present, involves a fixity that can no longer be changed. The future contains possibilities; but it is what happens in the present that determines which of the possibilities will be fixed in the ever-growing past. What occurs perhaps need not occur; but when it does, it remains always true from then on, part of the permanent fixture of the universe in its pastness. The fact that we can recognize that as absolutely true says something about us. Whitehead speaks of the "objective immortality" of contingent events and argues for the existence of God as cosmic memory.[3]

These features of time—no-longer, not-yet, and Now as the ever-flowing, non-temporally extended divider between them—remain fixed and apply to any moment of time. They are not in time but occupy "the standing Now," which perpetually intersects "the flowing Now." They are the eidetic features, the Forms of time.

But then past, present, and future not only *are* but are *manifest* to us human beings who live in time both unconsciously in our biological processes and consciously in our wakeful life. Manifest time, the time of consciousness, involves a certain temporal thickness in the flowing Now wherein awareness gathers the past and projects the future to understand and operate in the present. The registration of a sensation in the field of awareness—let's say, to recur to our original point of departure, the sound generated by reading aloud what the black patterns on white found on this page indicate—involves a retention of the first and subsequent instants of awareness throughout the duration of the experience and the immediate anticipation of what is to come. There is thus a certain "binding together" of time as *the lived Now* in any experience.

---

3. Whitehead, *Process and Reality: An Essay in Cosmology* (New York: Harper, 1957), pt. 2, chap. 2, §1, 135.

The conscious Now in the generation or reading of this page of reflections has a certain inner thickness by reason of our living it through. There is a sense in which the living Now is magnetized by the future insofar as we carry a sense of things in and through the projects in which we are engaged. In the immediate present, as our system automatically retains what we have just experienced, we automatically and non-reflectively anticipate the direction in which this sentence and the sequence of sentences are headed. Husserl refers in this context to automatic *retentions* and *protensions*, which constitute the *living present*.[4]

As you move through the text, the reading of the first page becomes progressively vague (unless you have a photographic memory) as does what you were doing before you began reading. The further one goes in life, the more does the past typically fade—except for moments of great importance. The fading trails off into infancy, the time of which is not retrievable. Since *infancy* literally means "not speaking," then it seems that memory begins to stand out through learning to speak.

As I said, the living present carries the aura of the just past and a sense of the immediately coming future; the process is automatic. However, we can stand back from it and deliberately go in search of the past and deliberately project the future. That is grounded in the fact that intellectual-volitional activity involves a distance from the Here-and-Now, being projected toward Space and Time as encompassing wholes by being projected beyond that by the notion of Being. Aquinas takes this up with the idea that we humans stand on the boundary between time and eternity.[5] Scheler claims that we act *down* into time from being projected beyond time.[6]

We can work to memorize certain materials. But there is a difference between rote memorization and retaining what we understand. In the latter case, instead of repeating formulas, we can speak in varying ways about the subject-matter involved. What is significantly

4. Edmund Husserl, *Crisis*, 68–69.

5. Thomas Aquinas, *Summa contra gentiles: Book II: Creation*, trans. James F. Anderson (Notre Dame: University of Notre Dame Press, 1956), chaps. 80 and 81, §12.

6. Max Scheler, *Formalism in Ethics and Material Ethics of Value*, trans. M. Frings (Evanston, Ill.: Northwestern University Press, 1973), 465–68, 468. See especially note 100.

retained in learning a discipline or a practical skill becomes spontaneously operative in any present. That allows you and I as readers, for
example, to recognize the print on this page as an instance of the English language. The immediate registration of the colors and shapes in
phenomenal space are mediated by what I have learned and retained
in my spontaneously operative memory.

Further, in conscious life we experience the constant *flow* of time
in the stream of experience within which differing contents from varying sources appear and disappear. The external world presents itself
as constantly affecting us in ever-differing ways through the flow of
sensation. Heraclitus noted that all things flow, and nothing remains
the same: "You can't step into the same river twice, for different waters
are always flowing."[7] Biology makes clear that our bodies are in a constant state of anabolism and katabolism, with three hundred million
or more cells dying and coming into being every minute. Modern
physics has shown that things are composed of elementary particles
that constantly irradiate their light spectra, so that what looks placid—
let's say a mountain—is actually composed of elementary processes;
and the mountain itself is rising, crumbling, or both.

At the same time, reveries or differing projects may solicit our
attention, or appetites awaken and place their demands upon us; feelings of vigor and balance may occupy the remote fringe of our awareness, or feelings of nausea and dizziness may overtake us; we may also
feel itches on our skin or pains in our joints. While we may be trying
to concentrate upon the eidetic features of time, all of these contents
are tumbling along in the streaming of our consciousness,[8] with the
differing contents rising up to center stage or falling back into the
more or less remote fringes of our consciousness or into oblivion.

How we anticipate determines how we gather the past in order to
focus upon the present where our projects are being realized. For
many of the current readers, the project is to understand the text with
a view toward the whole course within which it fits in order to con-

---

7. Heraclitus, "Heraclitus of Ephesus," in *The Presocratic Philosophers*, ed. C. S. Kirk,
and J. E. Raven (London: Cambridge University Press, 1966), no. 218, p. 197.
    8. The expression is one of William James'. See *The Principles of Psychology*, vol. 1
(New York: Henry Holt, 1890), 550–51.

tinue to take a curriculum that will lead to graduation and on into a career. Attending to the present is deepened by how far we project our future. Running ahead to our death rebounds upon the way we are present in any Now.[9]

There is another kind of temporal moment, which Plato called the *kairos* and which St. Paul made much of: that is, the opportune moment, the "window of opportunity" for certain kinds of occurrence.[10] We speak of that today in terms of outer space flights. There are certain conjunctions of terrestrial and celestial events within which such flights can safely occur and outside of which, depending upon their destination, they cannot succeed. So also with opportunities available for human action.

In his classic, *Being and Time*, Martin Heidegger places the consideration of time at the heart of his understanding of Being. The single star on his tomb represents his lifelong preoccupation with the question of Being. His initial focus was upon the human being, whose distinctiveness from other beings lies in his living out of the question of Being or the question of how we humans are involved in the Whole. His technical term for the human being is *Da-Sein*, or the place (*Da*) where concern with Being (*Sein*) as a whole and with one's own life as a whole appears in the midst of beings.[11] As the title to his main work indicates, he relates the question of Being to time, and as his special focus in *Being and Time*, human lived time.

The living Now involves the co-implication of past, present, and future, and this determines what he calls the "care-structure."[12] Care is the way one's heart is involved in a uniquely individual way. We always find ourselves engaged in projecting the future in terms of our care. What are the persons and matters that are near and dear to us? The care we have is the result of our past: the way we have been brought up and the way we have responded has determined how we currently find ourselves, that is, how we are disposed or "tuned."[13] Hei-

---

9. Much of this analysis appears in Heidegger's *Being and Time*, II, III, 61–66, p. 279–306; II, IV, 67, p. 307–12.

10. Rom 13:11–13; 2 Cor 6:1–8.

11. *BT*, Intro. II, 7, 32ff.

12. *BT*, II, III, 73, 349ff.

13. *BT*, I, VI, 40, 172ff.

Table 3-1: Being, Time, and What Is Now

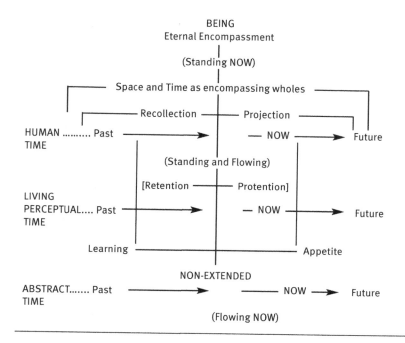

degger speaks of each of us, in any Now, as a *thrown project*, a past-future co-implication, but polarized by the future.[14] As such we are essentially *Being-in-the-World* with others formed by long traditions. When we awaken as mature individuals, we find ourselves formed in a way we have not chosen: we are "thrown" into the world.

As in Plato's Cave, living through our lives, we mostly think, act, and even *feel* the way *They* think, act, and feel. We are mirrors of those with whom we have been and are engaged. Heidegger speaks of this situation as *uneigentlich*, usually translated as "inauthentic," which suggests *phoniness* and which he does not at all intend. It is like *eigen* in German, *autos* in Greek, as the root of the English *auth-entic*, and corresponds to *proprius* in Latin. Less misleadingly put, the situation is that in which we have been *ap-propri-ated* by the They and do not fully appropriate what is manifest for ourselves. We orient ourselves

14. *BT*, I, V, 31, 135.

to the future primarily in the mode of curiosity, we relate to the past in an ambiguous way insofar it is not clear what is our own and what derived from others (what is shown or what is accepted), and we dwell in the present in terms of small talk or chatter.[15]

There is, however, a way to an "authentic" (i.e., an *appropriated*) existence, one in which a person comes with full responsibility to take a stance. This can happen when one's life as a whole comes before one's eyes, especially as one comes to reflect upon one's death, which is the ultimate limit to our Being-in-the-World. From this, a resolute stand toward the whole of our life becomes possible.[16]

Heidegger's descriptions follow, in a secular fashion, the religious practice he might have known from the short time he spent with the Jesuits. In the famous Ignatian Retreat, one enters into weeks of prayer and silence, beginning with reflection upon one's own death and the judgment that believers think will follow. During the Retreat, one focuses upon what Christians take to be the supreme Example of human life, Jesus Christ. Out of these prayerful considerations, one is expected to choose the way to follow, to decide upon one's personal vocation. For Heidegger, resoluteness involves "choosing one's hero" and retrieving the past in terms of the resolute projection of the future.[17] In the Ignatian approach, one's "hero" is Jesus Christ.

In so acting, one is able to transcend the clichés of everyday chit-chat and enter into genuine communication. It is out of this transcendence that the "sense of Being" (*der Sinn des Seins*) arises.[18]

Special occasions for deepening this sense occur in an encounter with a work of art. The German *Sinn*, like the English *sense*, has a double meaning: it refers to *sensation* and to *meaning*. In the working of the work of art, the sensory takes on focal significance; and with it, there opens the deeper lived meaning of the world within which it arose and now appears. The working upon us of the work of art opens up a World of meaning and "sets it upon the Earth," creating so much

15. *BT,* I, V, 35ff, 210–25.
16. *BT,* II, III, 62, 282–87.
17. *BT,* II, V, 74, 352.
18. Heidegger, "Introduction to 'What is Metaphysics?' (1949)," 217. See also *BT,* I, V, 34, 157–59.

"World space" that "even the ordinary appears extraordinary."[19] This lived sense of the Whole, mediated through the world within which the artwork is found as sensorily manifest and in which Heidegger sees the relation to Being as a question filled in a lived manner, is not a state but a temporal, orienting event. It would not be inappropriate to speak of such a moment as *kairos*, "the opportune time."

Here there is no mastery of Being after which we strive intellectually and practically; there is a being-apprehended by what always exhibits a surplus of mystery out of which the work and, indeed, we ourselves arise. Understood in this way, Being is a *Geheimnis*, a mystery.[20] It is curious that the center of this word is *Heim*: home. The *Ge-* indicates some sort of system or linkage as in *Ge-birge* or chain of *Bergen*, that is, mountains, or *Ge-stell* as framework or skeleton. *The home for human beings lies in relation to the surrounding, ever-retreating mystery of Being.*

What is fixed is the direction of the question of Being: it concerns the encompassing Whole. But how one's relation to it is concretely realized is plural. Indeed, how cultures relate to it is plural and historical. More generalized ways of seeing govern different cultures and different epochs, so that the meaning of Being as it occurs is itself historical.[21] That is, for Heidegger, the link between Being and Time.

* * *

But let us return to our original point of departure, focusing upon this page. The sentences we find are written in English. This situates writer and reader in the larger framework of a We that crosses generations. By convention, language fixes for ourselves and future generations the various eidetic features we apprehend and (like language) create, occupying the standing Now, vertically intersecting the horizontal flow of time. Language as a system is a-temporal—or better, omni-temporal, containing the continually repeatable sensory features of language constructed to hold our eidetic insights in place. Words are the media

---

19. Heidegger, *Origin of the Work of Art*, trans. Roger Berkowitz and Phillipe Nonet (unpublished manuscript, rev. P. Nonet, December 2006), 37, 47, 58.

20. Heidegger, "On the Essence of Truth," 134–35.

21. See Heidegger, *The End of Philosophy*, trans. J. Stambaugh (New York: Harper and Row, 1973).

through which we have access to the Forms, both those naturally available and those culturally constructed. Words are, like the Forms of differing natures, a-temporal or omni-temporal universals that stand in relation to the particular instances in which we might pronounce or write down the words that gather the Forms for us.[22] The linguistic tradition provides an inventory of the eidetic features, the essential distinctions, the Forms upon which we draw in speech, whether directed to others or articulated to ourselves in thought. Speech incarnates thought, and thought lays down its tracks in language.

As conscious, intelligent beings, we stand at the intersection of the flowing Now and the standing Now: the flowing Now of speaking and thinking and the standing Now of language and thought. It is language that situates us outside our individual privacy and within a common space of meaning that binds generations past, present, and to come. Language relates us to "the realm of Forms" both seen and constructed; its words are conventional stand-ins for the Forms apprehended in a given tradition. Language locates us in history.

* * *

The fact of language situates one's own inner temporality within the wider temporality of the history of our people, while regular human practice links it to the rhythms of the cosmos. Regular human practice is measured by the way the sun rises and sets relative to our revolving earth. Sundials allowed for more precision, breaking up the path of the sun into the regular points upon the face of the sundial that its shadow touches.

The mechanical clock abstracts from the presence or absence of the sun. Taking the temporal length of each revolution of the earth as the standard, the clock is based on the division of one revolution into twenty-four hours. And for convenience—not jamming the face with too many numbers—the face of the clock is divided into twelve-hour units that are subdivided into sixty-minute segments and then into sixty-second intervals. Like the choice of twenty-four hours, the choice of sixty for minutes and seconds seems arbitrary; but it has a history.

---

22. This is clearly following Plato's Line of Knowledge. Plato has Socrates present the idea that there are no forms without language in *Cratylus* 390 d7–e3. Rather than occupying some separate heaven, the Forms for Plato are present in language.

For one thing, the first mechanical clocks in the West only had the hour hand. This followed from the way the sundials were divided. The minute hand was added later, when people wished to coordinate their actions more exactly.

Going back to very early times, the Ancient Egyptians used twelve as a basic unit—a practice thought to be linked to counting three joints on each finger with the thumb. It was then applied to two twelve-hour segments: one for the day, the other for the night, giving us a twenty-four-hour division.[23]

Around 2000 B.C. the Sumerians developed a measuring system based upon the number sixty. Although it is unknown why sixty was chosen, it is notably convenient for expressing fractions, since sixty is the smallest number divisible by the first six counting numbers as well as by ten, twelve, fifteen, twenty, and thirty. It is from this that the hour is divided into sixty minutes and the minute into sixty seconds.

Breaking the measurement of time into units allows for more exact measurement of time than does the angle of the sun. The light of the day or its absence at night indicates which of the two twelve-hour segments are being represented at any given time. Digital clocks have indicators for a.m. or p.m. The military clock does not repeat the division into twelve-hour units but continues the count after twelve up to twenty-four, so that 2:00 p.m. is 14:00. The clock allows for accurate planning and for coordination of one's projects and of large and small numbers of people. The digital clock allows for the easy presentation of the military clock without having to indicate twenty-four hours on its face.

The calendar was devised in order to link us to our past and to keep track of it through records. The fundamental unit is the year, determined by the angle of the sun's orbit, from vernal to autumnal equinox. The year is divided into months that follow the lunar cycle, and the months are divided into weeks and days. The division of the month into four weeks seems to be arbitrary, while the division of the week into seven days at least parallels the seven days of creation in the Hebrew narrative. Here the calendar joins up with the clock.

---

23. The decimal system is thought to have had its origin in ten fingers for counting.

Each culture uses a significant event to determine the counting of the years. In the ancient Greek world, it was the First Olympiad in 776 B.C., which was the first time all the Greek cities gathered for athletic competition; in the Roman world it was the founding of Rome in 753 B.C.; in the West as a whole it was the supposed birth of Christ from which we measure Before Christ and In the Year of the Lord, *Anno Domini* (even though He probably was born four years Before Christ!). With the secularization of the West, dates are now indicated with C.E. for the Common Era and B.C.E. for Before the Common Era. The alphabetical characters make it possible that Christians can still understand them as indicating the Christian Era and Before the Christian Era. Since this method of measurement is now used almost universally, humankind is restricted to counting according to the Western understanding of the world and history.

Having a common dating system, though, allows us to place past events, monuments, and texts into a consistent historical framework. Having a common calendar allows the extension into millions and even billions of years in tracing the history of the cosmos itself. So we learn to move from our own inner temporality to coordination with others in terms of clocks and calendars and on to human and even cosmic history.

Time in general is a link between our inner ever-flowing awareness and the processes of nature and history into which we are born. It measures our time on earth and our linkage to those who went before and those who will follow. But the measuring principles are themselves beyond the temporal flow, as we as intellectual beings also are.

A NOTE ON CONTINGENCY AND ETERNITY

A contingent event (like the beginning of this sentence) that, before the fact, need not have existed but now does, is such that it is *forever after* true that it did. Isn't that intuitively obvious? Can one convincingly argue against the fact?

But what does one make of the *forever*? And what of the *intuitively obvious*? What are the conditions for the possibility in us of the ability for such intuition? How are we then related to time?

It means we are not locked into each of our temporal spans or into the coordinate time for events in the cosmos. In relation to things, we are positioned not only as subjects of direct encounter, but as oriented toward space and time as encompassing wholes. As we have noted several times, that is what makes possible language whose functioning units (semantic or syntactic) apply *wherever* and *whenever* their instances are found. Kant had seen that and claimed that space and time are a priori encompassing wholes.[24] That does not mean that space and time are only "in us," as Schopenhauer claimed.[25] Each encountered thing is located in *actual* space and time outside the one who encounters it and toward which space and time "in us" are emptily oriented.

There is a deeper ground that we have been evoking throughout this work. Reference to space and time as encompassing wholes occurs within our reference to Being as a whole, that is, to everything that exists, has existed, or will exist. The *forever after* introduces the notion of *eternity*. The past is fixed forever apart from the flux of temporal events, so that we ourselves, at the level of intuiting that as intellectual beings, are also above the flux. As Scheler noted in contrast to Heidegger, we act down into time while standing above it.[26] That exhibits the grounded difference between Heidegger and the speculative tradition, which sought to view things *sub specie aeternitatis*.

Noting that the past has "objective immortality" beyond its subjective disappearance, Whitehead suggested that the locus of the past is in God's memory, which forms His consequent nature.[27] But if that is so, then the most difficult of questions concerns the open future. Can there be an eternal encompassment of *all* time? If there is, then what about contingency and what, especially, about the freedom of self-determination? One runs into the problems that especially dogged Calvinists and Muslims, whose vision of God is such that He is the only true Agent.

---

24. Kant, *Critique of Pure Reason*, A22/B37, p. 74ff.

25. Arthur Schopenhauer, *The World as Will and Representation*, trans. E. F. J. Payne, vol. 1 (New York: Dover, 1966), 8–10.

26. Max Scheler, *On the Eternal in Man*, trans. B. Noble (London: SCM Press, 1960), 190n2.

27. For Whitehead, God is eternally existent as the ground of temporal being. *Process and Reality*, pt. 5, ch. 2, §1–7, 521–33.

One could attribute a qualified omniscience to God, as Richard Bernstein suggested: He can know all that can be known; but what cannot be known *in toto* before the fact are future contingents and, especially, free, self-determining acts.[28] One can know ahead of time what follows from the regularities of nature, but (as does Hegel's System) this gives only a kind of general framework of the future, not the actual events that will occur.

28. In a group discussion.

Chapter 4

The Heart and the Life of Feeling

A Phenomenological Sketch

I n our earlier exposition of the seven dimensions of human existence, we placed the notion of the heart at the heart of our experience. It is the source of the way we live within those dimensions and the way in which we are carried and conduct ourselves through time. Our first sketch provided the skeleton for our life; this chapter looks to the flesh-and-blood life, rooted in *the heart*, which works within that framework.

The notion of the heart plays a large role in poetry and in the Hebrew-Christian scriptures—and, indeed, in several different language groups. Besides referring to the physiological pump as an object of scientific examination and manipulation discovered through opening the chest cavity, consider the perennial and immediate access to it, which is found in such expressions as, "my heart was burning" with rage or "aching" or "crushed" with sorrow or "pounding" with fear or "throbbing" with love or "skipping a beat" in joy. Also consider expressions like the following: "You've stolen my heart." "I give you my heart." "Take heart." "He put his heart into it." "Try as I might, my heart just wasn't in it." "I hadn't the heart to tell him." "Eat your heart out." "Have a heart." "She's heartless." "Let's have a heart-to-heart talk." "He gave heartfelt thanks." "Heart of my heart!" "Sweetheart!" "I learned it by heart." "Give me ten hearty men." "He ate a hearty meal." "In your heart you know he's right" or "In your heart of hearts you know it." "Let's get to the heart of the matter." Or consider the scriptural and liturgical uses: "Mary pondered these things in her heart." "God speaks to the heart." "The fool says in his heart, 'There is no God.'" "Lift up your hearts." "Take away this heart of stone and create in me a new heart." "Create in me a clean heart, O God." "Thou shalt love the Lord thy God with thy whole heart."

My students and I were able to identify at least seventy different ways in which the term is used.[1] I thought we did well, but then I discovered that the *Oxford English Dictionary* has eighteen pages, with a total of twenty-one columns of distinctive uses! That must be the word with the most alternative meanings in the English language! It truly stands at the heart of human experience. And it bears many of these meanings cross-culturally, yet the philosophic tradition has devoted little attention to it.[2] I want to begin to give it the attention it deserves.[3] But before I directly address that, I want to once more review the way in which we situated it within the overall field of human awareness and its grounds.

* * *

As we noted in chapter 1, animals are monopolar, and humans are bipolar. Animals live extrovertedly within the Here-and-Now in automatic response to presentations in the environment guided by their fundamental instincts, which are geared toward organic flourishing. Though humans occupy the same Here-and-Now, they come to it from being infinitely beyond it. The field of human awareness is rooted at one end in the functioning of the animal organism, which produces the sensory field, and at the other end in the functioning of

---

1. See Table 4–1.

2. The polyvalent usage of the term *heart* would lend itself eminently to a Wittgensteinian family resemblance analysis.

3. I have provided an approach to the phenomena of the heart in the Introduction to my translation of Stephan Strasser's *Phenomenology of Feeling: An Essay on the Phenomena of the Heart* (Pittsburgh: Humanities Press, 1967). The Forward is written by Paul Ricoeur, who encouraged me to translate this work. See also Dietrich von Hildebrand, *The Heart* (South Bend: St. Augustine's Press, 2007), which I reviewed in *American Catholic Philosophical Quarterly* 83, no. 2 (Spring 2009): 303–9. See also my "Hegel on the Heart," *International Philosophical Quarterly* 41, no. 2 (June 2001): 131–44. I addressed the Baylor University symposium on Augustine's *Confessions* with a paper on "The Heart in/of Augustine's *Confessions*," and more recently the annual Heidegger Symposium at the University of Dallas with a paper on "The Heart in Heidegger's Thought." I dealt with von Hildebrand and Scheler in "Virtues, Values, and the Heart," in *Phenomenology and Virtue Ethics*, ed. K. Hemberg and P. Gyllenhammer (London: Bloomsbury, 2013), 132–46. I am planning to gather and supplement these studies in a future volume on the heart that will appear through The Catholic University of America Press.

Table 4-1: Ordinary Language Usage of the Term *Heart*

TYPE OF HEART	DEDICATED	TRANSFERRED	MISCELLANEOUS	
Bleeding, lonely, big, open, tender, good, hungry, longing, torn, heavy, troubled kind	Whole-hearted	Sweetheart	The heart has its reasons	Eat your heart out
	Half-hearted	Heart of my heart	Close to one's heart	Lift up your hearts
	Having one's heart in it	Dearheart	To your heart's content	Create in me a new heart
			Heart-to-heart talk	Change of heart
NEGATIVE	**VITALITY**	***TRANSCENDENTAL EXTENSION***	Disheartened	Heart in the right place
Of stone, cold, black	Coeur-age, stout-hearted, Hearty (men, meal, appetite)	Heart of the matter	Home is where the heart is	Take heart
Heartless	Young at heart		Heart and soul	Giving one's heart
	Lion-hearted	***LITERAL***	Loving with all one's heart	Taking to heart
		Pump—(mechanism)—learn by heart	Heartfelt thanks	Pour one's heart out
		Leaping for joy, soaring	From the bottom of my heart	Cross my heart
		Skipping a beat	Find it in your heart	No heart to tell or do to him
		Aching, crushed, broken,	Cry your heart out	In your heart you know
		Pounding with fear	Do your heart good	Heart-stopping experience
		Burning with rage, jealousy	In your heart-of-hearts	
		On fire with love	Wearing one's heart on one's sleeve	
		Racing, sinking		

the notion of Being, which grounds all our distinctively human functions. That notion is what makes the mind to be a mind as directedness toward totality, for Being includes all that is, and outside Being there is nothing. However, our orientation toward the Whole is initially empty: we exist, Heidegger rightly says, as the *Question* of Being.[4] We are always elsewhere, always beyond wherever we organically are; and whatever we focally consider, we are pre-focally aware of the Whole as beyond any horizon we might project.[5]

The notion of Being establishes a basic encompassing magnetic field that interplays with the magnetic field of attractions, repulsions, and neutralities established by our organic needs. The space of meaning between the sensorily given and the absent Whole is filled by the ways of thinking, acting, and feeling that each culture has developed over the centuries to establish another component of the magnetic field. Genetic structure limns the space of possibilities for each individual human. The culture within which she or he is born opens up the concrete possibilities for development. But as we come to make our own the possibilities we prefer, we create our own character, which percolates down into the heart. Heart is the total magnetic field of attractions, repulsions, and neutralities established by relation to the Whole, by genetic structure, by enculturation, and by one's own history of choices. This field is the locus of radical subjectivity and the default mode for our conduct of life.

In most of what we have listed above, the term *heart* is used metaphorically: just as the heart as a physiological pump is the center of the organism, so one's basic disposition is the center of one's conscious life. But I think the relation is closer than that parallelism. Besides referring to the pump, *heart* in the broader sense is not always a metaphor. The heart as an organ is intimately tied to one's emotional life, for, as I said, it pounds with fear, skips a beat at the presence of the beloved, is crushed with sorrow, is broken over a lost love, sinks in disappointment, is burning with rage, and leaps with joy. These are rather directly experienced phenomena of the heart. There are even

4. *Being and Time*, Intro., II, 6–7, p. 24–28.
5. See John Dewey, *Art as Experience*, 192–94.

reports that heart transplant patients begin to feel the kind of preferences felt by the original donor![6]

The heart studied in physiology is the "outside," relative to our visual capacity (unaided or instrumentally assisted), of what, "inside," is our emotional life. The consideration of the heart as a muscle, parallel to the brain and observable within the visual field, abstracts in both cases from its direct relation to conscious phenomena. It follows the abstractions that, by their nature, visual and tactual manipulation provide and that ground the scientific study of the heart as a muscular pump in the center of the chest. I refer to the findings of physiology as "abstract" because scientific seeing itself abstracts from the fullness of what is there. I cannot stress strongly enough that the appearance of the heart in the visual field, like anything else, is not the heart fully in itself but the heart actualized in its see-ability relative to the capacity for seeing. Such seeing cognitively traverses the apparently empty space between the eyes and the visual object to reveal those surface aspects of things that are relevant to organic flourishing. As we noted in a previous chapter, scientific seeing as such also abstracts from the potentialities that underlie the actualities; it also abstracts from the emotional expressivity of the whole body in relation to the presence of the person; and it abstracts from the common space of meaning occupied by experimenter and patient that appears through sound-generation in speech. As I said, these considerations are directly parallel to the relation between awareness and the brain. Descartes speculated on the pineal gland in the brain as the organ of thought. We need not speculate this way to see that matters of the heart are quite often both physiological and psychological. We noted before that Aristotle said the *physicist* describes anger as the warming of blood around the heart, and the *dialectician* describes it as the result of apprehension.[7] As Karl Rahner noted, *heart* is an *Urwort* (a primordial word) that expresses a nonarbitrary relation between one's emotional life and one's organic center.[8]

---

6. My general practitioner said that nurses who work with transplant patients are a treasure trove of stories about personality changes involved in transplant patients in general.

7. Aristotle, *On the Soul* 1.1.403a.30.

8. Rahner, "Some Theses for a Theology of Devotion to the Sacred Heart," in *Theological Investigations*, vol. 3, *The Theology of the Spiritual Life*, trans. Karl-H. Kruger and Boniface Kruger (Baltimore: Helicon Press, 1967), pt. V, 331ff.

In what follows I want to take a broader look and locate expressions relative to the heart within the overall life of feeling in its differing levels and forms. The differing types are overwhelming in their differences and relations, and each type requires detailed attention. We will have to restrict ourselves to a sketch, with no pretension to having covered all the bases, even in a preliminary way. Though all levels interpenetrate, so that our seeing is saturated with our understanding and feelings about things, we can still consider feelings in a hierarchy from obviously bodily based feelings (both localized and pervasive), through distinctively human moods, to the vast multiplicity of intentionally directed feelings in ordinary life that are linked to our basic dispositions, and on to what we will call *spiritual feelings* in the areas of aesthetics, intellectual life, love, and religion.

* * *

Begin first with the feeling that appears as literally touching (e.g., *feeling* one's way in the dark). Touching is usually associated with the hands, which can feel various objects. But the hands are not the organ of feeling as touching, like the eyes for seeing and the ears for hearing. Feeling has no localized organ; the whole bodily surface with its subcutaneous sensors is the organ of touch. One can touch with and be touched by any region of one's epidermis. What this presupposes is that, at the level of awareness, one is "in touch with" one's body as a functional whole and that awareness pervades the organism at a functional level as an expression of the way in which the underlying principle of holism pervades the organism in totality. That pervasive principle used to be called *psyche* or *soul* or *anima* as animating, building, and sustaining the organism and developing into animal awareness. I am not in touch with my brain or my liver or my pancreas, but I am in touch with the functioning wholeness of my organism. On account of this I have a sense of muscular tension, a sense of balance, and a sense of motion as I move across space, transitioning with a part of myself in moving my arms or as a whole in walking or running, and the like.

This pervasive sense is first of all a feeling of being awake, of self-presence as a psycho-physical whole. As we noted before, when the Reticular Activating System, the consciousness "switch" in the brainstem is "on," manifestation of one's surroundings plays in tandem with one's self-awareness as primary and pervasive feeling. As I said earlier, it is this feeling of self that founds the appearance of what is other in the environment. Unreflective self-presence is the basis for the manifestation of what is *other than oneself, precisely in its otherness*. There can be appearance, or manifest otherness, only if there is manifest sameness, nonreflective self-presence as the cognitive center to which what is other can and does appear *as other* than oneself. It is of crucial importance to underline this grounding feature of any appearance to awareness. Computers and robots simply have no self-presence and therefore no appearance of the other, even though they are causally impacted by the same light signals as organisms that can see and that eventuate in certain programmed responses in a robot, even the ability to learn adjustment to environmental challenges.

Further, to be aware at all, that is, to have feeling, there must be an *inner* extension binding past, present, and future. In an immediate flowing present, there is an automatic retention of the immediately past condition and *protension* of the immediate future to constitute the living now. The whole point of being aware is governed by the essential aims of the organism that is aware. As its essential modulations, feeling involves the emergence of appetite and the possibility of pleasure and pain in the future. Felt immediacy is further modulated through learning to pursue prey and flee predators. Appetite thus involves orientation toward the future and determines pursuit and avoidance; it also involves the functioning now of past learning.

Being in touch with one's body makes it possible to feel pain radiating from a definite location when the body is struck. It makes it possible to feel itches in spots where the skin is irritated. It also grounds pleasurable feelings such as the relief when one washes one's face with a cold cloth on a hot day or takes a hot shower in wintertime.

The arousal of feelings of hunger, thirst, sexual desire, and aggression is essential to sensory manifestness, because the initial point of sensory manifestness is to provide opportunities for and display threats to organic flourishing. So we have feelings of hunger, thirst, sexual desire, and aggression, the first three having specific loci in the organism. The mouth and the stomach are the loci of the feeling of hunger and thirst, the stomach itself being felt when the needs are very strong.

Sexual desire centers upon the genitalia. But, as the organism's natural tendency to reproduce itself, it follows the holistic life of the organism so that in sexual experience, one's whole bodily surface becomes sensitized. Sexual arousal culminates in the intensity of orgasm, which naturally accompanies the male depositing of the seed into the female body as the end of the organism. So sexual arousal, when acted upon, progressively pervades one's consciousness. Aggression also involves a reaction of the whole organism as it prepares to fight for the conditions of its flourishing and that of its mate and offspring.

Hunger, thirst, and sexual desire lead to feelings of pleasure when they are satisfied; when not satisfied, they can rise to the level of pain. As Aristotle noted, pleasure is the bloom on activity; it indicates a kind of excellence of functioning.[9] Of course, pain normally occurs when anything destructive happens to the organism. One might think that that God could have engineered it so that pain was replaced by a light going on or something of that sort.[10] What this fails to consider is that pain is the consequence of feeling pervading the organism. To eliminate the possibility of pain is to eliminate the possibility of pleasure: no feeling, no awareness.[11]

I said that sexual desire and aggression are feeling states that pervade the organism. There are other such states, such as vigor or weariness, but also nausea, dizziness, and the like. These supervene upon the pervasive feeling of readiness for holistic functioning, which normally pervades the organism as a functioning whole.

* * *

All of the above occurs at the organically grounded pole of our field of awareness; in human life it is, so to speak, "invaded from above" by distinctively human feelings. First, parallel to pervasive organic states, there are various good or bad moods: cheerfulness, sobriety, ambition, but also sadness, sullenness, lethargy, boredom, and anxiety. None of these as such is intentional in the sense of being

---

9. Aristotle, *Nicomachean Ethics* X.iv.1174.b31–3.
10. Somewhere Kurt Vonnegut made this observation.
11. In the *Phaedo* (60b) when the manacles were removed from the imprisoned Socrates, he remarked how good it felt and how pleasure and pain are intimately connected.

object-directed, like being angry about something or happy about something. They simply are states in which we find ourselves, without necessarily knowing the causes. One always has a peculiarly tuned state of mind.[12] There is here a certain relation to the heart, for it is the heart that is said to be glad or sad. In his *Confessions*, Augustine addresses his heart and asks why it is sad.[13]

Moods are ambiguous; they may be the result of native temperament. But upbringing, past choices, and present conditions may shift or modify a person's typical disposition. The traditional treatment of the *basic temperaments* as predispositions toward certain kinds of moods is relevant here. Traditionally, four temperaments have been listed, originally named by Hippocrates based upon the supposed dominance of one of four *humors*: blood in the *sanguine* temperament, phlegm in the *phlegmatic*, black bile in the *melancholic*, and yellow bile in the *choleric*. Though the physiological linkage is outdated, the analysis of temperaments is still useful. The sanguine is associated with cheerfulness and optimism, but also with superficiality; the phlegmatic with lethargy and inactivity but also with acceptance of troubling situations; the melancholic with seriousness but also with sadness and depression; the choleric with vigor, but also with aggression and anger. When we get beyond the antiquated notion of the humors as causes, the classifications still seem to apply psychologically, and they must have physiological causes: they follow from certain genetic constellations. They do seem to fit tendencies in different kinds of individuals. They can be considered arrayed as opposites along two intersecting axes that are the stuff of human life, namely, feelings and actions. Regarding feelings, there are the sanguine and the melancholy types, or the upbeat and the downbeat; regarding actions, there are the choleric and the phlegmatic types, or the vigorous and the lethargic. Particular states of mind modulate these four factors.

As I said, a sanguine temperament typically exhibits *cheerfulness*; some people are just naturally cheerful. This may be rooted either in physiology, in upbringing, or in both. One who has been loved and

---

12. In *Being and Time* Heidegger refers to this state with the term *Befindlichkeit*, or the state of mind in which one finds oneself at any given time. *BT*, I, V, 29, p. 134.

13. *Confessions*, vol. 1, IV.iv.1/160.

supported in favorable circumstances would be more inclined to dispositional cheerfulness than someone lacking these conditions. Or such a state may follow various kinds of successes. It may be evoked by beautiful surroundings. But it usually presents itself as an immediate, pervasive state that colors everything we do or undergo.

The melancholic person is characterized by *sobriety* or seriousness that may follow a sense of vocation and that keeps her or him focused upon her or his projects. Like cheerfulness, it too may simply be temperamental. The melancholy person may be inclined to a pervasive *sadness*, but sadness often follows naturally upon deprivation of various sorts. As a mood, it persists beyond consideration of the cause. Sadness may go all the way to what is somewhat misleadingly called *major depression*. I say misleadingly because such so-called "depression" is not just feeling bad; it involves basic rational disfunction. It shows itself in increased activity in the lower back quadrant of the right cerebral hemisphere in what is labeled "Broadman Area 25" and appears on a scan as intensely flashing light, as if there were some kind of short circuit in the brain.

The choleric type often exhibits *sullenness*. We speak of the *sullen* person as "carrying a chip on his shoulder" in the sense that he is spoiling for a fight, as it were, daring anyone to knock the chip off his shoulder as an excuse to get into a fight. Again, this may be based upon a choleric temperament, but it also may be caused by enduring difficult circumstances. In a positive sense, the choleric type is intensely task oriented.

Boredom is a mood to which the phlegmatic may be particularly prone. As a mood, it is not boredom *about* something in particular, but a general feeling of boredom regarding one's life as a whole.

But no matter the temperament, humans as such are subject to an underlying *anxiety*. In the technically limited sense of the term that Heidegger introduced, it is distinguished from *fear*. One is always afraid *of* something in the same sense as one might say one is *anxious* about something, like a final examination in school. But in Heidegger's sense, *Angst* or anxiety is a pervasive mood that underpins all of human life. It follows from the fact that we are always directed, via the notion of Being, toward the Totality and never in possession of it. And that relation to Totality grounds the ability to consider one's own life as a whole.[14] We are aware that we are "condemned to death," with only the time of execution hidden from us. Augustine reads this underlying anxiety from a religious standpoint as generating the longing of the heart for God for Whom it has been made and which will remain restless until it rests in Him.[15]

All of these moods can be more or less intense; but there is also that neutral state of feeling that accompanies everyday life. It has no particular feeling-tone as we go about our daily tasks in a routine manner. For the most part, we are on automatic pilot with no special mood except that neutral state of mind. But when it comes to choices, the default mode lies in the desires of one's heart. They guide a person, especially when the choices facing her or him have serious consequences.

But then there is the perdurance of such an ordinary state of mind in which our heart is no longer in what we do. Nothing speaks to us; nothing draws us out of ourselves and calls for our dedication. There is a feeling of great emptiness. Perhaps here it is identical with pervasive boredom. Or perhaps it is deeper: it may border on despair. In that case we have moved into the area of *spiritual* feelings—feelings in which one's relation to the Whole is at stake.

Now, when we transition to feelings that are directed toward something other than those things to which our bodily appetites drive us, we find a vast and bewildering multiplicity of feeling-types. We might arrange them schematically in terms of attraction and repulsion, expressed in liking and disliking, and culminating in various degrees of intensity of *love* and *hate* as the basic motors of human life, the basic way one's heart is oriented. Our loves and hates generate *hopes* and *fears*: hopes that we secure what we prefer and avoid what we find repelling; and fears that we might be overtaken by what we hate or dislike and fail to get what we want. These feelings play in tandem with feelings of power or weakness: power to secure what we desire and to avoid what we dislike, or inability to achieve either. The way things turn out might produce pleasure or pain, or, at a higher level, joy or sorrow. If we succeed in avoiding what we fear, then we

14. *BT,* II, VI, 40, 184.
15. Augustine, *Confessions,* vol. 1, I.i.1/12.

Table 4-2: Typology of Feelings

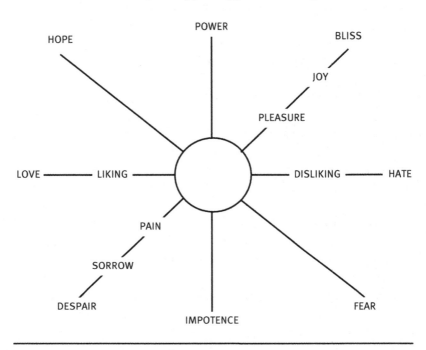

feel the pleasure of *relief*.[16] This gives us four intersecting axes with opposite feelings on each end: love and hate, hope and fear, power or weakness, and pleasure or pain.

Love, like *hate*, is multiform and leads into the consideration of spiritual feelings. One might say that the character of one's life is governed by the order of one's loves, by how one's heart is basically oriented. In a trivial sense one might *love* ice cream. But there is a plethora of feelings that are generated from interpersonal relations. At a level deeper than the love one might have of food, but still on a relatively superficial level, "I love you" might mean one is sexually fixated and craves libidinal satisfaction. It might rise to the level of an obsession. This state is what is negatively termed *lust*, which is often mistaken for sexual desire as such. Libidinal deformations are found

16. For a similar analysis, see Thomas Aquinas, *Summa theologiae*, II-I, q. 23, a. 4.

in *sadism* and *masochism*, in finding sexual satisfaction in maltreating the other or in being maltreated or in maltreating oneself. Sexual desire is a natural organic good; but in the human case it appears in a field of awareness that is able to consider the personal dignity of one's partner and, because we can know the universal as such, one is able to guide oneself by principle and not by a blind urge.

There is the phenomenon of "falling in love," which must be distinguished from libidinal fixation. A significant feature of the difference lies in the awe one feels before the other—a kind of feeling of the sacred. Some might be inclined to think that this is a disguise given by nature to lure the pair into reproductive activity, for sexual desire eventually follows as a matter of course. But as contrasted with libidinal fixation, where the person as such is only an occasion for one's own gratification, in "falling in love" the personal relation comes first, and sexual desire flows out from that as an expression of interpersonal relatedness. Being in love, one gives one's heart to the beloved.

"Falling in love" is more than *philia* or friendship, which does not have the magnetizing character exerted by the beloved, even though there may be some desire for the presence of the friend who is missed when distance or death separates. Friendship is akin to parental love in that it includes the desire to give up something of one's own for the sake of the other. Friends enjoy being with one another and sharing with one another.[17]

In yet another form, love as *eros* in the ancient sense expresses in the field of human awareness the directedness that rules all the living. Plato identified it as "the desire of the mortal for the immortal."[18] It is an awareness of a lack that seeks fulfillment. Maturity in all living forms, in plant and animal as well as in human forms, is found in the ability to reproduce, to keep as immortal as possible the kind of being that must die. Sexual desire is the next generation saying to the erotically aroused: "You have to die; let me live in your place." *Eros* and *Thanatos* belong together.

---

17. *Nicomachean Ethics* IX.iv.1166.a1–9. Three of Aristotle's twelve books in his *Nicomachean Ethics* (books V, VIII, and IX) are devoted to interpersonal relationships; justice through all interpersonal relations has one section, and friendship, the center of ethical life, has two.

18. Plato, *Symposium* 207d.

At the distinctively human level, one learns to pass on one's culture to the next generation and to defend it from attack so that it can be rendered as immortal as it can be. Such *eros* is exhibited in patriotic feeling: in love for one's country which rises to the level of being moved to self-sacrifice. If one is so gifted, one might be moved by the desire to do "immortal deeds" or produce "immortal works," that is, actions or products that will go down in the memory of posterity. But, by reason of our being directed toward the Totality via the notion of Being, we can also pursue the uncovering of the "deathless" order of the types that continue to be instantiated in things that must perish. One becomes a scientist, a mathematician, or a philosopher—all of which are driven by the peculiar *eros* that desires the immortal order of things, and ultimately the deathless Source of the cosmos itself.[19]

There is another form of distinctively human love that is said to imitate the divine: it is called *agape*. If *eros* is need-love, a sense of lack seeking fulfillment, then *agape* is gift-love as an overflow of goodness for the sake of the beloved.[20] This appears in the parent's love for the child and leads to parental self-sacrifice for the child's wellbeing. Its helplessness and the parent's realization of being its source naturally call forth such self-sacrifice. In the human case, the character of a biological source (a father or mother) is measured by how it reacts to objects of hatred. But without the presence of the thought of what one hates, hatred may go underground as a permanent disposition toward the object of hatred, awaiting its next avatar.

There are states that are variations on the theme of hatred. Possessiveness might displace love and may become *jealousy*, which, in turn, leads to suspicion and which subverts the love relation. One might also be filled with *envy* at the success of others.

There is a set of negative feelings in our relation to others that is directed toward oneself. One might feel *shame* at what one has done either before others or even before oneself. One might also feel *embarrassment* before others. Shame is distinguished from embarrassment

---

19. See the Ladder to Beauty in Plato's *Symposium*, 211e–212a.

20. Anders Nygren, *Agape and Eros*, trans. Philip S. Watson (Philadelphia: Westminster Press, 1953), 200–201. See also C. S. Lewis, *The Four Loves* (New York: Harcourt, Brace, and Co., 1960), 1, 17.

in that shame presupposes inner identification with the common values one has violated. One might feel embarrassed without doing anything wrong, as when a naked person becomes aware that someone else is watching. Such embarrassment is the reverse side of a sense of *modesty*. *Guilt* is in a class with shame and embarrassment. It has both an objective and a subjective form: one might be guilty of something and not feel guilty, and vice-versa: a scrupulous person might feel guilty about something that should not be a matter of guilt.

There is another family of feelings regarding other persons. *Empathy*, in one sense of the term, is the recognition of the inner state of others based upon their outer expression.[21] *Sympathy* or *compassion*, is different. The words in their Greek etymology, mean "feeling-in" and "feeling-with," respectively. Sympathy goes beyond empathy in that one shares the emotional state of the other whose feeling-state one recognizes with empathy.[22] *Benevolence* (etymologically, "well-wishing") goes beyond feeling-with in order to act positively toward the other. *Pity* is a negative emotion at the sad plight of other people.

Again, all of this may be experienced with differing degrees of intensity. When there is a high degree of intensity, we find that proclivities become *emotions* whereby we are moved by given objects. Being moved or "being touched" is linked to "having a heart"; for one who is not moved in appropriate ways is "heartless." There are spiritual states of "being moved" that involve a transformation of one's heart. Of course, being-moved might also involve negative feelings like being moved to disgust at ignoble actions.

Emotion can reach such intensity that we are overwhelmed. Such intense emotions are called *passions*, although the latter term is also used for all desires that might overtake us. In contemporary usage, following one's passions means pursuing whatever kind of positive action has one in its grip: pursuing a career, a sport, an art, and the like. Let us go on to sketch out the leading passions in the traditional sense of the term.

---

21. See Edith Stein, *Finite and Eternal Being: An Attempt at an Ascent to the Meaning of Being*, trans. K. Reinhardt (Washington, D.C.: ICS Publications, 2002), 378–79.
22. See Scheler, *The Nature of Sympathy*, trans. P. Heath (New York: The Shoe String Press, 1973), 45–47, 49–50.

* * *

"Ruling one's passions" usually refers to bodily-based desires. They are called *passions* because we are *passive* to them; they arise "from below," or from the organic pole of our being, and they threaten to rule us as conscious agents. We may be overcome by several different kinds of passions: in addition to *lust* as overwhelming sexual desire and to *gluttony*, there is *greed, lust for power, arrogance,* and the like, as negative states. Lust and gluttony are disorienting and do not allow one in their grip to focus one's powers. However, passion might also refer to states that focus us and give us power in certain directions. Richard III's lust for power took hold of him and, far from subverting his functional capacity, actually made him cunning. Saints may be ruled by *zeal* for God's work, which once again brings all their powers into focus. "Nothing great is achieved without passion," said Hegel, without "giving it our all."[23] Everything turns upon what we allow to take hold of us.

The ruling negative passions in the traditional lists of governing states of mind are called the *Seven Capital Sins*, whose opposites are the traditional virtues. They emerge within a religious tradition and are modulated in differing ways. But since such a list emerges out of the possibilities of the direction of human life, we can use them to focus upon differing feelings independent of the religious context. Of course, the context involves a particular understanding of each *vice* and its corresponding *virtue*. But even without a religious ground, there are dispositions that set one off-kilter. The Capital Sins refer to major dispositions that possess us. They appear as intense feelings and give rise to acts that fortify the disposition. The traditional list consists of seven: *pride, envy, gluttony, lust, greed, sloth,* and *anger.*[24]

Gluttony (including drunkenness) and *lust* are rooted in our organic needs, which are then allowed to govern one's actions. Lust is not sexual desire any more than gluttony is hunger or thirst. The vices involve a disorder, an excess that disorients one gripped by the pas-

---

23. Hegel, *Philosophy of Mind,* §474, 235.

24. As in considering temperament, a basic question is: Why these four? So in the case of the Capital Sins, the question is: Why these seven? We have not pursued these questions here, but they deserve an answer.

sion. The disorder would be the inability to govern oneself holistically. *Sloth* would follow a phlegmatic temperament. The feeling involved is a sense of lethargy, an inability to stir oneself to action, being defeated in the face of challenges, and weakened by the feeling of effort. *Greed* is a desire for ever more in the area of possessions that would include external goods and also power over others. As a vice it comes to govern one's life in such a way that one might fail to pay attention to helping others or to what might happen to others because of the steps one takes to secure more possessions or power; it may lead to cheating them in some ways or even eliminating them. *Anger* follows the blockage by others or even by circumstances that stand in the way of reaching what one considers important: thus, love and hate, hope and fear stand at the base of the feeling of anger.

Like hunger, thirst, and sexual desire, *anger* as such is not a vice. It is the natural response of the animal organism to what blocks its flourishing and that of its mate and offspring. It becomes a vice when one loses control. But it might also focus one's powers to seek revenge or to overcome obstacles. Anger can be a momentary state, can turn into an angry mood, and can settle more deeply into an angry disposition. A choleric temperament inclines one toward this disposition. Everything depends upon shaping such impulses to fit the circumstances. Humanly modulated anger is as natural and proper as animal-based aggression, such that there is something wrong with someone who does not experience anger on appropriate occasions, for example, when confronting flagrant injustices.

The term *pride* is used in both positive and negative ways and is very much affected by the kind of religious context within which it operates. In the Aristotelian list of virtues, *megalopsychia* or greatness of soul has a significant place. It is a disposition of the talented and successful to seek great things and to have their greatness recognized.[25] In the Christian understanding, that sounds like inordinate pride. One may say that an individual who lacks the disposition, who is slovenly and lives in filth and disorder or, as an adult, lives off others, has no pride or no self-respect and is lacking a sense of personal neatness and initiative.

---

25. Aristotle, *Nicomachean Ethics* IV.iii.1123b-IV.v.1136a.

One may justifiably be proud of one's own children and grandchildren when they reach various levels and types of success, but there is a line between being proud and bragging. When one thinks more highly of oneself than one ought, pride becomes *vanity*, and when one lords it over others, it becomes *arrogance*. Somewhere Architect Frank Lloyd Wright said that early in his life he was confronted by a choice between honest arrogance and false humility; and he chose the former.[26] Of course, honesty about oneself need not be accompanied by arrogance; and acknowledging one's shortcomings need not be false.

In the tradition, the Seven Deadly Sins are reduced to two: pride and concupiscence, the latter as disorderly desire. They follow from the two poles of human existence. Concupiscence arises from the disordering of hunger, thirst, and sexual desire and can be linked to the lack of initiative called sloth. Corresponding to the ontological pole, pride is setting oneself against the proper order of things in disordering anger, greed, and envy.

The virtues traditionally viewed as opposite the vices are *humility* opposite pride; *temperance* opposite gluttony; *chastity* opposite lust; *commitment* or, as an extreme, *zeal* opposite sloth; *generosity* opposite greed; *gentleness* opposite anger; and *admiration* opposite envy. *Humility* is not on the ancient lists of virtues. It emerges in Christianity. But there certainly is a disposition opposite to the negative forms of pride: accepting oneself for what one is, talented or not, and not looking down on others. Humility might become a vice if one regularly undervalues one's own achievements or even pretends to be less than one actually is. And if one has any significant achievements, humility consists in recognizing but not flaunting them. *Bragging* about oneself or one's offspring would be an exhibition of inordinate pride. One way of looking at humility is to consider it a willingness to be measured by objective standards, as pride consists in not allowing oneself to be measured. I would suggest that a deeper humility consists in allowing one's measures to be measured. Such humility might look like arrogance in relation to traditional measures, but it is the calling of the philosopher.

Again, these are dispositions issuing from felt tendencies to behave appropriately in situations. As Aristotle noted, virtue lies in a mean relative to the situation determined by practical wisdom that is itself made possible by virtuous disposition, the fruit of right upbringing. Furthermore, the noble man enjoys noble deeds; he who does not is not a noble man.[27] It is thus a matter of the heart. Problems with all of these vices and virtues arise from stereotypical understanding, which hides the reasons for praising one set and condemning the other.

The multiform life of feeling sometimes seems like a battlefield of conflicting feelings clamoring for our attention. This leads to some views that real life for a human being consists in reducing the life of feeling and in distrust of one's heart. Stoic philosophy holds up *apathia* or *ataraxia* as ideals: feelinglessness, unruffledness.[28] This is at least parallel to the Buddha's teaching that aims at *nirvana*, literally "the blowing out" of desire, the fruit of which is *serenity*. But there is also the compassionate Buddha, with a disposition to care for others. With Kant's emphasis upon duty, he seems Stoic; yet his whole critical project is grounded in awe. On his tombstone was written: "the starry skies above and the moral law within," which is a quotation from the end of his ethical work that is prefaced by: "two things fill me with awe."[29] Such awe is not foreign to Stoicism, as evidenced in Cleanthes' "Hymn to Zeus."[30] This brings us to a further consideration of the distinctive kinds of feeling that we might call *spiritual feelings*.

* * *

We have already noted such feelings in certain types of love and, on the negative end, in despair. We have taken note of awe, of being moved in a transformative way, and of having zeal for achieving the good and warding off evil. What distinguishes them is this: the recognition that something ultimate is involved, or what Paul Tillich calls

26. See *Simpson's Contemporary Quotations*, ed. James G. Simpson (Boston: Houghton Mifflin, 1988), no. 5547.

27. Aristotle, *Nicomachean Ethics* I.viii.1099.a12–4.

28. This originated with Pyrrho of Elis and was followed by Epictetus. See Epictetus, *The Discourses* I.4, IV.3.

29. Immanuel Kant, *Critique of Practical Reason*, trans. L. W. Beck (Indianapolis: Bobbs-Merrill, 1956), concl: 166. On Kant's Aesthetic, see my *Placing Aesthetics*, 117–58.

30. *The Stoic and Epicurean Philosophers*, ed. W. Oates (New York: Modern Library, 1957), 591–93.

the "Ultimate Concern." Spiritual feelings are aesthetic or religious or even intellectual and may shade off into one another.

First then, are *intellectual* feelings: intellectually one might be overtaken by *awe*, not as a temporary state, but as an underlying condition that propels inquiry. It is an awareness that suddenly brings to presence a haunting strangeness about our normal experience.[31] Originally impelled by it, one might lose sight of it and pursue only the problematic. It may generate *curiosity* that leads to a search for solutions to problems we encounter and to a feeling of satisfaction in arriving at the solutions. But whereas curiosity is stilled by the solution, awe lies at a deeper level. Awe is grounded in our being always referred beyond anything we can master to the always-encompassing Totality rooted in "the Mystery of Being."[32] Linked to that is the deep intellectual satisfaction in coming to be aware of the general lines of the entire context of our existence.

Here belong the kinds of experiences a scientist might feel when, for example, he not only looks and calculates but contemplates telescopic viewing with calculations of distances, being taken by the immensity of the distances involved. One could develop such contemplative awareness of the depth of time, the minuteness of the ultimate particles, the underlying complexity of even the simplest of things, and the unbelievable complexity of the human body. A deep sense of awe can emerge in this spiritual kind of "seeing" that is neither sensory nor intellectual but both, in the kind of fusion that touches and transforms one's heart.[33] It is this kind of vision that is the origin of lyric poetry.

Second, consider *aesthetic* feelings: they begin with pleasures of sense where one seeks one's own fine feelings and nothing ultimate is involved. Music in particular induces such a state of fine feeling. Aristotle said that music is the most imitative of the artforms when it comes to presenting *ethos* or felt disposition.[34] Indeed, music can induce the whole gamut of feelings.

31. See Heidegger, *What Is Philosophy?*, trans. J. Wilde and W. Kluback (Lanham: Rowan and Littlefield, 2003), 79–85, 185.
32. See Gabriel Marcel, *The Mystery of Being*, trans. G. Fraser, vol. 1 (Chicago: Regnery, 1960), 260–61.
33. See the preface "On Seeing" in de Chardin's *The Phenomenon of Man*, 32.
34. Aristotle, *Poetics* 1447a.13–26, 1448a.1–9; *Politics*, 1340a.5–25. See also my *Placing Aesthetics*, 77–79.

In the latter, the appreciation of the beautiful produces a feeling, but that feeling is not what is sought. It involves a decentering from desire in order to evoke appreciation, unconstrained by appetites. Beauty lies first of all in the character of the form of the sensory: the way colors, light and shadow, and the distribution of shapes are together harmoniously or the way sound is articulated through rhythm and harmony. But one might also learn to see beauty in the way the sensory surface expresses the underlying dynamics of natural processes, both in terms of current eco-systemic functioning and in terms of evolutionary background.[35] This involves a hollowing out of a space of meaning behind the actuality of sensory presence. One finds something similar in the expressivity of human behavior in and through the sensory surface. A rather plain face lit up with a smile is indeed beautiful. More profoundly, one finds the beauty of character that shines through the behavior of one who exhibits what otherwise might be an uncomely exterior. However, when distance between interior and exterior is extreme, when the exterior is extremely unsightly, as in Victor Hugo's Quasimodo, the beauty is more difficult to discern.

Distinguished from aesthetic awe is intellectual awe, which is evoked by encounter with magnitude, whether of size or of power. Aesthetic awe involves a feeling of our own tininess and impotence as a negative moment that also involves a sublime feeling of spiritual uplift, which Kant locates in our ability to think beyond any magnitude and in our moral call, which raises us above our animal-like feeling of fear.[36]

Not all spiritual feelings are positive. There are such states as despair and defiance. In *despair* one gives up on meaning and may be led to thoughts of one's own extinction. In spiritual *defiance*, one stands proudly against the order of things. There is the terrifying: "Better to reign in hell than to serve in heaven"—a line from Milton's *Paradise Lost*, which Jack London's captain in *The Sea-Wolf* cites approvingly.[37]

---

35. See Carlson and Berleant, *Aesthetics*.

36. Kant, *Critique of Judgment*, trans. W. Pluhar (Indianapolis: Hackett, 1987), §29/267ff.

37. John Milton, *Paradise Lost*, ed. M. Kelley, bk. 1 (New York: Walter J. Black, 1943), 100. It is cited in Jack London's *The Sea-Wolf* (New York: Grosset and Dunlap, 1904), chap. XXVI, 249.

In addition to intellectual and aesthetic feelings, there are distinctively *religious* feelings. As Hegel observed, religion involves a rising of the heart from the everyday to the Eternal and Encompassing, which is akin to intellectual awe.[38] Schleiermacher described a feeling of absolute *dependence*,[39] and Edith Stein called attention to an experience of being cradled in the arms of the Father, an experience that overcame the *Angst* her colleague Martin Heidegger described.[40] Rudolf Otto spoke of the experience of the numinous as *mysterium tremendum et fascinans* (a mystery that is both fearful and spellbinding), which, like Kant's sublime, evokes both negative and positive feelings.[41] There is a deep sense of *gratitude* for whatever gifts we have received. And there is, in addition, a feeling of great *sorrow* for having broken with God.

Essential to religious sensibility is a deep sense of the *presence* of God, "in Whom we live and move and have our being,"[42] which fills the empty space of reference to totality with something more than an inference or a conventional belief and calls forth *adoration* that might break forth in *praise*. *Sursum corda*: lift up your hearts. What is Beyond, Other, Encompassing, and Underlying can be experienced as such: perhaps as the Mystery, the permanently hidden that beckons us, as in Heidegger's thought or in Taoism; or perhaps as Personal Address, which involves the feeling of being called, as in the biblical tradition.[43] Here one lives at the level of what might be called one's *heart of hearts*, the native desire correlative to the drive toward the Totality, which underlies everything distinctively human. Again, there is a feeling of *peace and serenity* based upon total commitment to whatever God might send our way. It is not rooted in the blowing out of

38. Hegel, *Lectures on the Philosophy of Religion*, vol. 1, trans. E. Spiers and J. Sanderson (London: Kegan Paul, Trench, Trübner, and Co., 1895), 3–6, 17–19; Wood, *Placing Aesthetics*, 182.

39. Schleiermacher, *On Religion: Speeches to Its Cultured Despisers*, trans. John Oman (London: Kegan Paul, Trench, Trübner, and Co., 1893), xliv–xiv, lii–liii, 205–6.

40. Edith Stein, "The Being of the Ego and Eternal Being," in *Finite and Eternal Being*, 55–60; Heidegger, *BT*, I, vi, 170–79.

41. Rudolph Otto, *The Idea of the Holy*, trans. J. Harvey (New York: Oxford University Press, 1964), 12–40; Kant, *Critique of Judgment*, §23/245, §29/269, 271.

42. Acts 17:8.

43. Heidegger, *BT*, II, II, 251–53; Tao-te Ching, 1; Buber, *I and Thou*, 159–60.

Table 4-3: The Structure of Humanness

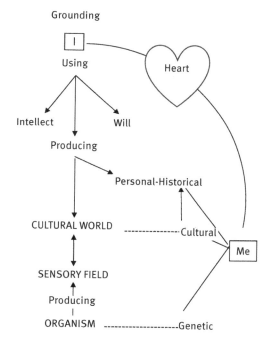

NOTION OF BEING

REFERENCE TO TOTALITY

Principle of Noncontradiction

Grounding

| I |

Using

Heart

Intellect   Will

Producing

Personal-Historical

CULTURAL WORLD ---------------Cultural

Me

SENSORY FIELD

Producing

ORGANISM ------------------Genetic

one's own desires, but in detachment from them. This detachment moves us, as the hymn would have it, "beyond our hopes, beyond our fears, from death into life,"[44] that is, from spiritual death to life in being overcome by our passion for eternity, identifying with the cosmic order, its Source, or both. The task of life is to align the order of our hopes and fears with a sense of the total context of human existence.

As we noted before, Augustine famously noted the restlessness of the human heart. It is rooted in the fact that we are referred, beyond

44. From Marty Haugen's "Shepherd Me, O God," a liturgical hymn based upon Psalm 23.

all limited modes of knowing, doing, and feeling, to the encompassing Whole as absolute Mystery. Whether or not we read that Mystery as personal Presence, it is what our hearts belong to by nature.

* * *

This is but a sketch of the wealth of felt experience that plays in our hearts. Understanding it gives us a stronger grasp of ourselves and furnishes the basis for a philosophic anthropology that does not simply privilege intellectual and volitional operations, for they themselves are rooted in the desires of the human heart. I would even go so far as to say, with Max Scheler and Dietrich von Hildebrand, that the heart is the real self—one's deep subjectivity—and the task of intellectual and volitional operations is to guide the direction of one's heart.[45] After all, even Aristotle said that virtue is about *feeling* aright regarding the good and the bad—provided it terminates in acting aright. In the virtuous person, feelings have been so ordered that they spontaneously move in the direction of the good.

---

45. Dietrich von Hildebrand, *The Heart* (South Bend: St. Augustine's Press, 2007). See also my article "Dietrich von Hildebrand on the Heart," *Quaestiones disputatae* 3, no. 2 (Spring 2013): 107–19 and my "Virtues, Values, and the Heart," 132–46.

Chapter 5

Phenomenology of the Book
A Study of Institutions

n chapter 1, we began by reflecting upon the book you are currently reading: the color of its pages, its shape, its smell, its "feel," and the sound it makes when the pages are turned. From a sensory point a view, a book is primarily something to be seen and handled. Seeing and handling each have their own essential features. Reflecting further upon the nature of sensory objects as such, and not just as visual and tactual objects, we found that each has five general characteristics: it is individual, immediately given in the Here-and-Now, actual, confined within its own boundaries, and in observable seamless continuity with its antecedents and consequents. The importance of this observation is shown by contrast when we reflect upon the nature of awareness, both sensory and intellectual.

Sensory awareness, in animals as well as humans, involves *a transcendence of the boundaries* of the organism by being cognitively "out there" with the objects observed. Our neuro-psychological system (functioning anonymously) gathers up the past and anticipates the future, having learnt from the past and having projected its goals; it therefore transcends the immediacy of sensory presentations. Intellectual awareness involves the presentation of *universals* as the types to which sensed individuals belong and the powers that underlie their sensory presentation. This means that intellectual awareness transcends the Here-and-Now of sensory experience to be implicitly aware of Space and Time as encompassing wholes, for universal notions are *potentially* applicable *any time* and *any place* their instances can be found and are capable of being recognized. Finally, through intellectual awareness, having the primordial distance from any situation provided by the notion of Being, we have the *freedom* to initiate new causal lines into the apparent seamless, visually observable continuity between antecedents and consequents. The way what is Ultimate is present to our hearts, how we dwell in relation to the object of Ultimate Concern, pervades our lives.

Viewing the situation in terms of the Flatland model, we found that, in addition to the four "outward" dimensions of space (3-D) and time (4-D), there are three "inward" dimensions of sensing (5-D), intellection (6-D), and reference to the Whole (7-D). The interplay of these dimensions displays three levels of determination that each of us finds operative right now: a genetically based level that limns each of our individual possibilities, a culturally introjected level produced by our primary caregivers and reenforced in many ways by the continuing impact of the surrounding culture, and the level of our current character formed from the choices we each have made based on the possibilities these three levels have opened up as we understood them. The operation of these levels percolates downward to establish the set of proclivities that form what a long tradition has called *the heart*, which determines how we dwell in relation to the Whole. The heart fits into the bipolar view of human existence by being a magnetic field of attractions, repulsions, and neutralities unique to each individual. It is the default mode for our everyday actions and choices.

In a previous chapter we therefore explored the "inner life" of the human being as the life of feeling guided by *the heart*. Now we will add a further consideration of *institutions*: we will return to the book to unpack those intentional strands that go beyond its founding sensory and intellectual presentations. Here we will explore what John Searle has called "the huge invisible ontology" of first- and second-person relations, which we began to explore earlier.[1] We will look to the interpersonal field, the distinction between nature and *techne*, the production and distribution systems in which it is embedded, the distinction between speech and writing, the nature of language, and the nature of literature.

LANGUAGE (I)

I am addressing you, my readers, through the English language, which I have learned from my parents. Language is the founding institution

---

1. Searle, *The Construction of Social Reality* (New York: Free Press, 1995), 3.

that lies at the basis of all institutions, for it is language that opens up the space for whatever we humans do and allows us to pass them on to subsequent generations.

All language is grounded in an *I* addressing a You within a common space of meaning developed through tradition. Induction into a language places one outside of one's individual privacy and into a common space of meaning. Thus, if someone says, "We are each locked within our privacy," we know perfectly well what that means. In that case, the content of the utterance contradicts the claim. But to be outside in the realm of public meaning is also to be outside in the environment through the sounds and sights that typically exhibit language to us "out there."

The saying is the generation of sound or its linguistic equivalent articulated so as to embody a meaning that discloses or fails to disclose the "something" about which one (an *I*) is speaking to another (a You). Intention of the speaker and disclosure of what is spoken about are important, but the rhetorical adjustment of what is said to the character of the hearer is also significant.

It is language that allows each of us to move beyond entertaining images and undergoing feelings within the privacy of our minds to articulating conceptually what we are thinking. Thought moves within language as it repeats common conceptions. In the case of introducing new insights, the initial thought is a sense of direction that seeks the right words that can best articulate and develop the thought. Finding the words clarifies the thought-direction for the thinker who can then pass it on to an audience. So language is not simply a way we communicate with others; it is the way in which we are able to think for ourselves.

The language employed involves words, which are sensory stand-ins for the apprehension of universal meaning—that is, meaning applicable to an indeterminate number of instances. The audile or visual or tactual (Braille) pattern is the observable outside that stands in for the meaning "inside," which inhabits the sensory as the human awareness inhabits the body—though only for human awareness. Each word that I am employing has been introduced as a convention peculiar to the tradition that carries it on. Given the geographical separation of initial traditions, the accumulated conventional sounds in one tradition are sharply differentiated from all other linguistic traditions, though there are distinct language groups such as the Indo-European group to which the currently employed language belongs.

Hearing someone speak in a foreign language, one only apprehends a flow of sounds. For one who lives in the language, the sounds are purely subsidiary to the communication that is going on in the common space of meaning. Words spoken, like the concepts they instantiate, are again like glasses: we usually look *through* them not *at* them. They are transparent media. But now we are reflecting upon them, making them the object of our attention.

Just as a word is an empirical stand-in for a universal meaning, each word as a sound or visual or tactual pattern itself is a cultural universal standing over against the indeterminate number of instances in which it can be employed. Over the history of its usage, a given word may have accumulated several different meanings. Each meaning, in turn, can be understood only in relation to the meanings that unpack it. Each word in a definition has a definition itself, and so on and so on, until one sees that the whole of our possible usages is a network of interrelated meanings that extends to everything about which one can speak. The dictionary lists all the words that are currently employed in a given language and constitute its semantics in which several meanings accumulate around a given word. Which meaning is involved in an actual discourse can only be discovered within the sentence (minimally a noun and a verb) in relation to its own referent.

As things might be defined in different ways, the network exhibits differences in definitional lines for different persons, groups, epochs, and cultures. One of the meanings that accrue to words is *metaphoric* meaning. Metaphor means a carrying (*phorein*) over (*meta*) of meaning from a literal instance to one related to it by reason of external similarities (so *metaphor* is itself a metaphor). It is commonplace to claim with Nietzsche that all language is metaphor—a claim that can only be sustained by so thinning out the notion of metaphor that it well-nigh evaporates. For Nietzsche, the transfer of the causal impact of light into visual awareness of color is the first metaphor, the transfer of sound into a meaning is the second, while the third is what I have been calling *metaphor*.[2] The first two suggestions do not pertain to meaning; they are themselves meaningless, though the latter is meaning-founding. They belong to the realm of causality, not to the realm of meaning and the space of reasons.

Metaphor is a favorite device of poets, who draw upon the transfer of highly charged emotive terms to the theme of their meditation. But again, when a term is being used metaphorically can only be determined by its use in a sentence aimed at some referent. The distinction between metaphor and simile seems slight: the latter adds *like*. But there is a great difference. A simile requires an intellectual mode of attention that abstracts from the emotional tonality surrounding the original usage of the word now used metaphorically. It is the emotional tonality upon which poetry draws.

The other side of the meaning of the word is its sound. The concatenation of sounds in spoken language is another feature drawn upon by poets, who ideally produce a texture of sounds that matches the referent of the poem in the disposition it creates.

The putting together of words in a sentence so as to refer to something is governed by the syntax of the language: a set of universal rules that determine the different grammatical functions presented in declension of nouns and conjugation of verbs together with their supplementary functions (e.g., adjectives and adverbs). The semantics and syntactics of a given language together form a universal structure—or a system having a kind of atemporal existence—drawn upon in the temporal event of discourse, which, over time and in the innovations of genius, leads to a glacially slow transformation of the structures in what then appears as their quasi-atemporality. The linguistic system is atemporal with regard to the event of speaking or writing, but it is temporal with regard to the very long-range picture. The system changes over time, but at a glacial pace.

So, whether it is written or spoken, discourse is rooted in an *I* addressing a You by uttering a sentential set of meanings that refer to the objects about which the discourse is conducted. Just as a word, or even a phoneme or a letter of the alphabet, is a universal over

---

2. Wood, "True and False in Nietzsche's *Truth and Lies*," *Existentia* 25, fasc. 3–4 (2015): 201–13.

against the individual instances of its utterance, so the sentence is a universal so related to the individual instances of its own utterance. The meaning of the sentence can be translated into different languages, so that meaning, though it always requires sensory instantiation, is not tied to any given language. However, the network of meanings that unpack a given word that translates into a foreign language is not one-to-one the same as the network of what appears as the same meaning in a different language. Finally, the truth of a given sentence is determined by its manifesting or failing to manifest the actual character of its referents.

The space of meaning grounds linguistic manifestation as each word reverberates both sonorously and in terms of the interplay of literal and metaphorical meanings. And though it may seem that language is only an instrument we employ, more deeply considered, it is a mode of manifestation that holds us in its grips. We are taken up into the meanings afforded by language.[3]

Language indicates two essential features of being human: thought comes to itself as it *incarnates* itself in words, and the words we use bear witness to our essential *sociality*. For Aristotle, the defining characteristic of the human being is that it is *zoion politikon*, or a political animal: that is, one who lives off of tradition, who flourishes through institutions long in the making. For Aristotle too, the human being is *zoion logon echon*, commonly translated as "rational animal"; but *logos*, before it is "logic," is language.[4] The human being is a linguistic animal and therefore a political animal and therefore a rational animal. Rationality is the inward ground of humanness, which can only be activated through its sociality and its incarnation in speech wherein we are sensate beings suffused and suffusing with meaning.

* * *

The wakeful life of the human being takes place largely in the interpersonal realm, whether directly or indirectly. In my writing this book and in your reading it, there is present a relation between I and You rooted in language. As I said in the beginning, in generating my

3. Martin Heidegger, "A Dialogue on Language," in *On the Way toward Language*, trans. P. Hertz (San Francisco: Harper and Row, 1971), 35–36, 40–41.
4. Aristotle, *Politics* I.I.1253a.4.

text, I am, in my absence, now indirectly present to You reading my text in my future and in your present. Let us first consider *You and Me*. Let us consider our present state as the terminus of a long maturation process, viewing ourselves unfolding like the unfolding of a plant from seed to flower presented in a few minutes through time-lapse photography. And here we should not only intellectually follow the meanings involved but should meditate on the process so that our whole past becomes a sort of "vision," drawing near to us, touching us. This is the sort of awareness expressed in lyric poetry.

So, as I write this and you read it, we are both differently tuned but occupying the same linguistic world. And, since you are reading *this*, we occupy the peculiar subworld of philosophical exploration. Of course, the script or a book is not a You. But it is expressive of the meaning apprehended and articulated by Me *vis-á-vis* You and read by You *vis-á-vis* Me. And it is that expression you are attempting to reanimate, by reading, from the dead letter that is fixed on the page.

In prose we have the exhibition of the apprehension of linguistically formulatable meaning shorn (for the most part) of any explicit symbolic references. But the lived character of our relation to objects is more easily recognizable in poetry, which, as we noted, rests upon the emotive reverberation of words in linguistic meaning and in meaningful sound. Our lived relation is also recognizable in the arts generally. Though both prose and poetry originally appeared in speech, they now appear in writing and thus in books. Let us look more carefully then at the book, which is the focus of our current labors and anchor of our exploration of the nodes of inter-subjective relation within which it functions.

THE BOOK ONCE MORE

Consider again a book lying on the desk before you. Any book will do. In fact, you do not even have to consider a real book; an imaginary one will do. The reason is that we have already achieved an eidetic inventory: an implicit but functional list of the essential features of the nature of a book that enables each of us to pick one out when we see it. We might say, in a preliminary way, that a book is a set of bound pages containing writing, images, or both.

Spontaneously we focus upon it as something to be read; but that focus presupposes several pre-focal elements that give us access to it. It is seen; it is there to be handled; its pages generate sound when turned; it may give off a peculiar odor; and it could be—though not advisedly—tasted. That is, it is an *empirical object* correlated with our sensing capacities. Secondly, it is a *material object,* where the term *material* initially refers to its accessibility to the senses.[5] As such it presupposes certain supportive substructures of potentiality that are not immediately given in the field of sensory experience. Furthermore, it is embedded in various traditions: the tradition of bookmaking, the tradition of purchase and exchange, and most significantly, the literary tradition. It is a *technological object*, an *economic object*, and finally, a *literary object.* It is the latter way of showing itself, sitting atop a hierarchy of structures, that is typically focal.

The book shows a hierarchy like one's own awareness of it that (1) is embedded in a spatiotemporal matrix, (2) possesses an organically articulated substructure, (3) senses, and (4) reads the book, in that hierarchical order. The words on a page are also correlatively so embedded, articulated in print, capable of being seen, and aimed at being read. The words are placeholders for the activation of communicative meaning accomplished by readers who exhibit that parallel hierarchy.

We have dealt with the sensory fields and the levels of awareness in chapter 1 and reinforced and developed them in subsequent chapters. Here we will consider the distinction between nature and *techne*.

TECHNICAL PRODUCTION

The book's feature of having been technically produced supports its book quality. *Techne* is set over against *phusis*, or nature, which it partly imitates and partly completes.[6] Men made spears in imitation of the protective function of the horns or teeth or claws or beaks of animals, and in so doing completed what was lacking for defense and attack in unaided human nature. Further, through *techne* we have

---

5. For a development of this theme, see my "Five Bodies and a Sixth: On the Place of Awareness in an Evolutionary World," in *The Beautiful, the True, and the Good*, 312–23.

6. Aristotle, *Physics* 2.8199a.15.

learned to form the built environment as a second nature within which we dwell.[7]

In the case of the book, the wood pulp and the chemical components that constitute the ink and glue are made from materials provided by nature. The processing of these components into a form suitable for the artifacts constructed from them to fulfill humanly projected purposes requires the physical abstraction of components of nature and their analysis and resynthesis. Such abstraction, analysis, and synthesis are not merely mental but also require our acting upon external nature, handling it in various ways. In fact, merely looking at things, no matter how carefully, will not yield nearly as much knowledge about them as will our actively manipulating them and in the process seeing what we could not otherwise see.[8] Though one should not disparage "armchair" philosophizing such as we are now exercising, since it makes explicit what is presupposed but usually not reflected upon in our scientific and technologically aided probing.

Eye and hand go together with the abstraction of regularities, the projection of purposes, and the reformation of things. Things so treated are no longer simply empirical objects but are so reconstructed as to serve our ends; they become instruments, new organs that extend those organs given by nature, such as our eyes and our hands. An empirical inspection of the parts that go into the construction of instruments will not tell us what the instrument is: only the purpose will tell us what it is and why the parts are shaped the way they are.[9] The instruments are correlated with the development in ourselves of

7. See the last chapter, which deals with the built environment, in my *Nature, Art-forms, and the World.*

8. That is Hegel's observation in his treatment of the master-slave relation. In working with things, the slave discovers properties of things not available through looking alone, and he develops capacities for *manipulation that would* otherwise have lain fallow. Hegel, *Phenomenology of Spirit,* 111–19. Alexandre Kojéve made this the center of his interpretation of Hegel's view of history. *Introduction to the Reading of Hegel,* trans. J. Nichols (Ithaca: Cornell University Press, 1969), 20–25.

9. See Socrates' discussion of the 100 parts of a wagon in *Theaetetus* 307a. See also Robert Pirsig, *Zen, and the Art of Motorcycle Maintenance* (New York: William Morrow and Company, 1974), 94–99. This contains a similar observation of the parts of a motorcycle. Memorizing the shape of each part will not in the least reveal the character of the bike until one knows the purpose and how the parts serve the purposes and thus have the shapes they do.

new powers to understand and manipulate in view of our deliberately projected ends. In working over nature, we add acquired skills to our native powers for seeing and apprehending.

As we noted previously, our natural powers, developed habits, and the built-in capacity of artifacts to serve our needs are concrete universals; that is, they are not simply individual aspects of individual organisms or tools, but *universal* orientations toward the *kind* of things correlative to them. Here I emphasize *universal* and *kind*. Thus, seeing is a native power oriented by nature toward *all things* of the kind we call colored. Natural powers and natural kinds go together. An individual aspect of individual organisms, seeing is a universally oriented power. It and its universal correlate, color, are natural kinds of powers and generic aspects whose instances are *individual* aspects of *individual* things as objects of *individual* acts of seeing by *individual* organically situated seers. Nominalism is given the lie by attention to such powers and their correlates. Individual things presented in their sensed individuality are the locus of powers of acting and being acted upon, and as such are not simply individual as over against the universals we use to describe them; they are *individual* clusters of *universal* orientations, both active and passive. And since there are natural powers, there are *natural kinds* that are correlative to them. Each entity is a peculiar cluster of such powers, constituting its actual or possible relations to things in its actual or possible environment.[10] And native powers are found in the kind of things that are produced as instances of a given kind of organism—in our case, the human kind. It is the task of scientific inquiry to develop methods for discovering the powers that each kind of being possesses—which it can only do by becoming ever more technologically sophisticated, putting the object through various tests to see how it reacts.[11]

Developed skills in intelligently manipulating nature raise our native powers to a higher power, establishing new universal orienta-

10. Plato in his *Sophist* suggested that the definition of being is the power of acting and being acted upon (247e). See also my "Individuals, Universals, and Capacity," *The Review of Metaphysics* 54, no. 3 (March 2001), 512–14.

11. This is why Heidegger claims that the essence of modern natural science is technological. *The Question Concerning Technology and Other Essays*, trans. W. Lovitt (New York: Harper, 1977), 25.

tions, since the ability to manufacture one book entails the ability to produce an indeterminate number of books. And, like any artifact, a book has the power to have its meaning activated an indefinite number of times.

PRODUCTION OF THE BOOK

A book does not exist by nature; it exists as a result of the peculiar technology of book production, which has a history. And here we move for a time beyond phenomenology to de-sediment our initial access to things. Think again of Kurt Vonnegut's *Slaughterhouse Five*, in which, as we have previously noted, he presents a vision of the bombers that created the massive firestorms in Dresden during World War II moving in reverse: the bombs sucking up the fires, the planes sucking up the bombs, running backward and returning to their base and then to the factories that assembled them and to the factories that produced the parts, and then to the plants that processed the raw materials extracted from the earth. Meditate this way on all the current humanly produced structures that surround us: our bookshelves, walls, homes, rugs, windows, desks, computers, clothing, eyeglasses, etc. All of the current built environment is the sedimented result of a whole history of coming into being that stretches back to the cavemen and beyond. This history involves, among other things, the progressive unveiling of different properties of the materials involved in the production process that further empowers human existence. Current artifacts present a functional surface that not only conceals underlying natural powers, but also conceals the depth of the historical process that produced them.[12] In a way, such meditation develops that "thinking as thanking" central to Heidegger's thought. Gratitude and appreciation can arise out of such meditation.

So we look at the book's antecedents. Initially there were clay or stone tablets, then papyrus followed by velum rolled up into scrolls, and finally thinner paper sheets laid flat and bound together in a codex. Clay was worked by means of a stylus pressed into a moist surface that

---

12. See the postscript to this chapter on pp. 147–149 for further meditations upon the built environment.

was allowed to dry and was then rendered hard by being heated to a high temperature and afterward slowly cooled. Stone tablets had to be rendered smooth and were then worked with hammer and chisel. Papyrus was formed from reeds bundled together, and velum from the hides of sheep scraped smooth. Early so-called "books" were not like our books as the bound gatherings of flat pages; instead, they were scrolls that were rolled up papyrus or velum. A book like the Bible ("The Book") was not an original physical unity, but rather a set of scrolls. The title *Pentateuch* for the first five books of the Bible means "five scrolls." To get them all into one "book" (*biblos*) required many centuries of bookmaking technology, beginning with papermaking. (It also involved the authoritative determination of the canon in the second century A.D. by Jews for the Hebrew Bible and around 400 A.D. by Christians for the Old and New Testaments.) But even after bookmaking, the Torah or the Pentateuch is still available in synagogues in a single, very thick scroll where one must labor to find passages by unrolling in one direction while rolling up in the other.

Bound pages have been typically covered with stiff stock to preserve the interior, produced at first by the labor of handwriting. In more recent times, paperbacks have replaced hardbacks. Also in recent times with the widespread development of literacy, the production of newspapers, magazines, and pamphlets as variations on the theme of books are tied to their typically dated character and thus to their ready disposability. Hence their lack of any durable cover, even the relative durability of a paperback. Magazines are like books, only usually thinner and shorter. But some books, especially children's books, are not as big as some magazines.

Papermaking involves producing wood pulp mixed with a solution that makes it stick together and permits it to be smoothed out, dried, and cut, and to endure over long periods of time. Paper was thin enough to allow a stack of pages to be bound together to make books as we now know them. But, by reason of the comparatively crude paper technology, the first books or codices were large and heavy and of limited length compared to contemporary books.

The development of papyrus, velum, and paper had to be correlated with the discovery of properties of certain liquids that would lay down a track, dry, and remain for long periods of time without fading. One wonders how many experiments had to be conducted to find an ink that would endure on paper over long periods of time, for it takes long periods of time to discover that. (The same holds for paint colors.)

The time involved in writing by hand upon manuscripts was shortened immensely by the invention of mobile type and processes of ink application that allowed an indefinite number of reproductions of identical characters. More sophisticated machine-production magnified the speed of production, while the development of the computer eliminated the need for typesetting from original manuscripts. Word processing significantly reduced the time of composition, since one could add, delete, and reposition text without having to type the whole thing over several times to reach the final version. It also led to the development of e-books, which can be downloaded in increasingly greater numbers from some of the world's greatest libraries. (We will reflect further upon e-books when we consider the electronic revolution.)

The amount of time involved in hand-copying made the early process of book production labor intensive and thus quite expensive, so that only the rich or certain institutions like monasteries or churches could afford a book. That is why they were often chained up like telephone directories in public phone booths.

Rapid mechanical reproduction allowed widespread dissemination of texts and thus aided the transition from an essentially aural culture to a predominantly visual culture. The former involved dependency upon a speaker and heavy reliance upon audile memory. The latter allowed the spatial and temporal separability of the reader from the writer, with the reader able to read what, when, and where he wished from texts produced far away and in different eras. This promoted a thrust toward individualism as well as increasing reliance upon the text, which Plato called an *external memory*, a supplement to natural memory.[13] The introduction of the printing press in the West extended literacy and stimulated the Protestant reliance upon individual belief. Literacy was a step in the direction of "seeing for oneself" and not being wholly dependent upon others to tell one what to think and do. It took

---

13. Plato, *Phaedrus* 275a. Ironically, it is *in writing* that Plato recorded his objection to writing.

readers away from the face-to-face relations involved in speech acts and stimulated private withdrawal to read and thus possibly to think for oneself. It thus laid the psychological basis for new research into nature and history by breaking from past conceptions.[14]

Of course, the various media are subjected to the general flux of physical things. Whatever form emerges—including our own human form—eventually falls back into the elements that entered into its composition. The various media for the preservation of the written word have greater and lesser capacities for enduring. Stone is the most enduring ("set in stone"), paper the least (and within that genus, non-acid-free paper the very least). The judgment of import preserves what is considered valuable by copying it into another medium or another instance of the same medium, so that writing from millennia ago can still be read in contemporary copies.

The transmission process was occasionally halted by the destruction of great libraries at the command of fanatical Muslim leaders who claimed either the insidiousness or the superfluity of all but the Koran: a book was insidious if it disagreed with the Koran, superfluous if it agreed. (They did not seem to consider another option: a book might deal with something—let's say, subatomic physics—of which the Koran says nothing.) Significant works are also translated from their original version to reach a wider audience. In fact, through translations, a given book may reach a universal literate audience: the meaning of a text can be activated an indeterminate number of times.

The actions of the Muslim leaders call attention to the effort made throughout the ages to control what is accessible to a given reading population. Fascist book burning was a more recent attempt. The former Catholic Index of Forbidden Books (thankfully no longer in effect) was also an attempt in that direction: something like four thousand books were on the Index when it was rescinded by Pope Paul VI in 1966. Censorship of any sort is a variation on the same theme.

Let me underscore the basis for such historical considerations: it is aimed at a meditation that gains an appreciative sense of the his-

14. Of course, these observations were made decades ago by Marshall McLuhan, *The Guttenberg Galaxy: The Making of Typographic Man* (Toronto: University of Toronto Press, 1962), 156–58.

torical sedimentation behind the artefacts in our current environment. Everything that surrounds us in the built environment takes on a new dimension of depth. It is another way of attending to the being, and not simply the appearance, of the present state of things.

THE EXCHANGE SYSTEM

The book is lying on the table, its production process hidden by its pastness but sedimented in the product. The distribution and exchange process that allowed me to purchase the book is also hidden. In earliest times one would have engaged in bartering, haggling with the seller for what she or he would accept as having value equivalent to the book. Prior to printing, the equivalency would have been significant, given the labor-intensity of writing by hand. Now, thanks to printing and to print-reproductive machinery, the price of books is significantly down. Now also, thanks to the emergence of a money system and a free market, something like a thermostatic process operates to set monetary equivalents in quantitative terms external to the goods exchanged. This also has the advantage of not having to bring nonmonetary equivalents to the exchange. One just brings along cash or, easier still, today one brings one's checkbook or credit card. Mail service and online purchasing makes exchange extremely easy and rapid: one goes to one's computer, contacts one's book dealer, orders the book, and pays for it by registered credit card.

All of this takes us away from face-to-face or even live voice-to-voice relations. The system operates impersonally, being held in place by functionaries producing and exchanging in a linked process. Most of them must feel they are at least relatively well paid for their services, otherwise the system would break down owing to lack of performance. We know what happens when garbage collectors go on strike.

But of course, a similar though not identical thing happens in the anonymity of the relation between author and audience. Though we know the name of the author, our relation as readers to her or him is indirect and nonreciprocal. We indirectly get to know something of the author from her or his writing, but she or he knows nothing at all about the vast majority of the individuals in her or his audience.

SPEECH AND WRITING

Books are produced for the sake of the exhibition and preservation of *writing*. Writing translates the flowing temporality of sound involved in speech into the fixed spatiality of visual presentation. According to an old Roman adage, *Verba fluunt, scripta manent*, "Words flow, writing remains." It actually reverses the process whereby the flow of sound establishes a location in the brain as it impacts the nervous system, translating the temporality of sound production and reception into the spatiality of cerebral position. Various movements of things impact our nervous systems through various organs and inscribe their resultants within our brains, which retain the results within their spatiality. This original static inscription is re-translated into audile mobility in speech and is re-inscribed through the temporal process of writing into spatial form—this time, not in the internal medium of the brain, but onto an external medium, right now onto the page that I am writing and you are reading. Such a move fixes the flux in a manner that is more exact and more comprehensive than automatic fixation in the brain, which does not usually allow of fully exact and total recall. Not everything that we hear is remembered or well-remembered—particularly the non-focal aspects accompanying focal events. Writing remedies that. The audio recorder does so as well, and in so doing provides a fuller reproduction of speech, presenting not only the words, but the aural dynamics of the original speech acts, which writing is not able to capture. Video recording adds gestural meaning. But then again, writing has it over audio or video recording in that one can more rapidly revisit what has been written, can scan it to focus upon certain sections, can underscore and make notes in the margins, etc.

Writing down one's own thoughts makes greater complexity possible. We can see immediately what we cannot fully recall. Musical notation performs the same function, not only preserving works from earlier periods, but also allowing for the development of the complexity of scores for the symphony orchestra. Higher mathematics, because of its extreme complexity, is only possible through writing. But that is true of science in general and of the more complex sorts of technology. It has been estimated that if a team of two engineers, working a forty-hour week, began drawing up plans for the Boeing 747 aircraft at the time of Christ, they would not have finished until the 1960s.[15] And they have now produced the much more sophisticated 787. The current Airbus A380 has 4 million parts. Also consider the Hadron Collider: 10 million parts assembled by ten thousand scientists and engineers and operated by four thousand scientists! So much for the alleged superiority of oral tradition—at least for the development of music, mathematics, science, and technology.

Writing distances the reader from the writer. Writing removes language from the face-to-face situation where speech acts are generated in relation to a comparatively small audience. Writing opens out to a potentially universal audience, that is, to anyone capable of reading the language in which the text or translation was written. It allows for recurrent visitation of the same text to draw upon its virtualities. In the situation of speech, one interested in what has been said would have to go back to the original speaker or members of the original audience to recover what one had failed to remember, provided they remembered it better than the inquirer—or get it from intermediaries and therefore some steps removed from the original occurrence. Prior to the invention of writing there is thus a double dependency: upon the presence of the person delivering the original speech and upon subsequent recurrence to others. Writing frees the reader from these face-to-face dependencies and, once again, promotes in the individual a certain independence from the community, while establishing a new, anonymous community of readers. It allows for the distinctive modern state of *public opinion*.[16]

Translation of speech into writing involves the *identically same meaning* instantiated in a radically different medium. In fact, we find here a hierarchy of relations. The sentence specific to a given language is a kind of universal over against its embodiment in a text or in voice. The empirical features of each medium are widely different: in sound for speech, in visual objectivity for writing, in a tactual medium for

---

15. Somewhere, possibly on a TV interview, John Kenneth Galbraith made this claim.

16. On the emergence of *public opinion*, see Hegel's *Elements of the Philosophy of Right*, trans. R. Nisbet (New York: Cambridge University Press, 1991), §§315–20.

Braille, in visual signing for the deaf, or in semaphore signaling or Morse code. In addition to these diverse kinds of media, there are also their individual instances. I used the word "are" in the last two sentences and have produced it again in this sentence. The instances are separated in space and were generated in different segments of the time of writing as they are now read in different but linked segments of time by one who is attending to what I wrote.[17]

I could also write the same thing with a different typeface. And the actual sound of its pronunciation might vary considerably: for example, in my ordinary way of speaking and in the deeper voice I produce when I have a cold, or when a typical woman speaks the same thing said by a typical male or with a different accent by people in different parts of the country. The sentence thus differs from its individual utterances that involve greater or lesser difference in empirical features in each utterance. But it is the same word, or the same sentence that is identical in the difference of its media and its individual instances of appearance in any of the media. Of course, the impact of the medium qua medium makes a difference in how the message affects us. But we typically discount certain features of the empirically given—the difference in voice or the difference in media—in order to get at the identically same word, not a *similar* word, but the *identically same* word.

We could translate the ethnically specific sentential universal into another language and thus would have to distinguish the sentence from the propositional meaning. But we must add that we cannot have the propositional meaning without some ethnically specific embodiment, without its being resident in some language. This says something important about the mind-body relation: we cannot have uni-

17. It is instructive to the reader to try to pay attention to the general features of what is being written, but also how these features are involved here and now as he or she reads what is written. I take this to be the point of Plato's having most of his *Theaetetus* read to an audience—reported, of course, in writing. And I also take that to be the point of Plato's narrations of the routes of oral transmission of past events that open both the *Symposium* and the *Parmenides*. See my "*Doxa* and *Eros*, Speech and Writing, with Special Attention to Plato's *Symposium*," *Existentia* 18, fasc. 3–4 (2008): 247–61. In his *Phaedrus* 274d–275b, Plato has Thamus attack the invention of writing by Theuth because it would establish a *hypmneme*, or an exterior memory that would lead to the atrophy of real memory. Thamus was also to give a positive assessment, which he never did. That is our clue to look to *the thing itself* to see, for example, that it is through writing that Plato mediates the attack, so that we later (even in translation) have access to the dialogue.

versal or intellectual meaning without embodiment in individuated sensory materials, though the intellectual meaning is not restricted to any particular embodiment, whether in different sensory media at different times and places, or in any particular language or any given person. Meaning is the intellectually apprehended "inside" of the sensorily apprehended utterance that appears to outside observation in seeing, hearing, or touching. What cannot in principle be translated adequately is poetry, for it depends upon the sonority of the particular language and the connotative value of words that play in the relation between words and sounds in different cultures.

But then the whole point of forming sentences, at least in the immediate context, is ultimately to make claims about the character of the objects about which we speak. And so, in addition to the propositions necessarily embedded in a given language and uttered in different media and in different empirical instances, we have judgments about the truth or falsity of the propositions in relation to what is manifest through each proposition.[18]

So we have *utterance*, or individual instantiation in an empirical medium (aural or visual or tactual) at a particular point in space-time; *expression* (sentence, word, letter) peculiar to a given language, of a cultural eidetic or set of universal meanings; translation of the same sentence or word into another language, involving *propositions* that are identical in the different languages used to express them; and, finally, the *judgment* about the truth or falsity of what is said.[19] In the latter case, provided it is true, such a judgment points to what is fixed from the moment of its occurrence ever after. Even if the statement about it is false, the fact of its falsity becomes a permanent fixture of the universe. As I said previously, it is odd that we who are supposedly trapped in language could recognize that with absolute certainty.

MODES OF WRITING

Consider next the discovery of the *modes of writing*: hieroglyphs and cuneiform at first, then *alphabetical writing*. The latter involved a par-

---

18. I am focusing only upon constative or declarative sentences. One would have to adjust the presentation for interrogative, optative, and imperative sentences.

19. Bernard Lonergan makes these observations in his *Insight*, 271ff.

ticular stroke of genius, discovering, in the first place, that all the sounds generated in a given language could be reduced to a set of elementary phonological units, and then, secondly, inventing a set of inscriptions that could capture that in a visual medium. Paul Weiss (whom Mortimer Adler called "the wisest man of the twentieth century") noted that his first philosophical experience was when, at six years of age, he was introduced to the alphabet. That everything you could say could be captured in combinations of just twenty-six characters: that was astonishing! It is even more astonishing than Mendeleev's discovery of the Periodic Table of the Elements (upon which deconstructionists and extreme relativists should meditate).

But perhaps more astonishing is the invention of *speech*. I was struck when I heard that human beings are conjectured to have been on the earth for some 1.75 million years and that writing occurred a mere five millennia ago. What were humans doing for the million-plus years before writing? Among other things, they invented and developed the most sophisticated instrument ever devised: language, an extraordinary structure that allows us to communicate with one another about anything and everything—indeed, that allows us to think for ourselves in an articulate fashion about anything and everything.

At first, writing imitated the constant flow of speech by not putting spaces between the words or the sentences and not using punctuation marks. The sequence of words was recorded in differing ways. Our writing from left to right is inverted in Hebrew writing, which begins at the right side of a page and moves to the left. There was also what was called *boustrophedon* or "ox-head" writing, that is, writing that moved in one direction on a given line and then in reverse direction—word by word—on the next line, just as the ox moves his head in one direction and then in another. Writing forward and then backward and then forward again unduly complicates the process. (Fortunately, boustrophedon writing did not catch on.)

In more recent times, typewriting has increasingly replaced handwriting. There is the obvious advantage of increased clarity, especially given certain forms of handwriting. There is also the neat aesthetic of regular dark characters in perfectly straight lines with straight margins. But what is lost in the substitution of typing for handwriting is the exhibition of character found in handwriting. Graphologists attempt to make correlations between handwriting style and the dispositional peculiarities of the person writing. However, there is no one-to-one correlation, for one thing because certain styles may have their roots in physical motor problems. Nonetheless, handwriting is an aspect of the overall gestural style of a specific person. In reading it, one comes into closer contact with the writer.

THE ELECTRONIC REVOLUTION

With the electronic revolution, writing and reading have undergone and are undergoing significant changes. (I mentioned some of this earlier but will expand upon it here.) It has hastened the shrinkage of space and time until we are in instant contact across the globe, both in an audile mode and in a direct visual mode: we can immediately hear and see people from different parts of the world. Large international corporations can have meetings of the boards in different countries where the physical table around which they gather is visually extended on one end by a screen that projects a life-sized video of board members gathered in another country around a similar table such that the tables appear continuous. The discussants can even "high-five" each other at the end of the conference by touching the image of the physically absent participants reaching out to touch their respective screens.

A letter that once took months to transport by boat, weeks by pony express, and days by regular mail is now instantaneously delivered via email. Email follows the trail blazed by the telegraph and telephone. The former involves the translation of printed words into shorter or longer electrical impulses to give us another form of writing (Morse code). The telephone involves the hidden electronic mediation of the telephone system that translates the voice into electronic signals and retranslates the signals into sounds at the receiver's end, putting us into immediate relation with the vocal presence of our interlocutor. Voicemail abstracts from presence to give us the past voice of the one who answers.[20] One does not have to write to communicate with

20. My sister-in-law has kept her late husband's voice on the answering machine so we can maintain a more vivid remembrance by calling up to leave a message.

another at a significant spatial, and therefore temporal, distance; one can speak directly or by recording. And now with Skype one can actually see one's interlocutor at the other end of the line.

With voice-recognition software, there is not even a need to type what comes to be written on the computer screen; one speaks into a microphone and the words are translated onto the screen as a written message. For a relatively small amount, one can replace the significantly more expensive human transcriber and speed up the process of written production. Voice recognition software can be a huge advantage for those who write professionally. That is a step forward that follows the invention of the word processor.

Word processors have lifted a great burden from the writer. Previously, one who had to correct a mistake or add material early in a manuscript of several hundred pages had to type the whole thing over. Now one just inserts the new material, and the processing program automatically changes the pagination without any additional work on the part of writer. This enables subsequent modifications even after the text is printed.

Another aspect that helps writers is the instant availability of materials through the use of search engines. Not too long ago I was looking for a passage in Aristotle that I was sure could be found in two places. Hauling out the books, I spent two hours searching in vain. But then I went to a search engine, typed in the quotation involved, and immediately had what I sought. Online availability extends to journals and now even to whole libraries. A search engine becomes an index that not only *indicates* the place a given bit of information can be found but actually *brings one to* the place sought.

E-books are rapidly displacing paper books. Instead of underscoring or making marginal comments, one can make remarks in subtexts that can be revealed or hidden as one wishes. More recent versions of e-books allow for finger manipulation of the pages.

In research one can bypass the process of journal-submission to go directly to colleagues in the field. The process of journal production involves peer reviews that are sometimes delayed considerably. It also involves manuscript backlogs, printing and distributing, processing replies to the paper after it is available, and further time for production and distribution of the reply. The advantage of the journal process is peer reviewing so that readers do not have to sort through manuscripts of lesser value. But now journals have themselves moved online, so that the production and distribution process is considerably sped up and costs are substantially lowered. Especially in natural science, going directly to known experts eliminates the mediation of the journal to allow research to be quickly evaluated and to allow the researcher to be apprised of current research relevant to her or his project. Projects can be developed simultaneously by spatially separated teams of researchers. The shrinkage of the time of research presentation, critique, and development has been raised to another power.

The electronic revolution is creating a new social space, or rather, sets of social spaces formed around common interests and involving instantaneous communicative interchange. We have entered and are increasingly developing an era of what Marshall McLuhan decades ago termed "the global village" created by the formation of an integrated external electronic "nervous system" for the whole planet.[21] The Arab Spring that unsettled the Middle East was made possible by instant communication afforded by modern means.

The shrinkage of space and time and the creation of new social spaces through the development of media, beginning with writing, have from their inception involved distanciation from the bodily presence of other people and hence an abstraction from indwelling in a specific place. The mechanisms involved create a presence-in-absence.

READING

Books are produced so that they can be read. Let us now consider *reading*. In our culture it begins with learning the alphabet, then being able to sound out each individual word. Reading reaches a new level of development when one no longer reads aloud. Even in the late

---

21. McLuhan, *The Guttenberg Galaxy*, 21, 31–32. Teilhard de Chardin used this to create the myth of the Omega Point, with the electronic revolution providing the physical basis, or an external nervous system, for the Mystical Body and the Second Coming. Pierre Leroy, "Teilhard de Chardin: The Man," introduction to *The Divine Milieu* by Pierre Teilhard de Chardin (New York: Harper and Row Publishers, 1960), 26, 35–37.

fourth century A.D., Augustine was surprised to see Bishop Ambrose reading without moving his lips.

Reading this chapter, we work from an immediately available mastery of reading. When we first learned how to read, we may have learned phonetically how to pronounce each syllable. We had to concentrate on the syllables and sound them out. Once they were promoted to subsidiary awareness as a functional possession, we could read the sentences fluently aloud, the sound helping the association, while looking past the printed page to the meanings it exhibits. The next step in mastery entailed reading without sounding out and thus being able to read more rapidly. The individual words almost disappear as we get into the flow of the meaning they incarnate. They are strictly subsidiary to following the focal meaning.

But of course, reading aloud slows down the reading process immensely. Silent reading progresses to the point that one can read sentences rather than words and can speed-read texts or skim for general meaning. However, the former is merely the optimum of reading flexibility. One should not speed-read philosophy, except perhaps for the first reading to get the general lay of the land; after that, one needs to learn to ponder each sentence. There actually is no such thing as philosophic reading, only rereading and rereading and rereading.

Reading aloud, even to oneself, adds another dimension to silent reading. The oral reading of poetry in particular is more important than simply reading silently, for poetry is itself song and not just message—or rather, its sonority is central to the message. Since this is the case, one should also never speed-read poetry; in fact, one should typically read poetry aloud since the sound evokes the How of our relation to the object of the song. Poetry depends upon the empirical articulation of the message. It functions through its music to make what is merely understood—let's say in a prosaic summary—a "real presence" by bringing it "nearer" to the hearers, affecting the way they inhabit their worlds. Not only the melodiousness of the words but the dynamics of loud and soft, slow and fast, and the emphasis put upon particular words draws upon *the whole person* and not simply the detached intellect. In addition, words themselves have emotional reverberations that are enhanced through the development of metaphors. With all these devices the poem is able to touch *the heart*, the center of one's subjectivity, the way one is existentially "tuned" and inclined to respond.

Further, drama—for example, a Greek tragedy or Shakespearean play—calls for full embodiment through enactment. Drama thus appeals focally to the eye and the ear, presenting the full dynamics of human action in the gestural style as well as the words employed by the characters.

Being read to, as distinguished from reading for oneself, establishes a greater closeness of reader to audience. Even though the audience in a typical American parish is usually literate, the Scriptures are still read to them. In addition to appealing through the sound of the language, such reading takes each member of the audience out of her or his privacy, so that she or he is deliberately dependent upon the reader, establishing a new mode of community in and through the new mode of presence through speech.

Reading a significant piece of literature involves following the recipe of the words to construct for oneself—or have constructed within oneself—the imaginative world of the text. It also involves multiple rereadings. In a first reading, one might "just read" and follow along. One might be intrigued by the characters or the plot or the deep view of life a book presents. One might then revisit it again and again as something endearing. In reading Shakespeare, the vision of life, the action, and the wonderful diction might become a part of one's life.

In rereading to *study* a work, one might look to the overall structure of the whole, which at first is perhaps not fully apprehensible. Through rereading one sees how the parts fit into the whole in such a way that the character of the whole is more fully revealed. Rereading involves a tacking between the parts and the whole as a dialectical relation. In a novel, rereading involves closer attention to each of the characters and their interrelation in action and diction. One moves from mere reading to real studying, thus taking away not merely impressions and a few *bon mots* for cocktail parties, but real learning, a real assimilation to one's own thought processes. And that only happens when one has an encounter, not simply with the words of a text and through them with the opinions of an author, but with the things about which the book speaks. Especially in a text from an era or in a cultural orbit other than one's own, one has to learn to enter into the standpoint of the text and, by applying it to one's own context, attempt to stretch and fuse one's inhabited horizon with that of the text.[22] Along the way, one can come to dwell in the aura of a text, that is, the peculiar tone that binds together the whole. This is most clear in poetry where the musical accompaniment, the music of the words, or both, provide the emotional cement that holds the parts together.[23]

LANGUAGE (II)

Speech and writing are two modes of appearance of language. And what is proximally most important about a book is that its empirically available surface is expression in a language. Language begins in the situation of the face-to-face, of an *I* facing a You and establishing a We. Actually establishing a We in conversation depends upon a broader We that forms the tradition of native speakers that individual speakers have been inducted into and that links current speakers with past and future speakers. Language operates in terms of syntax or the way in which grammatical structure is taken up in referring to the object about which one speaks or writes.

Considering the book, there is a distinction between the book and its properties, between what can be done to it and what it can do, between its present, past, and future existence, between the universal terms used to describe it and its own individual existence, etc. In the first case we have the linguistic distinction between nouns naming different subjects and adjectives or what can be "thrown to" (*ad-jectum*) or predicated of a subject: "The 'book' is 'rectangular,' with a 'blue' cover."

22. This is a major point in Hans-Georg Gadamer's hermeneutics in *Truth and Method* (New York: Crossroad, 1982), 273–74, 337.
23. Edgar Alan Poe said the poem began with a particular mood that led him to pick a word that best presented that mood. That became a focal point for constructing the whole. In his example, *The Raven* began with a mood of utter despair, and the word that best presented that was "nevermore." The name of the dead beloved thus became Lenore. All the rest, Poe said, was a matter of technique. But the whole construction is guided by the mood. "The Philosophy of Composition," in *Selected Prose and Poetry of Edgar Allen Poe*, ed. T. Mabbott (New York: Modern Library, 1951).

In many languages nouns and adjectives are *declined*, which means they "fall" or "decline" into various cases (from *casus* meaning "fall"). On the one hand, they fall into singular and plural instances. On the other hand, they fall into the cases called nominative (book as subject of a judgment), genitive (of or belonging to the book), dative (to or for the book), accusative (book as object of action, for example, being read), and ablative (by or with the book). Where language does not build these distinctions into the various endings of the noun or adjective, it supplies them by means of different prepositions, as we have shown in English in the previous sentence. So we have cases or "falls" from the first person nominative singular into the various modulations. Some languages often add masculine, feminine, or neuter types of nouns, determined by their endings.[24] The kinds of articles (in English, *the* and *a* or *an*) that preface the nouns indicate whether they are determinate singular or indeterminate singular.

Concerning what can be done by or to a subject, there are the passive and active verbs: "The book is being read and informs us of certain details." There is also what can be attached to the verb, namely, the ad-verb—for example, "The book is read 'avidly' and it 'richly' informs us." Verbs have tenses (that is, the way they are temporally tensed or "stretched"): past, present, and future forms. Forms that the verbs take on constitute the conjugations of the verbs, that is, the way they are "conjoined" or "yoked" (Latin *jugati*) to the forms that modulate them. The conjunctive modulations work in terms of person and number, that is, in terms of first person (singular: I, or plural: we), second person (you, singular or plural), or third person (he, she, it or, in the plural, they).

In our present exposition, the sentences we are generating are declarative in character; that is, they testify to the truth of the claims about the referents of the sentences. But I might include interrogative sentences—for example, "Is what I have said thus far defensible?" The statements could also be imperative, that is, issuing a command: "Pay

---

24. It is interesting to speculate why gender assignments apply to nongendered things. Perhaps the Latins called the moon *luna* (a feminine ending) because of its soft lighting. On the other hand, they called a sailor *nauta*. It is difficult to understand what could be feminine about a hearty seaman, except as ironic!

attention to what I am saying!" Or they could be optative, presenting a wish: "If only reductionists would reflect upon what I am saying." Or, finally, they could be subjunctive: "I might have chosen a different topic for this chapter."

As we have noted previously, the first and second person (I read, You read) stand for the anchors of language in the face-to-face situation. That gets modified, through writing and later through the invention of the telegraph, the telephone, and the video phone, to different forms of presence-in-absence. But there is always an *I* addressing a You, as in this book the writer is addressing his absent audience (which is only metaphorically so, since no literal "audition" goes on unless the reader reads aloud). As I said in the beginning of this text, right now, I as writer am addressing You as reader, but as an anonymous reader: one usually unknown to me, who is indirectly joined through this reading to what I hope is a larger number of readers, the vast majority of whom do not know each other or me personally. And what we speak or write about, apart from each other, is a third person object: He, She, It, or They. But when I and You join together, a We is constituted: in the present case, We who pursue philosophy.

These observations about the basic structures of language are extremely important in dealing with the human being. There has been for a long time a mighty attempt to reduce first- and second-person functions to third-person functions. Thus, it is assumed that the activities of speakers can be reduced to such objects as brains and computers. But those who are doing so always involve an *I* addressing a You and, together with their coworkers and readers, refer to a We, freely choosing to pursue the truths in their science. As we have said several times, following John Searle, third-person ontologies are rooted in first- and second-person ontologies.[25]

There is the further observation that in addressing a You, we might really mean "It" (as Martin Buber put it), that is, object of my desire, means for my ends, and thus only of instrumental value to me. How does one properly address a You? As Kant put it, morality involves treating humanity (i.e., rationality, involving a capacity to

---

25. See John Searle, *Rediscovery of Mind*, 117.

intend and find means for reaching certain ends), whether in oneself or others, as an end and not simply a means. Morality goes beyond instrumental value. But for Buber, a book can also be either an It or a Thou.[26] In the first case it becomes a matter of information or object of analysis and critique. In the second case, it addresses You in a manner that might lead to one's transformation; it can change one's heart. Of course, most books do not have such power; but poetic works constitute a special domain of transformative power.

* * *

Let us return to the notion of Being involved in the claim of what is the case. From one point of view, "Being" is, as Nietzsche observed, "the last trailing cloud of evaporating reality."[27] As we develop definitions—for example, in our treatment of the human being as rational animal—we find that they are embedded in hierarchies of identities and differences, moving from the immediately given to progressively more encompassing universals. In developing definitions, we progressively abstract from content. So as our concepts become more encompassing, they also have lesser content, and thus become increasingly thinner. Thus *organism* is of wider extension than *human being*, but it also must abstract from the differences between humans, animals, and plants to be able to cover them all. At the top of these hierarchies of abstraction we find *thing* and *attributes*, which we may describe as *being in itself* and *being in virtue of another*, respectively. A book exists *in itself*, and its color, size, and weight exist *in virtue of* the thing whose properties they are. One more abstraction (abstracting from *in itself* and *in virtue of another*) and we have isolated the empty notion of Being. This notion exhibits, we maintain, the original emptiness of the mind, but it is a notion that aims at filling. It is thus in light of this empty notion of Being, which covers everything, that we can consider any individual instance as an instance of being and of its type, both of

26. Martin Buber, *I and Thou*, 172. Kant developed his position in *Groundwork of the Metaphysics of Morals*, trans. M. Gregor (Cambridge: Cambridge University Press, 1998), 45/4:433. All references to Kant's ethics outside of his critiques shall be taken from the *Akademie Edition* (see https://korpora.zim.uni-duisburg-essen.de/Kant/verzeichnisse-gesamt.html). Any numbers following the / are thus from said edition.

27. Friedrich Nietzsche, *Twilight of the Idols* in *Twilight of the Idols and the Anti-Christ*, trans. R. Hollingdale (Baltimore: Penguin, 1968), III, §4.

which refer us beyond the given individual to apply to all instances of the type in question, and, indeed, to all instances of being—that is, to everything, and beyond its appearance, toward its full reality which recedes as it juts into the field of awareness.[28]

Duns Scotus refers to a common generic notion that applies univocally to all that is: being outside of nothing. But *Being* is peculiar in that it is not an ordinary genus, for in principle it includes everything—all principles, all things, and everything about everything. And here it functions, not univocally, as with being-outside-of-nothing, but according to metaphysical analogy. Read hierarchically and against the notion of a possible Fullness of Being, everything that is has an essence that limits the degree to which it can exhibit the fullness of Being. Of course, such a reading involves an *onto-theo-logy*, which is a theology developed in terms of the logic of the notion of being, forbidden as heresy in Heideggerian circles.[29] That the notion of Being is initially an empty reference to the Whole refers to the mind. Thought and Being are one: empty thought and empty Being, but aimed at the Fullness.

The verb *to be* has a most irregular conjugation. This suggests that it is not simply an empty word. Consider: "I read; you read; he, she, or it reads; we read, you (plural) read, they read." But: "I *am*; you *are*; he, she, or it *is*; we, you (plural) and they *are*." Also consider: "I read" or "you read" (past tense); but "I *was*" and "you *were*"; "I will read," but "I will *be*"; "I will have read," but "I will *have been*." Then there is the participial *being*, used also as a noun, for instance in the translation of the word *ontology*, which is a Greek derivative that means a "study of Being." *Am, are, is, was, were, be, been, being*—what surprising irregularity! Study of the Sanskrit roots has indicated meanings like *to live, to emerge*, or *to dwell*. But, of course, these original meanings have been erased and all we have left are relatively empty forms.[30]

28. See my "First Things First: On the Priority of the Notion of Being," in *Being and the Cosmos*, 33–62.

29. Martin Heidegger, "The Onto-theo-logical Constitution of Metaphysics," in *Identity and Difference*, trans. J. Stambaugh (New York: Harper and Row, 1969), 42–74. Heidegger said that if he were to do a theology, *being* would not be a term he would use. But that is because he has a special meaning for *Sein*.

30. I owe these observations on the verb *to be* to Martin Heidegger's *Introduction to Metaphysics*, 73–76.

What they originated in was an animist view of being that has been progressively abandoned while its forms remain in the conjugation of the word *being*.

However, it is the functioning of the notion of Being that sets off human beings as the beings that have language—or better, as the beings that are had by language. We are embraced and encompassed by the meanings lodged in the language we employ. Reference to the Whole via the notion of Being makes each of us an *I*, able to abstract ourselves from everything that can be made an object of observation and reflection, including everything within ourselves: it makes us *condemned to choose*. But we are also, at the same time, *condemned to meaning* by the language we speak and that we also find in books.[31] Forced to choose by our orientation toward the Whole, we can only choose among the options available in the worlds we inhabit.[32]

ORAL TRADITION

We are headed toward a treatment of what typically appears in a book, namely, literature. But literature arises from oral tradition: literature is oral tradition transformed through preservation of the temporality of speech in the spatial medium of writing. So we will first treat oral tradition.

To begin with, the young must be inducted into the practices that are linked to the physical survival of the group. A kind of master-apprentice system is set up through a show-and-tell method, with the master showing and telling his apprentice how to perform the set of functions that belong to his craft. It was only since the French Encyclopedia in the eighteenth century that we have manuals of such instructions, complete with plates. Denis Diderot, coeditor with d'Alembert of the famous French Encyclopedia, visited the various workshops, committed the instructions of the masters to writing, and

---

31. Merleau-Ponty, *The Structure of Behavior*, 24.

32. It was Hegel who grounded the necessity of free choice in the orientation to the Whole via the notion of Being. Hegel, *Elements*, §§4 and 5. Freedom as self-determination is rooted in the ability to abstract from everything, and that possibility is given at the beginning of the Logic in the absolutely empty notion of Being. See *Introduction to the System*, §468. See also Hegel, *Hegel's Science of Logic*, 69–73.

commissioned drawings of the tools, the objects worked with the tools, and the steps in the process. Now we can teach ourselves certain crafts by following what is said and shown in a book.

Secondly, the young must also be inducted into the character of their people and their meaning systems. Storytelling transmits knowledge of the special events that display the people's character: that hunt, that trek, that battle, that war, that flood, that plague, and the like. Gifted with the power of abstraction, the rhapsode as storyteller selects from the concrete character of the events and their context only what is dramatically relevant, following the operation of memory that retains explicitly only that which is *memorable*. He thereby compresses the time of action into the significantly narrowed time of narration. He develops mnemonic devices such as meters and rime schemes, often displaying prodigious feats of memory which atrophied with the development of writing. Plato remarks in his *Phaedrus* that the invention of writing would lead to such an atrophy, for we come to rely more and more upon this *external memory*.[33] Such an external memory is massively developed in the computer with whose word-processing program I am composing this text.

The rhapsode does not only abstract, but he also paces, organizes, and highlights various aspects of the narrative. At the height of his craft, he learns to build dramatic suspense and to bring the work to a fitting close. He establishes a whole that is like an organism, being so arranged that everything that needs to be there is there, and nothing is there that does not need to be there. The rhapsode learns to rise above the everyday use of language, which allows us to glance, stereotype, and routinely respond to what we might encounter. He develops elevated forms of language, even introducing foreign terms to let matters of great import stand out from the routine world. He discovers metaphors that draw the emotional aura of a literal term to an object that in some way resembles the metaphorized object. Thus, he speaks of a great warrior as a lion. An accomplished rhapsode also knows how to suffuse the whole with a certain tone that gains expression as he develops the sonorous possibilities of the language: he sings. And

33. Plato, *Phaedrus*, 275a.

he also often learns to accompany his recitation with a stringed instrument. At the height of his art, he makes even the ordinary appear extraordinary. Literature, in fact, arose out of such practices.[34]

LITERACY

Perhaps it was not such epic poetry that was the first form of writing. More likely, it was a matter of keeping records for some king who established an extended kingdom, recording commands in given situations and laws to cover all like situations, as well as recording the chronology of the dynasty and its memorable events. The literacy of the leaders helped them to coordinate people spread over long distances by eliminating the spatial and temporal confinement of the face-to-face relation for writers and readers. Writing emerged with the emergence of the great empires. World history begins with these empires. Writing made possible universal laws for large masses of people. What it coordinated was the work of the leaders, who, in turn, coordinated the work of the masses under them. Only they or their scribes and the subordinate leaders they addressed were literate. It was not until the early nineteenth century that universal literacy was an expressed policy set in place by the newly emergent democratic societies. Mass circulation of newspapers and journals of opinion multiplied rapidly at roughly the same time. New media create differing social forms.

Writing was also used by merchants exchanging goods to record their sales and inventory. Some such writings from the Middle East are still available from many thousands of years ago because of the character of the medium upon which they were written, namely, clay tablets. They would have perished earlier because, after a significant lapse of time, there was no need or desire to preserve them. They were only important for a specific time, however valuable an historian might find them as an indication of key aspects in the life of a people. With chronicles and laws as also with legends celebrated in poetry, something central to the identity of a whole people is involved; and so they have been copied, recopied and transmitted, at times disseminated to distant

---

34. These observations are basically those of Aristotle in his *Poetics*, trans. W. Fyfe (Cambridge, Mass.: Harvard University Press, 1973). See especially 1451a on *organicity*, and 1456b–1459a20 on diction.

places and recopied again, creating the problem of the *critical edition.* Manuscripts copied from an original center are sent by horse or mule or camel and boat to far removed places, where, since they are important sources of meaning, they are recopied and sent on to further distant places. Copyists may misread some words, may skip a line, or may even add their own material as a mode of anonymous "immortality." This creates divergent manuscript traditions developing in widely separated geographical areas. Beginning with the Renaissance, scholars have traced the trees of transmission of key manuscripts in order to reconstruct the original text as closely as possible. This is true for the Bible and the Koran; it is true for the works of classical antiquity in general. It is true for written works of other cultural traditions as well. Because of the labor of those who produced the critical editions, we can read the Bible or Plato today with some confidence that we are reading the original words of the writers—or, more usually, a translation of those words, which indicates that meaning to a large extent transcends particular linguistic traditions.

Actually, the same is true for oral tradition.[35] Stories may be told and retold with significant variation by different rhapsodes. They may follow different migration routes. And thus, through both geographical and chronological separation, variant traditions coexist in different places. But then, in the transition from oral to written communication, or in the transmission of different written traditions about the same events, a redactor may come to bring various strands together, with greater or lesser success at integration. For example, in the Bible, in the beginning of *Genesis* we have two different creation narratives, one following immediately upon the other.[36] We have three lists of the *Decalogue* that vary in some significant ways: two in *Exodus* and the other in *Deuteronomy.*[37] And in the Greek tradition, Homer is thought to have been a compiler of different oral traditions.[38]

---

35. Some claim that oral tradition can better preserve exact terms than written tradition because the penalties for innovation are at times severe.

36. Gn 1:1–2:3, 1:3–2:3.

37. Ex 20:2–17, 34, 12–26, as well as Dt 5:6–21. We are repeating what has become traditional in the Christian tradition.

38. G. S. Kirk, *Homer and the Oral Tradition* (Cambridge: Cambridge University Press, 1976), vii.

In understanding works that come from other cultures, like the ancient Near East from which the Bible came, one must understand the peculiar literary form of a given text and the way it was used in the life of a people. If in the distant future someone from another planet came upon a book of Aesop's fables, she or he might think that at some time in the past there were talking animals on this planet. Just so, not understanding the kind of literature found in the biblical *Genesis*, being ignorant of the common literary forms of the Fertile Crescent at the time of the original writing or oral tradition, one who does not understand mythopoetic thought regularly thinks that what we have is literal description, rather than a story that has significant meaning. Furthermore, not understanding how the biblical authors understood historical writing and being ignorant of the findings of geology, archaeology, and astronomy, one might think (following a construction of a biblically based chronology by Bishop Usher) that creation happened in 4004 B.C. To cling to a literal reading is *literally* to misunderstand what is being said and to miss the real import it still might have for us today.

LITERATURE

Let us next consider literature, according to its own etymology in *littera* (letters), as a form of writing. There are many kinds of writing. Viewed in relation to literature, one might first consider a laundry list or a shopping list. A random list has no quality even remotely approaching literature except as writing. However, if one arranged the lists according to categories, let us say by the order of spatial sequence of different types of food in a particular grocery store, one has achieved at least one of the components of literature: it must be organized.

At a different level there is the letter sent by one person to another. A business letter is organized and executed in a crisp and efficient way, but one would not see it as literary. A personal letter, however, could convey a certain mood and may be written with a certain flair and thus may take on a quasi-literary quality. A collection of such letters might be considered literary.

Then there are journals that are of varying sorts, either personal or public. Of the former, one type would be a diary that records different events in one's life and perhaps reflects upon them; another would be a series of ongoing, loosely related reflections that develop various themes that might be antecedent to a more fully organized work or set of works. The public type would be the professional journal concerned with various kinds of issues pertinent to different professional interests. This is an extension of meaning of the French *journal* or "daily" from the regularity of a sequence of days, to a regularly appearing publication as a weekly, a monthly, a quarterly or an annual.

Then there are newspapers and news magazines. They are each divided into various sections, most of them reporting on current events, some of them containing editorial comments on those events as well as various forms of advertisement. They emerged in the eighteenth century following the spreading of literacy and the development of public opinion among intellectual elites. They developed into more popular forms with the movement toward universal literacy in Western societies. Magazines continue to proliferate in various genres focused upon specialized topics.

In the development of an intellectual elite, formal types of writing such as the essay and the treatise emerged. A treatise is highly organized either as a single essay or as a lengthy exposition of a single theme with its related subthemes. In Aristotle we see the beginning of the treatise form: only what we have are largely lecture notes more or less formally organized. One would still not consider such works—or many other forms of writing we have considered thus far—as literature.

The early philosopher Parmenides' work *On Nature* begins with a proem that presents an allegory, and the whole is written in hexameters. Aristotle remarks that it still is not poetry, although he does not say why.[39] But with Plato's dialogues, we have a hybrid of literature and philosophy. A Platonic dialogue, in its best instances, like the *Statesman* or the *Republic*, is literary. As we observed earlier, The *Statesman* presents the image of weaving that we can use to describe a Platonic text (from *textus*, meaning "what is woven") as the interweaving of two modes of showing: there are the hard-twisted strands

---

39. Aristotle, *Poetics* 1415a.37.

and the soft-twisted strands. The former involve an *apodeixis* or "showing from the top down," as in geometric demonstration and in that dialogue's own hierarchical divisions covering the field of experience as a whole.[40] As Plato puts it in his *Phaedrus*, when carrying out the divisions, one should learn to "carve along the [eidetic] joints" of what is given in experience "and not hack through like a clumsy butcher."[41] The soft-twisted or fuzzy strands consist of the *paradeigmata* or "showings alongside," as in metaphors, allegories, diagrams, and myths that are placed alongside the literal focus to let certain aspects stand out. And the whole takes on a dramatic cast with the interplay between interlocutors. When Plato met Socrates, he burned the tragedies he had been preoccupied in producing up to that time, but in the construction of his dialogues he carried over the poet's art into "the soft weave," which, together with the hard weave, binds the fabric of his thought together.[42]

A story would have more of a literary character than would a philosophic dialogue, although we should distinguish the stories told in history and biography from epics, dramas, and novels. The former set can take on literary qualities, depending upon the depth of the accompanying reflections, the character of the diction, and the overall organization. The latter set would be what we call *literature* in the honorific sense of the term. Such works exhibit the qualities we sketched above in discussing the oral tradition mediated by a rhapsode.

Literature in the high sense of the term has appeared in different genres. Basically, there is prose and poetry, with the latter distinguished by the emphasis upon musicality and *atmospherics*, that is, the sound-properties linked to the dispositional evocations underscored especially in the employment of metaphor.

In antiquity Aristotle's prose was considered by Cicero—to the great surprise of the readers of Aristotle today—the work of a stylistic master.[43] Unfortunately, we have no examples of it; all we possess are

---

40. Plato, *Statesman* 279a–283a.
41. Plato, *Phaedrus* 265e.
42. Would that he had preserved such works.
43. Cicero, *Academics*, in *On the Nature of the Gods, Academics*, trans. H. Rackham, bk. II, Loeb Classical Library 268 (Cambridge, Mass.: Harvard University Press, 1933), chap. 38, §119.

his unpolished lecture notes.[44] In modern times, history and biography can exhibit style in their use of language. The novel and the short story are distinctively modern developments. *Modernity* underscores the current *mode* of doing things (even eating pie *á la mode*), while *novel* originally meant something new. The novel is modern, *the* new literary form. It involves a widening of the kind of characters treated, focusing upon ordinary people in apprenticeship, domestic tragedy, and the like, over against the classical tradition's focus on socially elevated characters. It can be the locus of differing literary forms within it.

Poetry has been typically divided into epic, lyric, and dramatic, with the latter divided into tragedy and comedy. Epic paints a broad canvas as it depicts agents that exhibit an *epoch* and not simply individual characters. Drama focuses upon characters in interaction, either at a high level (kings and princesses and the like) and portraying serious matter, or at a lower level where characters are closer to or at the lowest level of the ordinary and the action is frivolous or is so treated in comedy.[45] Lyric poetry focuses upon the individual, upon characters (most often the beloved), animals ("The Windhover"), and artifacts ("Ode to a Grecian Urn" or "Tintern Abbey"). Here the music of the words and the general atmosphere becomes part of the message, establishing a participation in, a special "nearness" to, the object of the poem. Actually sung, it displays the mood more deeply; and accompanied by instrumental music, like the soundtrack of a movie, it brings the hearers even more deeply into the mood of the piece.

Literary forms typically involve fictionalizing, and some overly literal-minded people claim that creating fiction is a form of lying. Aristotle saw more deeply: fiction is more philosophical than history, for history only presents what happened, while fiction involves an understanding of what *could* happen, even though it does not. It thus involves, like philosophy, an understanding of the universal: typical characters in typical situations doing typical things, though with sig-

44. It is surprising that texts that had made their way from Greece to Rome and that must have been widely disseminated geographically have disappeared.

45. The classic treatment is in Aristotle, *Poetics*. It seems odd that, even though he wrote on comedy (writings we no longer have), he didn't treat of the lyric poem.

nificant variation in individual cases where the action occurs.[46] A great novelist expresses a deep understanding of human nature as focused in individual characters. Even fantasy fiction displays certain universal qualities like quest, nobility, the slide into animality, and the brooding presence of evil always lingering on the horizon, as in the *Hobbit* stories.

We might follow up the rough hierarchy of written forms we have considered by pointing out the relation between content and aesthetic form. At the lower levels the focus is entirely upon the content with minimum attention to aesthetic form. In a letter one might attend to the aesthetics of visual presentation. The treatise generally does not attend to style, although again we note Cicero's testimony to Aristotle's polished works. As we go up the line we are following, aesthetic form becomes more and more prominent in poetry, until we reach purely instrumental music (which abstracts sonorousness from the spoken or sung word), in which aesthetic form is itself the content.

Aesthetic form happens because of the way we as live creatures: we are related both to our own biorhythms and our material environment. Part of the work of the work of art is to reconnect us as rhythmic beings with that total rhythmic environment.[47] The other part of the work is to reconnect us with our tradition and our contemporaries through the content mediated and the mode of mediation through distinct genres. Focus upon content emphasizes the object of attention; poetry emphasizes how the object is present, how it touches us, involves us, and becomes a significant presence for us.

The work of literature that presents a story has several levels: first there are words and their interconnections that express meanings; then there are characters with their action and diction that display their character; and then there are ideas and attitudes. The plot ties it all together. Finally, there is the world-atmosphere that pervades the whole. Coming to understand the work involves at the deepest level coming to sense the atmosphere that is the hidden cement that tightly binds the various parts. One can then come to see how that sense is articulated in the various levels.

46. Aristotle, *Poetics* VIII.1451a.1.
47. John Dewey emphasizes this in *Art as Experience*, 14ff, 147ff, 162ff.

One learns to understand works by studying the classics as models of fine literature. Classics are works that have drawn sensitive and reflective people throughout the ages that followed their inception. Over time, certain works emerged that reached canonical status: in the loose sense with classic literature and in a strict sense with the biblical canon. It is to the former one looks to learn about human behavior through stories, to learn about the togetherness of the concepts that situate us in the cosmos through philosophy and theology, to become more sensitively alert to things, and to be especially touched and transformed through lyric poetry. If one is a believer, then one looks to the Bible for understanding (truth), guidance (goodness), and inspiration (beauty).

The comparison of classic works grounds literary criticism. It teaches us to recognize quality by making explicit the criteria that emerge from such comparison. One learns to distinguish the merely titillating, as in Stephen King's manipulative horror stories, from the profound, as in all of Shakespeare's works.

One problem with the approach through the study of the classics is the tendency to close the canon, at least to the types of literature permitted, and to formulate "eternal rules," as in Neoclassicism. However, when the classics first emerged, they were novelties. There is a parallel in music: when Stravinsky's *Rite of Spring* was first performed in 1913, a riot broke out and the composer had to leave the music hall through a back window. Of course, this ballet is now part of the standard repertoire. What that should teach us is to be on the alert for the emergence of new works that might attain to classic status and redefine the criteria of excellence. And that leaves the question of how one recognizes such works as candidates for such status. The development of that question would take us beyond the limits of the present inquiry, but it would involve the capacity to discern the form that unifies a given work. In the contemporary era of so-called "deconstruction," the very practice tends to let the capacity to detect form atrophy, and thus deconstruction becomes self-fulfilling, tending to keep its practitioners permanently locked within their presuppositions.[48]

48. For further reflection on the arts and our relation to nature, see my *Nature, Art-forms, and the World*.

* * *

Reflection upon the nature of the book yielded the essential features of a wide variety of interconnected regions of experience that are presupposed in reading a book: *its appearance in the sensory environment*, the *I and the You* of writer and reader as *dwelling in a common world* formed (among other things) by a *production system* that is linked to an *exchange system* through which books are distributed, with all of this and more mediated by *language* which is expressed in *speech* but is also retained since about 7000 B.C. in *writing*. The acme of writing is contained in *the canonical text*.

Study of classic texts frees us from contemporary preferences. Study of a wide variety of classics from different periods frees us from the preferences of a given thinker or tradition. Such freedom is not for its own sake, but for granting us the distance and the tools to assess where we are and to discern something of where we might and perhaps should be. Books are the tools for the rational liberation of the human being.

Our exercise provided a structural analysis of the field of human experience and the peculiar sorts of historical sedimentations underlying our current access to the things in our environment. The results should be carried into all our reflection, questioning, and argumentation, for these results constitute the permanent framework within which all our activities occur and the proximate test for the adequacy of all our modes of theorizing about regions we might explore and the character of the Whole toward which we are, by our nature, oriented.

POSTSCRIPT: FURTHER MEDITATION ON THE ENVIRONMENT, NATURAL AND BUILT

In his Preface to *The Phenomenon of Man* entitled "On Seeing," Pierre Teilhard de Chardin calls for the development of "new senses" based upon the scientific uncovering of the vastness of space and time, the interrelatedness of things, and the immense complexity of their substructure. The new senses involve meditatively bringing together the immediate sensory environment with the scientific knowledge involved in each case. It aims at a move from juxtaposition of the immediately given and the scientifically known, to interpenetration and a sense of deepened presence.[49]

As we noted earlier, in recent decades there has been a development in the aesthetic consideration of the environment led by Allen Carlson, who has been at the forefront of a movement that downplays the immediate aesthetic access to the sensory presentations of living things in favor of a scientifically mediated awareness, progressively developing, of ecosystemic connections, underlying substructures, and evolutionary history.[50] We can come to see each organic type as having an evolutionary history that goes back to the first emergence of life within the history of the generation of the solar system. This concretizes the view of the Whole toward which the notion of Being directs us, which makes possible a sense of depth behind the immediately given, that is, a sense of astonishment at the difference between what is immediately experienced and reflectively thought.

The built environment is similar in this respect. And here we apply Vonnegut's image to that environment. Go into the medicine cabinet. See whatever you focus upon as coming from the store where you bought it. Think of the store itself as linked with many thousands of connections to the supply chains that produced and distributed the products. Think of them in turn as the result of the processes that produced them, and behind that think of the history of the coming to be of the various phases of the technology involved in the product's historical development.

I find material for such reflection by watching the television show "How It's Built," which shows the technological apparatus involved in producing the simplest things we use. I find another dimension in the show "Impossible Engineering," which, in showing the construction of some highly complex building, bridge, ship, factory, or the like, also shows something of the history of the inventions that made it possible today. Think of that as going back to the time of the cavemen who invented the first implements. The history of technology and the link

49. See the Preface to *The Phenomenon of Man*.
50. Carlson, "Appreciation and the Natural Environment," in *The Aesthetics of Natural Environments*, 63–75.

to the products of today's technology in daily use is indeed awesome, a rich field for meditation.

Meditation upon both the living and the built environment serves to expand our vision and deepen our appreciation for the things around us that we take for granted. As Heidegger noted, thinking (meditatively) is thanking for things: it is appreciative awareness.[51] Kierkegaard said that we are like corks floating on an ocean seventy thousand fathoms deep.[52] Think of that not only in relation to the natural environment, but also in relation to the built environment.

51. Heidegger, *What Is Called Thinking?*, 138–45.
52. Kierkegaard, *Concluding Unscientific Postscript*, 289.

Part II
Moral-Political Extensions

Chapter 6

Aspects of Freedom
Choosing and Functioning[1]

Armed with the phenomenological investigations we have conducted regarding the field of experience, we now turn to a notion that lies at the base of modern political theory: the notion of freedom. Like justice, love, and happiness, freedom is one of those highly charged value terms that can be and is employed to move hearts, but that is also notoriously ambiguous. In the late 1950s, when Fidel Castro was leading the Cuban Revolution against the Batista regime, a television interviewer asked a young college student why he supported Castro. The young man replied, "Because he brings freedom." When asked further what freedom meant, he responded, "I'm not sure. But Castro brings it, and I'm for it!"

In a sense, however, people have a fairly clear conception of what they mean by the freedom they desire. Negatively, they do not want to be pushed around or told what to do by others. Positively, they want to be able to do what they choose. In Kantian terms, they want freedom from heteronomy (being governed by others) and freedom for autonomy (being self-legislating)—though the self-legislation they seek is often quite unlike anything Kant had in mind.[2]

But there are difficulties with such seemingly straightforward notions. What if some of the things people choose to do are self-destructive?[3] Such actions then serve as negative examples for others, promoting a principle that is destructive of individuals as individuals, rendering them unfit for participation in common life, thereby contributing to its

---

1. This essay appeared first in a commemorative issue, dedicated to the memory of Fr. Robert Lechner, a true "free spirit" and founding editor of *Philosophy Today*. 35, no. 1 (Spring 1991): 106–15.
2. Immanuel Kant, *GMM'PP*, 41, 58/4:429, 449; *Critique of Practical Reason*, I, i: 33–34.
3. Plato, *Republic* I.331.

unravelling.[4] What if what people are told to do are necessary conditions for individual and collective existence or wellbeing?[5] To what extent can or ought a society coerce an individual for her or his own good? To what extent can it coerce an individual for society's good? To what extent can a society demand a good example from its members? What constitutes the wellbeing of a society and of individuals within it? What are the relations between the two? Such questions are basically political. But when we raise the question of wellbeing, I will claim that we are pointing to questions of a metaphysical nature regarding the foundations of free actions in the structure of humanness. It is upon those questions that we choose to focus our initial and major attention here.

* * *

In immediate experience, freedom presents itself as the capacity to do this rather than that, without coercion: to get up from my chair rather than remain seated, to speak or not speak, to say this or that. A minimum of disengagement from the sheer immediate is involved— freedom-*from* the *now* and freedom-*for* the next moment.

When we pass beyond spontaneous immediacy and attend to matters even slightly remote from the immediate situation, I must be able to distance myself sufficiently to make judgments about the options available for choice: factual judgments of the existence and availability of the options, as well as judgments of desirability, of consequences, of value, and of the means available for reaching a chosen goal.[6] To make choices on the basis of these judgments and to be able to carry out the choices in action, I must have a minimum of awareness. I cannot be semiconscious or drugged, drunk or half-asleep. There must be a conscious self-possession that stands at a distance from whatever is nonconscious. Consciousness itself thus seems to be a certain freedom-from the immediate, involving projection of the future as necessary conditions of freedom-for choice.[7]

4. Aristotle, *Politics*, I.2.1252a15ff: Plato, *Republic* I.351c.

5. Paul Ricoeur, *Freedom and Nature: The Voluntary and the Involuntary*, trans. E. Kohak (Evanston: Northwestern University Press, 1966), 37ff; Bernard Lonergan, *Insight*, 596–98.

6. Jean-Paul Sartre, *Being and Nothingness*, trans. H. Barnes (New York: Harper, 1965), 433ff.

7. See my *Path into Metaphysics*, 33ff.

The movement from experienced desirability to the judgment of value is a move to the formulation of *principles*, which implies an anticipation of Time (and Space) as a whole, for a principle has the intentional structure (whatever my personal intentions in considering it) of applying *whenever* (in time) and *wherever* (in space) one might find its instances. A principle is a universal intention, even if it is formulated provisionally. Its ground lies in our prior natural openness to the whole of Space and Time to which we refer in our formulation of any principle. That involves a freedom-from the more extended *now* of any possible action.

Placing that observation within its fuller context, note that there are four strata or dimensions to our being: (1) the supporting stratum of the biologically unconscious, (2) the stratum of immediate sensation and desire, (3) the stratum linked to judgment and the formulation of principles, and (4) the stratum of *dwelling in the totality*. If the unconscious biological level is not blocked and is therefore freely functioning, then the conscious level can emerge for its own free functioning. For the former to occur, proper nutrition, rest, and exercise are necessary conditions. In sleep, consciousness must abdicate its free legislation in order to be able to get it back upon awakening. But even here it is necessarily dependent upon biological function: upon chemical balance and upon the holding open of the "consciousness switch" in the Reticular Activating System at the base of the brain.[8] Freedom as conscious self-determination is necessarily dependent upon the free functioning of the biological substratum.

Here we have two significant meanings of freedom: freedom of choice or the self-determination of consciousness, and freedom of functioning. In the latter case, there is requisite freedom from whatever would impede the free flow of a nature. In this latter sense, freedom is a transcendental notion, covering the free fall of bodies, the free unfolding of the plant, the free flight of the bird, the free unfolding of one's personal powers, the free movement of the soul of the mystic to God, and the freedom of God Himself.

---

8. Dean Wooldridge, *Mechanical Man: The Physics Basis of Intelligent Life* (New York: McGraw-Hill, 1972), 139–42.

The mystical relation will figure importantly into our considerations here, for it involves, I claim, a lived articulation of the fourth and founding stratum of our being. It is actually rooted in our everyday capacity to make responsible judgments. Judgments, we noted, involve a minimum capacity of distantiation from the most immediate *Now* linked to a capacity to grasp principles that intend an indeterminate number of here's and now's, that is, that exceed the Here-and-Now in the direction of the whole of Space (any *here*) and of Time (any *now*). But the judgment does not only involve a comprehension of universal meanings, it also involves the bringing into play of the notion of Being.

Seemingly the emptiest of notions—the minimal being-outside-of-nothing that all things share—it is also the fullest of notions, outside of which there is nothing to anything, for all-that-is is being. All things share it, and it includes within its scope everything about each thing.[9] It involves *in us* a reference to the totality of what-is (whatever that turns out to be) and consequently an inward distance from anything less than the totality. That distance, that being inwardly pried loose from anything less than the totality, that primordial freedom-from anything partial, makes freedom of choice both possible and necessary. The other side of freedom-from the partial is necessary directedness toward the totality.[10] And the upshot of both sides—distance and necessary reference—is the *necessity* of choice: being "condemned to freedom," as Sartre puts it.[11] Even not choosing is choosing to drift, to let oneself be carried by processes—biological, psychological and social—that factually enter now into the constitution of what we call our self.[12] The exercise of freedom of choice is thus grounded in two sorts of necessity, two elements of nature that set the frame for our distinctively human freedom: (1) the necessity of the free functioning of the biological processes that make consciousness possible

    9. Lonergan, *Insight*, 348–74. Talk of "beyond being" only makes sense if there has been a prior restriction to what one understands by being. But being refers to everything and to everything about everything. Being is what is the case; there can be nothing beyond that.

    10. See Aquinas, *Summa theologiae*, I, q. 82, a. 1, ad 3; art. 2, ad 2.

    11. Sartre, *Being and Nothingness*, 481ff.

    12. See Karl Jaspers, *Philosophy*, vol. 2, trans. E. Ashton (Chicago: University of Chicago Press, 1970), 160ff.

(consider the distortion of consciousness caused by chemical imbalance), and (2) the necessary directedness of the humanly conscious being toward the totality.

Freedom of choice is likewise linked to the scope of the options available, though there is an exercise of choice in the hypothetical mode: if things were otherwise, then I would do x. The actual options available are tied to the breadth of awareness that brings the options (*as options*) into awareness. The actual options are likewise tied to the habit-structures that elevate them from merely being theoretical options for humanness-as-such and make them real options for *our* society and real options for *me*. We can avail ourselves of them because we have secured the precondition of habit-formation along the lines of the options. Freedom for the options theoretically available in the society and for humanness-as-such (which never coincide) requires a freeing of the mind from narrow ways of conceiving. Such is the function of *liberal education*: a liberation from narrowness and a freedom-for broader, richer options of conception and therefore also of choice.

But such a freeing must also learn to appreciate the kind of freedom of action that the narrowness of a tradition produces.[13] Secure in her or his vision of things and not torn by the anxiety produced by the realization of alternative visions of reality and value and consequent lifestyles, an individual is capable of throwing her- or himself into the concrete form of action she or he chooses within these structures. Submitting to the discipline embodied, let us say, in a long tradition of engineering, she or he frees her or his capacity to discover and create within that field.

We might note here that technical traditions are relatively independent of lifestyle—beyond resisting those undisciplined lifestyles that make prolonged concentration and effort impossible. Technical traditions are relatively independent of ideology as well. Werner Braun did equally well as a rocket expert for the Nazis and for the Americans; and a rocket expert who is a "free lover" or a murderer could theoretically do equally well in rocketry as a more ascetic type who respects his neighbor.

---

13. Paul Ricoeur, *Freedom and Nature,* 163ff. Kierkegaard, *Concluding Unscientific Postscript,* n287.

A tradition, like a person, is a sedimented result of past decisions among possibilities provided "in the beginning" by natural conditions. The initial structures and urges of human nature and the initial surrounding conditions of nonhuman nature provided a limited set of options from which humans were forced to choose. Culture widens the options—some cultures considerably more than others—both in terms of technical control of the environment and in terms of social institutions. An "open society" like ours theoretically attempts to secure a maximum of options both technically and socially.

Which among the options should we actualize? The question shows that we tend to view decision positively. But the notion of *decision* also embodies a negative view: a decision is a "cutting-off," not only of deliberation, but also of other possible options. "What should we choose?" implies "What shall we cut off?" Hence the experience of "the dizziness of freedom" brought about by the awareness of myriad possibilities.[14] And hence the tendency to be caught in the nonfreedom of hyper-reflection where "the native hue of resolution is sicklied o'er with the pale cast of thought."[15]

Further, choices made bring consequences in their train and lead to other choices—perhaps the choice to go back on a given choice because its consequences turn out to negate other choices or their consequences that are considered more desirable than the choices in question or vice versa. Free choices have necessary consequences, whether or not they are foreseen or foreseeable. And because of the complexity of things, the consequences of free choices run into necessary conflicts and compel further choices. One gets trapped within the network of the consequences of one's own choices, as tradition likewise traps itself and those within it in similar networks. Because of ignorance of consequences and circumstances, the ends intended are not reached concretely, or they are discovered to be undesirable because of their consequences (e.g., in the cases of drug or alcohol or, indeed, sexual addiction).

14. Kierkegaard, *The Concept of Dread*, trans. W. Lowrie (Princeton: Princeton University Press, 1957), 55.
15. William Shakespeare, *Hamlet*, ed. Sylvan Barnet (New York: Signet Classics, 1998), 3.1.84–5.

At each level of our being, there is a specific sort of freedom that is a function of a sort of "institutionalization." Freely functioning metabolic routines (and they can only function freely in rhythmic interplay with the whole of our biology) make possible the free development of motor habits at the level of behavior: hand-eye coordination brings the third dimension into focus; tongue, teeth, lips, and palate coordination, linked to semantic and syntactical habits, brings objects into focus through linguistic identification, tying them to regular patterns of behavioral response. We are free to speak of the world and of our options in it when we have established in ourselves the routines of language and those motor-habits which support and surround the Lifeworld opened by language, which necessarily occurs through the mediations of others who taught us language and guided the establishment of our early behavioral routines.[16]

At another level, I become free to play the piano because I have submitted, or been submitted, to the discipline of recurrent practice, of accepting the commands of a master and thereby of a tradition whose structures make possible the freeing of the possibility I might have of learning to play well. Reversing conventional wisdom, art historian Henri Focillon claimed that art develops only under the constraint of conventions, and that when total "freedom" is allowed, what we get are only imitations![17] However, the compulsions of a tradition are not enough if I will ever be a real virtuoso. Somewhere along the line I must choose to commit myself fully and not simply be compelled to undertake and undergo the process of development.

But I may not have been submitted to discipline. I may have been allowed to grow up "freely," that is, submitting myself to whatever happens to well up within me in interplay with whatever allurements play upon me from my environs. But whereas metabolic routines function freely in their togetherness "automatically," the routines that emerge when we allow impulses to have their freedom

---

16. See Maurice Merleau-Ponty, *Phenomenology of Perception*, trans. C. Smith (London: Routledge and Kegan Paul, 162), 176ff.

17. See Henri Focillon, *The Life of Forms in Art*, trans. C. Hogan and G. Kubler (New York: Zone Books, 1989), 62. Friedrich Nietzsche made the same observation in *The Will to Power*, trans. W. Kaufmann and R. J. Hollingdale (New York: Random House, 1967), §809, 428.

tend toward a chaos of directions or lack of direction, toward being dragged this way and that, and eventually toward various forms of addiction. Undirected and undisciplined by insightful people at the earlier stages of our being, we are unable to open up the space of reflective distance from the Now of our urges and are thereby unable to measure the consequences of our actions, set long range goals, and work at the integration of the patterns of thought and action.[18] One freely chooses to consume alcohol or drugs and enjoys the feeling of freedom that results—until compulsion sets in. Then *it* frees itself and *I* am forced to come along for the ride, like it or not. Now no longer do I live but *it* lives in me. Though I am now fully compelled and can no longer direct myself, there is still one personal freedom left: the freedom to choose my attitude toward my addiction. And that may lead me to let others impose a discipline upon me to permit me to arrive once again at least at an average level of freedom of choice and action.

Peter Weiss's powerful play, *Marat/Sade*, comes to mind. The anguished cry for "Free-dom! Free-dom!" continually arose from the lips of one of the chained inmates of the asylum in which the play within the play was set. Out of pity, his chains were removed—whereupon he pounced upon the first female he encountered. The inmates marched to the tune of "We want our rights and we don't care how! We want a revolution now!" and ended up destroying the whole context of their existence. The words that rolled from the lips of a drooling inmate: "Man is a mad animal!" displayed a terrifying wisdom. The bars, chains, and bludgeons of the institution kept the mad animal from destroying others and eventually himself.[19]

Returning to the example of the pianist, note that there are two sorts of mechanisms at play in relation to freedom of choice and execution: skills and compulsions. Consider here the distinction between the two.[20] Skills are associative motor habits gained through distance from the now, which narrows our possibilities sufficiently, projecting a definite goal and holding ourselves to repetitive acts until

18. Lonergan, *Insight*, 607–33.
19. Peter Weiss, *Marat/Sade* (New York: Pocketbooks, 1963), 53.
20. Ricoeur, *Freedom and Nature*, 231–49, 355ff.

the habit becomes second nature. As I type, my thought translates itself onto the screen with scarcely a thought of the way my fingers operate the keys. When I am not at the computer, the skill passes into absolute unconsciousness and rises again when I choose to compose an essay or a letter. There is a calm assurance and complete command by the will, which exercises absolute sovereignty (as long as the chemical-neurological system is properly functioning!).

But contrast that with compulsions and revulsions. Here certain associative mechanisms are called forth by thoughts, persons, things, and situations that take over our wills and drive us one way or the other. Think of phobias, fixations, and scrupulosity. Consider the sad sight of us humans when we are driven by fear or rage or avarice or lust. Think of those who prey upon the compulsions of people: pimps and drug dealers, but also advertisers. Consider here both cynical and well-intentioned religious leaders. Perhaps nowhere in human experience are neurotic fixations more operative or is one more tyrannically under the spell of the Superego than in religion. For here the modes of thought and conduct are tied to an articulation of the meaning of the Whole toward which, by our nature, we are, at first, emptily directed.

But think also of the kind of compulsion for excellence that drives a performing artist or the passion for understanding that grips the scientist or the thirst for wisdom that overcomes the philosopher or the desire for the presence of the Other that overtakes the lover or the yearning for the Face of God that consumes the saint.[21] Consider the revulsion one might feel in deceiving another, in harming innocent children, or in destroying others. Those compulsions and those revulsions are, one would think, salutary.

Also consider the emergence of a fully rational pattern of experience: the detachment to contemplate the whole order of actual and possible existence, to measure and weigh, to order and shape, to establish and refashion rules in accordance with the rule-generating orientation of an intelligence fully alert to all the significant parameters of

---

21. See G. W. F. Hegel, *Reason in History*, trans. R. Hartmann (New York: Macmillan, 1953), 29: "Nothing great in the world has been accomplished without passion." Also consider Platonic *eros*: *Symposium* 209ff and *Phaedrus* 244ff.

human existence.[22] What discipline or institutions make possible such a habit, one that can break through compulsions and revulsions, and that can crack the tyranny of both the Id and the Superego? Here is a freedom more fully deserving of the name. It is the object of truly liberal education.

The freeing of the rational pattern of experience has its grounds in the openness of our intellect toward the whole order of what-is, in the manifold ways in which that order reveals and conceals itself through the changing perspectives that emerge throughout cultures and history. But if the rational pattern involves reflective recognition of its grounds, then it also involves its own surpassing (without cancellation) toward the full mystery of Being.[23] And that also means orientation toward the full being of any Other, person or thing, context or possibility, that is concretely present within the field of our experience.[24] Hence the possibility and necessity for the opening out of a passion for excellence in creating from possibilities, in pursuing the order of nature, in loving other persons, in seeking wisdom, and in searching for God. Our autonomy as rational agents involves a dialectical relation between the disciplined emergence of the rational pattern of experience from the impulses of our animal nature as well as the motor habits of a tradition, and being gripped by passion or the good, the true, the beautiful, and the holy. In that dialectical interplay, the wildness of the passion for the beyond of Being is tamed by rational disclosure of the actual, and rationality is pulled out of its tendency toward complacent self-enclosure by the passion for the mystery of Being.[25] Passion may generate some of the finest and noblest aspects of human existence, but it may also be marred by fanaticism and extreme partiality. Religion, fit within the whole context of human experience, necessarily calls for the rational pattern

22. See Aristotle, *Nicomachean Ethics* VI.v, on the intellectual virtue of *phronesis* or practical reason as the pivot of human life. See also Lonergan, *Insight*, 173ff and 595ff.

23. See Martin Heidegger, "On the Essence of Truth," 125ff.

24. See Wood, *Path into Metaphysics*, 54ff, 91ff, 108ff, 313.

25. See the preface of Pope St. John Paul II, Encyclical Letter *Fides et ratio* (September 14, 1998): the human spirit soars on two wings: faith and reason. One without the other only circles around itself and never takes off. See my counterpart to this work: *Ratio et Fides*.

of experience as a critical, relational aspect of its own unfolding in manifold contexts.[26]

If our character as free agents is grounded in our reference to the Whole, then reference to the Whole also gives the basic teleology of our nature. By nature we seek to understand "what it's all about" and to be "at one with the All." The most significant freedom, indeed, the final freedom, is the freeing of the possibility for that union, so that the soul moves toward the Meaning-Center of things like the stone falls toward the earth. The mystic rests in the mysterious Ground of Being, in principle freed in the center of her or his being. But that is still not final freedom for our nature, since the multiple possibilities and multiple demands of our nature and our situation call for moving out into our many tasks, letting contact with the Center stretch out over all the scattered aspects of our experience.[27] Only contact with the Ground prevents those multiple possibilities and demands from tearing us asunder and thus imprisoning us in plurality rather than bringing plurality to unity.

Institutions and whole societies are geared toward the freeing of certain potentialities that are distinctively human. However, not only the regular sequences of nature and culture, but also the internal or external contingencies of nature, along with the contingencies of social relations, produce contexts within which potentialities, even high-level potentialities, can be blocked. Because of sickness, because of a need in others to whom we are committed, something deep within us must remain chained. Hence suffering, both physical and emotional.

What freedom is possible here? As in addiction, there is the freedom to take up a certain attitude. But further, there is the freedom to sustain a line of conduct, however difficult. The development of an attitude of acceptance toward our inevitable sufferings and frustrations frees us for final freedom, that is, the freedom for integration into the whole of Being, provided acceptance is combined with a continual striving to remove the source of suffering lest acceptance become sheer passivity or masochistic addiction. Now, the whole of

26. See Bernard Lonergan, *Method in Theology* (New York: Herder and Herder, 1972), pp. xi–xii, pp. 127–33.

27. Martin Buber, *I and Thou*, 176ff.

Being is not some completed set of eternal principles and absolute ideals, but the concrete texture of interplay between the myriad sets of individual relations in which we are enmeshed and the vision of possibilities and ideals that draw us forward and upward. Saying "Yes!" to Being is accepting that complete real context. The Taoist returning to one's destiny; Stoic and Spinozist acceptance of necessity; Nietzschean *amor fati*; and Hebrew, Christian, and Muslim resignation to the Will of God/Allah, all give expression to this final dimension of freedom.[28] Acceptance of suffering through natural and social contingencies and through our commitments to others makes us more sensitive, more open, more understanding, and it helps us identify with others and thus be more deeply present to Being, to the real structure of actual existents.

* * *

Most of our comments thus far have been directed to the freedom of the individual: his options, actual choices, effective action, potentialities, levels of nature, skills, compulsions and revulsions, reflective distance, rational pattern, and final freedom. But all these aspects of individual freedom are deeply tied to the institutions within which he has been raised and to those which constitute his current environment. We must also consider the freedom of these institutions and, indeed, the freedom of the complex of institutions that constitutes a nation-state.

The human individual, to begin with, is largely an overlay of culturally induced and sustained habits developed upon a biological substratum. "The self-made man" is so based on his having been made in a certain way by his significant others, who, in turn, have been shaped and sustained by others, etc. The significant others are the vehicles for the transmission of a set of practices and of the institutions sustaining them that constitute a way of life. The individual may take the shaping institutions for granted, neither choosing them nor rejecting them, but considering them given, like the terrain. He may come to treasure them, being thankful for what he has been able to be, for the powers

---

28. On Taoism, see Tao-te Ching, 16; on Stoic freedom, see Epictetus, *The Discourses* IV.1; on Spinoza, see *The Ethics*, pt. V, prop. VI and XXVII; on Nietzsche's *amor fati*, see *The Will to Power*, §1041, p. 536; Hegel *Elements*, §276, p. 223.

he has been able to free within those institutions as the unquestioned base. But due to the emergence of choice and behavior patterns that stand opposed to the prevailing institutions, the individual may find the range of his choices restricted and his freedom to act them out impeded or canceled. He seeks liberation from them. Turning against them, he becomes an impediment to *their* free functioning. That means he stands in the way of the freedom of those who choose to sustain the institutions by reason of the values embodied in them.

In the case of non-choice, we meet the inertia of institutions. We just never thought about it: "That's the way we do things." Being inertial by disposition, at least at a certain level of our being, we may be angry at those who would impede, modify, or overthrow a given institution or order of institutions. Other dispositional tendencies automatically turn to change. Dispositional conservatives and dispositional liberals are both incapable of fundamental, critical reflection. Both want freedom of choice and action, but they are in conflict at the level of institutions and the values they embody and express. Both are enslaved to their dispositions, incapable of fully freeing the rational pattern of their experience.

The conditions for the free functioning of institutions lie either in persuasion of individuals or in their coercion.[29] Some mix of the two would seem to be always involved, though the proportions vary. Institutions that promote the subtler potentialities whose freeing requires great effort over long periods cannot be sustained by sheer coercion, though some measure of coercion supports one who is persuaded of the value of participating in a given institution but is hampered by a weak resolve. Mixed with persuasion, some measure of coercion can serve to fix the intellectually wavering or even to convert those initially opposed. Everything depends upon the right mix for the right individuals. Though sheer coercion cannot keep people at the higher tasks, sheer coercion, practiced even to the point of terrorism, can keep people at routinized tasks for surprisingly long periods.

In situations of accelerated change, particularly change brought about by the increase in technical knowledge, it is of crucial impor-

---

29. On Platonic *peitho,* see *Timaeus* 51; see also Alfred North Whitehead, *Adventures of Ideas* (New York: Macmillan, 1933), pt. I, V, pp. 69–86.

tance to the society that the rational pattern of experience be freed. Rationality involves an ongoing attempt to balance a view of the sorts of institutions that promote and that are compatible with the highest powers of humanness within the actual institutions in a given context. The prudential blending of the two prevents either attempting to impose on a situation structures it cannot possibly bear or acquiescence in the *status quo* without regard to how it serves or impedes the freeing of the higher human powers.

The complex of institutions we call a nation-state may also be impeded in its free functioning, whether by threats from within or by challenges from without. One needs a mix of coercion and persuasion to prepare for the common defense by conscription and taxation. One needs a mix of coercion and persuasion to ensure the provision of the basic necessities and to prevent some members of the society from encroaching upon others. Some freedoms are sacrificed through persuasion or taken away by coercion for the sake of others. One needs a mix of persuasion and coercion to provide a stable context for the rearing of the next generation—together with provision of biological necessities and national defense, which is one of the basic requirements of any long-term life-group. One needs a method of passing on information, techniques, and practices to the next generation. One needs, in the long term, the emergence of Institutions that promote the rational pattern of experience.[30] Economics, the military and the police, institutions of marriage and child rearing, and training and education: each primary institution requires decisions about its initial form and its requisite modification under altered circumstances. Through the individuals who sustain it, each such institution seeks its free functioning. Part of the problem is that each of these institutions and institutional complexes admits of differing forms that are largely matters of choice. The freedom of those who initially chose them and the free functioning of those who are carried by them are inhibited by the desires and choices of others who would do otherwise. A liberally educated person seeks to adjudicate the competing claims and does so in terms of the values embedded in the institutions.

---

30. G. W. F. Hegel, *Philosophy of Right*, trans. R. Nisbet (New York: Cambridge University Press, 1991), §432.

But how does one evaluate the values? Since the peculiar complex of such institutions varies from nation-state to nation-state and from epoch to epoch, one needs to establish a certain critical distance as a first priority. That would establish an evaluative criterion for nation-states: Do they promote critical distance?

One must distinguish here between internal and external critique. Internal critique is directed toward functional rationality: does the institution in question meet the goals toward which it is directed? Do the values embedded in the institutional complex clash with one another? Can we harmonize the values with one another and in their institutional embodiments? External critique measures the society in terms of how its institutions succeed in freeing the potentialities of its members, horizontally in terms of the extension of its perquisites to all its members and vertically in terms of the way it allows for the freeing of the highest potentialities. It seeks criteria to establish the right mix between those two demands.[31]

The highest potentialities involve freeing the rational pattern, that is, the capacity to assess and bring coherence into the overall pattern of individual and collective action, for everything turns upon that. But that is also linked, as I claimed previously, to freeing the peculiar human passions for the pursuit of beauty, excellence, truth, love, and mysticism. How can an institutional complex be conceived so as to maximize the freeing of these potentialities? How can we learn to arrange our lives so that we may reach toward what I have previously called "final freedom"? In this ideal-typical state, the original empty directedness of our nature toward the whole of being, a directedness which grounds freedom of choice, is filled in a manner that gathers the whole of our being in relation to the Fullness of Being. Such freedom provides the deepest lived context within which we are enabled to carry on the individual and collective tasks posed by our distinctive character as human beings living in the peculiarities of the concrete institutional complex in which we find ourselves called upon to think and act.

* * *

31. Jürgen Habermas, *Knowledge and Human Interests*, trans. J. Shapiro (Boston: Beacon Press, 1971), 274ff.

Freedom is a multifaceted concept. It has its roots in nature. Each nature has its positive free functioning, which involves, negatively, freedom from obstruction. And obstruction may be either external or internal, based upon hostility from without or imbalance from within. Distinctively human nature involves a pre-reflective reference to the Whole of Being, which pries us loose from any element of nature within as well as without, and forces us to choose our way. Out of the sedimented choices of others, culture appears as second nature and as the matrix for the emergence of new members. Submission to nature and human culture both within and without, linked to our reference to the Whole, opens up an indeterminate set of possibilities for choice, and thus sets in motion an actual or possible chaos. Our task is, as Nietzsche would have it, "to compel the chaos within us to become form."[32] But not every form is desirable. I have contended that there is a measure for adjudicating various forms of human life through the founding reference to the Whole that gives a final *telos* to the process. It involves an individual and collective way of life that is open to the Whole, to the Mystery of appearing and receding in and through each encounter. Freeing that potentiality is the most significant freedom we can achieve. But its freeing is dialectically tied to the freeing of the rational pattern of experience, individually and collectively, so that with the materials available in ourselves we can form flexible institutions that are finally open to the Mystery of the Whole along with respect for the integrity of individuals.

32. Friedrich Nietzsche, *The Will to Power*, §842, p. 444.

Chapter 7

Moral-Political Extensions
Preliminary Sketches[1]

Being human develops in and through the way the *I* relates to the You, the We, the It, and the Others. Those relations constitute the moral-political domain and operate in terms of institutionalization. We have learned to reflect upon the moral-political through the explorations presented in the philosophic tradition, which contains a kind of moral-political phenomenology that I will explore in this chapter.

In this first part we will reflect in a general way upon intersubjectivity. We will go on to assimilate the tradition of virtue from Plato through Aristotle to Aquinas. In relation to the latter, I will attempt to show a rational grounding of the Ten Commandments in natural moral law. As Lessing said, revelation was given from without as a command and not rationally grounded, but it was given in order to be rationally comprehended.[2] We will go on to assimilate Kant to that tradition; and we will conclude with some reflections on happiness.

INTERSUBJECTIVITY

The human subject is not entirely self-contained. She or he arises in an already articulated historical context, is assimilated to, and develops in relation to those who mediate that context. The human individual is constituted by intersubjectivity. There is a primordial intersubjectivity: the relation of the human subject to other subjects-of-being directly encounterable in and through sensation and indirectly infer-

---

1. I should again emphasize *sketches*. Drawing upon several thinkers (especially Aristotle, Aquinas, and Kant) I am laying out a framework. I point in directions grounded in my seven-dimensional view. Obviously a great deal more could be said about the issues and the thinkers.

2. Gotthold Ephraim Lessing, *The Education of the Human Race* (London: Kegan Paul, Trench, and Co., 1883), §§65–67.

able through intellection. But what mediates that access is the fundamental product of reciprocal, human intersubjectivity: language.

Of course, one does not begin with language, except in the sense of the expressive music of another person's voice. It is typically through the mother's voice and her loving touch that an infant gains a sense of security. One remains *in-fans*, or nonspeaking, until one learns to use language.[3] Such use is initially functional, tied to negotiating the sensorily present environment in terms of felt need. A significant question concerns when one learns to move beyond that, for at that point and not before, one becomes a center of responsibility.

Through encountering household rules, one learns that one does not have to follow impulse and can then give rules to one's own life in order to "compel the chaos that is within to take on form."[4] One finds the beginning of a lifelong struggle between acting as an appetite-driven animal or as a self-determining, rationally free human being.

It is through language, action, and example that the developing child's primary caregivers induct her or him into the practices and institutions of their culture. This sets the basic context within which we can each discover, develop, and measure our native capacities. I cannot emphasize too strongly that, in its invention of differing practices, culture is the context with which capacities (otherwise lying fallow within the gene pool) can be developed. How many classical pianists were there at the time of Moses? How many baseball, basketball, or football players? Even Andrew Carnegie, steel magnate and one of the late nineteenth- and early twentieth-century "robber barons," claimed that he owed his success to the system that made it possible and that any decent person should pay it back in the form of philanthropy.[5] So much for the myth of the "self-made individual" who owes everything to her or his own initiative.

3. See Chad Engelland, *On Ostension* (Boston: MIT Press, 2014), 176–77.
4. Nietzsche, *The Will to Power*, §842, p. 444.
5. See his *Gospel of Wealth* (New York: Applewood Books, 1998), 15–16. Andrew Carnegie claimed that one who died with his estate intact was a disgrace, for he owed what he was able to become to the system that made it possible. He did not pass anything on to his children. (He had already positioned them to succeed financially.) The money went back to the system; hence one hundred Carnegie libraries, Carnegie Mellon University, Carnegie Hall, and the like.

In addition to hunger and thirst, the onset of adolescence brings a new natural desire, *libido*, with greater or lesser insistency, depending upon the nature of a given individual. It drives the individual into relations with the other. The realm of intersubjectivity that emerges at this time is full of ambiguity. The other person easily becomes merely an occasion for self-gratification. But at the same time, as Plato made clear, *eros* can also emerge, which is linked to but distinctively different than libido. Underlying sexual experience is *eros* as the desire of organic nature, condemned to death, to seek immortality through reproduction.[6] That is what underlies sexual arousal. It is the next generation saying: "You have to die. Let us live in your place." But *eros* in the human being is linked to the ontological pole of reference to the Whole and thus to the whole of each individual within the Whole. One learns to regard the individual other as having its own integrity, beyond its sensory showing and its occasioning sexual gratification. The higher experience involves a feeling of awe, setting at a distance one's own needs to acknowledge the integrity of the other, even possibly experiencing something of the sacred. The other changes from It, as object of one's own gratification, to Thou as term of reverence.

The love of the mortal for the immortal is further modulated in the human case by the desire to do great deeds or perform great works within the institutional framework of a given culture, thereby affecting future generations. One learns to love the laws and institutions that will carry on a way of life into the indefinite future. But *eros* is further transformed through seeking the deathless order of the Whole in terms of the invariant laws that govern the cosmos: logical, mathematical, scientific, philosophical, and maybe even theological laws.

* * *

Let us return to the immediate situation. As an example of a shift in the character of intersubjective relations, take the case of the ophthalmologist who greets her patient, briefly discussing the patient's family, the weather, the latest sports event, etc. Then she gets down to work. Her attention is now focused upon the eyeball mechanism that

---

6. This section follows Plato's observations given through Socrates and Diotima in his *Symposium* 210a–212c.

she knows in terms of the typical structure and functioning of the visual system: how light passes through the pupils and the lenses to affect the rods and cones of the retina; how the electrical signals this produces pass, through a series of electro-chemical switches along the optical nerve, to the visual cortex in the back of the brain, which grounds seeing. She has learned to recognize typicality of function and deviation from typicality; and she knows how to bring the deviations back to normality of function. But this is available by *abstracting* from the expressivity of the eyes, the face, and the gestural style of bodily comportment generally. She moves away from the concrete expressivity of the lived body and of language in the interpersonal relation and into an attention to the impersonal mechanisms that ground seeing. This move is the basic move of empirical science.

We have already noted John Searle's observation that third-person ontology is grounded in first- and second-person ontology: neutral scientific investigation of impersonal things is grounded in the concrete relation of persons.[7] Martin Buber claims that *I-It* relations involve a turning away from *I-Thou* relations.[8] Science abstracts from life as lived in the encounter between concrete human beings, though what science discovers—for example, the way the nervous system operates—makes possible the sphere of the interpersonal. Science does not occupy that sphere in what it does, but only in the relations of person to person in their work and in their lives generally.

Buber also remarked that in any dyadic relation between persons there are actually eight *persons* involved: I as I appear to you and you as you appear to me are the most obvious. But there is also I as I *want* to appear to you and you as you *want* to appear to me. And there is I as I appear to myself and you as you appear to yourself. But finally, there is I as I fully am and you as you fully are, which is more or less hidden from each of us. Interpersonal relations are a game of mirrors, of appearance and reality.[9] And in such complex relations, it is no wonder that misunderstandings constantly occur.

7. Nagel, *Mind and Cosmos* (Oxford: Oxford University Press, 2012), 212. Searle, *Rediscovery of Mind*, 117.

8. Buber, *I and Thou*, 68–69.

9. Buber, *The Knowledge of Man*, trans. M. Friedman (New York: Harper, 1965), 77.

Sartre underscored the struggle between subjectivities. "Hell is other people": you assimilating me into your world; I assimilating you into my world. We are each like vampires, sucking the lifeblood out of each other's world.[10] In this he is influenced by Hegel's description of the master-slave relation. Each human being is by nature a light that opens upon the Whole; she or he is, in a way, all things, as Aristotle would have it. More than one such light constitutes a contradiction—both cannot be the Whole—that must be resolved. A struggle ensues. One who becomes master is willing to risk his life in the struggle with the other, while the slave, as that other, fears for his life and so surrenders. That more primitive relation plays out in other forms after the institution of law. For Hegel, the developmental upshot of that struggle arises when it dawns on them that they are each the locus of a single light: the light of rationality. From then on, each person can gain recognition as a rational and thus free subject, the locus of dignity and responsibility.[11]

Responsibility occurs within a set of institutional practices. Though they differ widely from culture to culture, the question emerges as to their measure. To get at this we will take a roundabout approach through the grounding feature of human being: the relation to Being that orients all our thinking.

NATURAL MORAL LAW AND THE VIRTUES

If we apply the notion of Being to beings, we see that each being, by being of the kind it is, is directed toward its own end. This is clear; or at least it should be clear, but it is heavily contested in the case of living beings, for they are governed by the drive to develop, sustain, and reproduce themselves. Set in an evolutionary context, the elemental situation at the Big Bang contained the potentialities to eventuate in self-replicating beings, sensorily aware beings, and rationally aware beings, subsuming, in their rationality, the two previous levels.[12] At

10. Sartre, *No Exit and Three Other Plays*, trans. S. Gilbert (New York: Vintage, 1949), 47.

11. Hegel, *Phenomenology of Spirit*, §§128–96.

12. For a development of this, see the concluding chapter of my *Being and the Cosmos*: "The Cosmos Has an Inside."

the level of the emergence of rationality, the cosmos has produced the conditions for its own self-manifestation and can reasonably be construed as aimed at that manifestation from the start.[13] A living being is evidently teleological: it is an organ-ism, where the "-ism" indicates a system, that is, a system of organs or instruments for serving certain purposes, ultimately the mature flourishing of the organism and its carrying on its kind into the next generation through reproduction. Each organism seeks the full actualization of its native powers, which is realized when it reaches the reproductive stage.

Let us return to the tendency of all living beings that Plato described as "the love of the mortal for the immortal." *Eros* and *Thanatos* belong together: death is overcome, in a way, through reproduction, keeping the species as immortal as it can be. So each living thing has its own good that it seeks by nature: the full actuality of its being as the kind it is and the continued existence of its kind. Because of this, organisms can succeed or fail. When there are living things, other things (living and nonliving) become values and dis-values in relation to the goals of the organism as its own inner goods. The whole eco-system is a circle of organisms and nonliving entities, which each function in its ecological niche as a good for others and as good in itself. So being and goodness are in some sense convertible. The more actuality in its own kind a thing has, the more being it has: as a seed progressively actualizes its potency, it possesses more of its being, until it reaches full maturity in the ability to reproduce.

As far as rational agents are concerned (and here we gloss on Aquinas' notion of natural moral law), truth-seeking, as the mind's own specific good, follows from the initially empty notion of Being as the imperative for intellectual development. That is the highest level of the general imperative: "Do good and avoid evil." (Or rather, it shows itself as the highest insofar as it involves the deepest imperative for Aquinas: "Worship God.") What good and evil mean are specified by what fosters, inhibits, or destroys the intrinsic ends of the human being.

13. Thomas Nagel recently made that claim referring to German Idealism. His basic position is that the mind that can get at objectivity and even *eternality* in mathematics and logic cannot be explained in terms of mechanisms of adjustment to environment. The mind is the cosmos waking up to itself, and its self-manifestation is construed as one of its goals. *Mind and Cosmos*, 85.

There are several basic natural imperatives built on the levels of human structure. At the organic level, the imperative is: *Preserve the conditions of your own life*; at the sentient level: *Reproduce and care for offspring*. But at the third, the distinctively human level, there are two imperatives: *Live in community* and *Seek the truth*.[14] The last two are reciprocal: the search for the truth is an enterprise that can only be carried on successfully through thousands of years of accumulated discoveries. And the possibilities hidden in the human gene pool can only be tapped when the appropriate communal institutions are developed. As we noted previously, at the time of Moses there were probably as many potential classical pianists or professional basketball players as there are now. The difference is that there were no modern pianos, no classical repertoire, and no conservatories for teaching advanced technique in piano performance; nor were there the rules of basketball and gifted coaches who encouraged people with the appropriate talents to hone them to perfection. As Aristotle noted, the human being is a *political animal*, that is, one who flourishes only on the basis of tradition, one who is indebted to remotely past generations for its concrete possibilities of development.[15]

The personal conditions for flourishing are what come to be called *the cardinal virtues*, each a hinge (Latin *cardo*) of a full human life. (Here we refer to the line from Plato through Aristotle to Aquinas.) As Nietzsche was fond of noting and as we cited before, any significant human achievement depends upon bringing order into the chaos of natural appetites. Though animals may safely follow their instinctive urges and so fulfill their own wellbeing (and their role in the ecosystem, or both) as well as that of their offspring, in attempting to do the same, humans only become chaotic. And the reason lies in the ontological pole of our being: referred to the Whole via the notion of Being, we are pried loose from anything less than the Whole and are "condemned to choose."[16] We are given over to ourselves to shape what

14. Aquinas, *Summa theologiae*, I, q. 94, a. 2. Actually, Aquinas speaks of this imperative as searching for the truth about God. But as the *Summa* itself indicates, that involves becoming aware of the whole order of things.

15. Aristotle, *Politics* I.1253a.

16. Jean-Paul Sartre, "Existentialism is a Humanism," in *Existentialism from Dostoevsky to Sartre*, ed. and trans. W. Kaufmann (New York: Meridian Books, 1956), 295.

is given in us by nature. It is up to us to shape our appetitive life in the light of our higher commitments. So the premise of all significant human achievement is temperance or *sophrosune*, which Aristotle etymologizes as *sozein phronesin*, or preserving your *phronesis*, that is, the capacity for intelligent self-direction.[17]

That capacity is the pivot of the whole of one's life. It is learning to keep one's balance in surfing through the contingencies of life. It is the capacity for sizing up situations and finding the right thing to do. It presupposes temperance or self-restraint typically learned through disciplined upbringing. Parental orders teach the young child that it does not have to follow its appetites but can direct itself according to rule and give itself rules. That is the condition for the rational development of the child, freeing her or him from being governed by appetites so that she or he can be free to govern her- or himself.[18] Some parents seem never to learn that, without rules, when one gives in to every whim of the child, the child is "spoiled," unable to lead a life harmonious in itself and in harmony with all rationally functioning beings.

The exercise of *phronesis*, which is distinct from cunning, depends upon the virtue of *justice*, the fixed disposition to give each person one encounters his or her due.[19] Of course, what that means must be determined by the practices of a community, which can be subject to critique in terms of consistency of principles and applications and consistency of a community's principles with those that are required for maximum rational flourishing.[20] The notion of justice should be extended intellectually as the fixed disposition to give each interlocu-

17. Aristotle, *Nicomachean Ethics* VI.v.1140b12.

18. After presenting the program of "education" (actually training) in the *Republic*, Socrates says we will turn the pupils over to themselves as *free men*, that is, not slaves of appetite, and thus capable of directing themselves. Plato, *Republic* III.412a–413a. Hegel claims that rationality involves "breaking the natural will" (where the will is one with appetite) through obedience to orders. Hegel, *Hegel's Philosophy of Mind*, §396, *Zusatz*, p. 60.

19. On *phronesis*, see Aristotle, *NE* VI.1140a25–1145a12; on justice, see *NE* V.1030b10–1131b.

20. See Terry Pinkard, *Hegel's Naturalism: Mind, Nature, and the Final Ends of Life* (London: Oxford, 2012), 55–56, 144–45; and Robert Pippin, *After the Beautiful: Hegel and the Philosophy of Pictorial Modernism* (Chicago: University of Chicago Press, 2014), 68–69. Hegel provides the conceptual tools for analyzing normative functioning and normative change.

tor and each position its fair reading, keeping oneself open to being corrected in misunderstanding another or overlooking significant principles or applications that might emerge from dialogical encounter.[21] Indeed, the notion of justice should be extended to giving each thing that exists its due. Further, acting rightly in situations also requires the fixed disposition to overcome whatever hardships may stand in the way; hence the need for *fortitude*. Thus, the four cardinal virtues—practical wisdom, temperance, justice, and fortitude—constitute the foundations of a rationally free human life.[22]

As a final note on virtue, notice that there is a basic distinction between virtues and skills. Both are *habits*, that is, ways in which we *have* (Latin *habere*) ourselves in hand. But contrary to a skill, which is dormant unless put into action, a virtue occupies what Dietrich von Hildebrand aptly calls a "super-actual substratum" of human life.[23] Like a skill, a virtue is present even when one is asleep. However, when one is awake, moral virtue is always operative in sustaining the direction of the field of awareness. It is automatically set in motion by situations without having to be deliberately called up, as in the case with skills. Thus, if we have the virtue of temperance, then it is always operative, governing one's intake of food and drink and one's sexual life. Above all, practical wisdom is always operative, always sizing up situations.

THE TEN COMMANDMENTS AS SECONDARY NATURAL LAW PRINCIPLES

Virtuous existence occurs in terms of the ends set by the levels of human structure, which we have already mentioned: preservation of one's own life, care for one's offspring, living in community, and seeking truth. The further application of these natural imperatives can, by the exercise of reason, lead to variations on the traditional Ten

21. See my "Nature, Culture, and the Dialogical Imperative," in *The Beautiful, the True, and the Good*, xix–xxxii.
22. Plato, *Republic* IV.427d–434c is the classical locus of their first appearance in philosophy.
23. *The Nature of Love*, trans. J. E. and J. H. Crosby (South Bend, Ind.: St. Augustine's Press, 2009), 46.

Commandments.[24] These are imperatives that follow from those built into the levels of human structure.[25]

In seeking the truth, when we consider the overall framework set up by the notion of Being, the question that emerges is: Is the totality of being the sum of finite beings, hierarchically arranged? Or is there something beyond the finite, an In-finite Being? This question emerges because we can always ask before any putative limit to the cosmos, whether there is something that stands beyond the limits. Stephen Hawking proclaims that asking whether there was time before the Big Bang or space beyond the expanding universe are meaningless questions.[26] But they are not meaningless, and that is because we are oriented toward Space and Time as indeterminately encompassing forms that we bring to bear upon experienced, narrated, or inferred spaces and times; and that orientation, in turn, is rooted in our being projected toward Being as a whole, even beyond Space and Time. Because we are oriented toward the Totality, we can always ask if what occurs within Hawking's stipulative limits is all there is.

There are three a priori forms that we bring to bear upon experience: the notion of Being as referred to totality and potentially infinite, and Space and Time as indeterminately encompassing perceived forms. Because of the functioning of the a priori notion of Being in us, we can ask whether there is something beyond any putative limit, indeed, whether there might be something beyond the totality of finite beings. Is there something which, positively and in its own nature, corresponds to what we grasp negatively as absolutely in-finite possibility? *Absolutely infinite* is set over against finite infinities such as the various number series. The question then emerges of how finite being can *be* at all, since being as conceptualized is potentially infinite in an absolute

---

24. There are actually three versions of the list in the Torah: Ex 20:2–17, 34, 12–26, as well as Dt 5:6–21. We are repeating what has become traditional in the Christian tradition.

25. In his *Sane Society* (New York: Holt, 1990), 269–79, 304–6, psychologist Eric Fromm cited the example of a community of disparate beliefs that tried to determine what conditions must be met for them to establish a long-term, multigenerational community. They came up with the Ten Commandments. But since some of them were atheists, they had to omit the first three, which dealt with God.

26. Stephen Hawking and Roger Penrose, *The Nature of Space and Time* (Princeton, N.J.: Princeton University Press, 1996), 19–20, 98.

way. And the answer then presents itself: only because absolutely Infinite Being continually gives being to everything finite. Because we are oriented toward the Infinite, finite being presents itself as needing a cause of the limitation of being whose nature is absolutely infinite.[27]

When we think of infinite being, we think of it as contrasted with finite being; that is why we call it in-finite. However, if we think of *absolutely* infinite Being, it would necessarily have to include finite being, or else it would be limited to one side of the finite-infinite distinction. (Here Hegel comes into play.)[28] If there are *gods*, they would be *angelic beings*, good or evil; they would be great but still finite beings, themselves grounded in the single absolute, infinite fullness of Being. There can only be one such Being, since by its nature it includes everything else, which is necessarily finite.[29] Such inclusion means both that, as absolutely Infinite Being, It completely transcends all finitude, and yet it is completely immanent in each thing. It is right to call it *God*. As Augustine said, He is closer to me than I am to myself.[30] And according to St. Paul, "In Him we live and move and have our being."[31] As correlate to our reference to Being, He would be "He Who Is" and "He Whom my heart seeks."[32]

As absolutely unrestricted, such a Being would have to be omniscient, omnipotent, and all-wise. Nothing escapes Him because His knowing and choosing sustains creatures in being, and thus He is all powerful. And the interrelatedness of things shows something of His infinite wisdom. As the ground of all finite Being through Whose generosity we exist, such a Being deserves our praise and thanks.

---

27. Hegel claims that the existence of relative nonbeing is a contradiction that can only be resolved by grounding finite being in Infinite Being. *Hegel's Science of Logic*, 128.

28. *Hegel's Science of Logic*, 143–50.

29. Aquinas, *Summa theologiae*, I, q. 7.

30. Augustine, *Confessions*, vol. 1, III.vi.I/120.

31. Acts 17:28.

32. "He Who Is" is the common translation of the Burning Bush revelation. Martin Buber claimed that the Hebrew says, "I shall be present . . . [a]s which I shall be present." *Moses: The Revelation and the Covenant* (New York: Harper and Brothers, 1958): 51–52. The flip side to that is, "Pay attention to the signs of the times," or what Buber called the epiphany of the Thou. Interestingly, that is what he claims happens in the introduction of the gods of the brook, the grove, and the mountain; they are *moment gods*, which the Hebrew Bible identifies as words spoken by a single voice: that of Yahweh, Whose speaking brings and sustains being in beings. Buber, *I and Thou*, 56.

So, following out the imperative to seek the truth, we come to two primary commandments as the first of several imperatives derived from the deepest stem of human existence (namely, human rationality): first, *There is but one God Who gives us being* and thus *He deserves our worship*, that is, our appreciation and gratitude. There is nothing that could be called *God* as the fullness of being besides this One: there are no strange gods besides Him. Now, the third commandment, to *Keep holy the Sabbath*, would not be a natural law imperative, but something peculiar to the Hebrew tradition; however, it spells out for a people a way to situate worship of God as a primary response.

The seven commandments that pertain to inter-human relations spell out the conditions for the possibility of living in community in such a way as to pass on the developments that emerge from past generations. So the first commandment in this regard would be: (4) *Honor your father and mother*, that is, respect them and through them the tradition that they have mediated to you, the tradition that gives you your concrete possibilities of development. Respect them by carrying it on—though properly doing that might also involve critique of aspects of the tradition, developing through philosophy the institution of critique and application. Along with acknowledgment and worship of God, this is the only other positive commandment.

Then, if we are to live in community, we certainly cannot (5) kill each other or (6) take our neighbor's spouse for ourselves or (7) steal from one another. Indeed, we should not even *think* about (9) committing adultery and (10) stealing, for the thought is father to the deed.

There is one more commandment relating to the neighbor: (8) *You shall not bear false witness*, that is, lie in such a way as to harm your neighbor. It is linked to another commandment that pertains to our relation to God: (2) *You shall not take the name of the Lord your God in vain*. I take that to mean the following: do not swear by God in bearing false witness against your neighbor and compound the evil by directly falsifying your relation to God.

Keeping the totality of these commandments makes one a just person. However, with regard to one's neighbor, the commandments are negative: they establish a fence around an area of action. We might add that what happens within that area is found in the two great commandments of love that sum up the *Torah*: Love the Lord, Whom you justly praise and thank, with your whole being; and love your neighbor as yourself.[33] The second is the way to the first: "How can you love God Whom you cannot see if you do not love your neighbor whom you do see?"[34] The second presupposes proper self-love, for one cannot love one's neighbor *as oneself* if one has contempt for oneself.[35]

These articulations constitute principles of human development rooted in permanent features of human existence. They are developments of what comes to be called *natural moral law*. The Decalogue contains secondary principles as applications of the imperative built into the trilevel structure of humanness.[36]

The command to preserve one's own life and to live in community together govern such things as traffic laws. How can automobile traffic be governed in such a way as to maximize not only the efficiency of moving from place to place, but especially the safety of those who travel? One thing that must be decided is on which side of the road to drive. There are two reasonable possibilities: in North America the makers of our tradition decided to drive on the right side; in England and in parts of its old empire, tradition-formers decided to drive on the left. These are thus two opposite laws governed by the same imperative.

The deepest level of human activity is seeking the truth that governs all the rest. Such seeking is directed to the ongoing pursuit of understanding the underlying reality of ourselves and the things we encounter in individual sensory actuality. Underlying that actuality are the natural powers of things, and underlying the sensory actuality of other humans are their states of mind and humanly developed skills, both practical and theoretical. Following out the truth-imperative launches natural science as an ongoing, expansive, and methodically self-corrective process. One might say that the modern specification of the natural law imperative to seek the truth, as formulated

33. Mt 22:37–40 refers to the Torah: Dt 6:3 and Lv 19:18.
34. 1 Jn 4:20–21.
35. One might rationalize contempt for others with its parallel to contempt for oneself as following the commandment.
36. Aquinas, *Summa theologiae*, I, q. 94, a. 2.

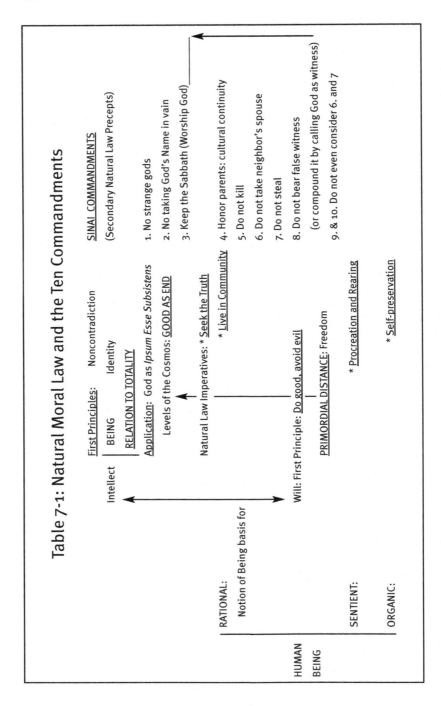

Table 7-1: Natural Moral Law and the Ten Commandments

by C. S. Peirce, is: *Do not block the path of inquiry.*[37] This is a distinctively modern development that had to fight a long uphill battle against the religious establishments that thought they were in possession of the final truth of things and consequently limited the things people could say, read, and write—and, with God as the inner Spy, even what people could think.

Now the imperative involved in ongoing scientific inquiry has to be understood as itself operating within the principles that specify the dignity and rights of human beings. That is what is involved in the battle over abortion and abortifacients. Even though a fertilized ovum presents itself as a relatively uncomplex cell, and detailed scientific investigation uncovers nothing but its relative complexity, it nonetheless has a set of powers (unobservable in principle) that have been set in motion and that will terminate, unless inhibited, in an adult capable of reproduction and of freely directing itself. Failure to respect this being-underway is what is involved in opposition to abortifacients, to destroying fertilized ova for embryonic research, and, in the case of infertile couples, in opposition to artificially producing embryos that are implanted in larger numbers than the desired birth, so that the weakest will be destroyed.

This opens a vast area that is beyond the scope of this presentation. One can see, however, that arguments can be launched for proper procedure in such areas on the basis of natural law, not as a religiously sectarian enterprise, despite the fact that it is appropriated and even developed by the Roman Catholic Church. Arguing from religious revelation and tradition is not proper to the public forum; arguing from natural moral law as understood above is the only legitimate basis for public policy arguments in a religiously pluralistic or fully secular society.

KANT AND THE MORAL TRADITION

As we said, the Ten Commandments for the most part build a fence of negations around the community. What goes on *within* the negative

---

37. C. S. Peirce, "The Scientific Attitude and Fallibilism," in *Philosophical Writings of Peirce*, ed. J. Buchler (New York: Dover, 1955), xxxi.

boundaries is made clear in the New Testament as love of God recip-
rocally tied to love of one's neighbor on par with one's love of oneself
that summed up the teaching of the Torah. Many consider Immanuel
Kant to have overcome the philosophic tradition in favor of a new
principle for ethics: *the categorical imperative.* However, I would claim
that he is, rather, *deepening* that tradition along the lines of love of
neighbor as oneself.

The categorical imperative is distinguished from the hypothetical
imperative. The latter has the form of *If-then*: "*If* you want to be happy,
then do x and stop doing y." Kant understands that as characteristic
of the eudaemonist or "happiness" tradition that found its classic statement in Aristotle's ethics. Kant calls such imperatives *counsels of pru-
dence.* They are similar to what he calls *rules of skill,* such as, "If you
want to build a bridge, then follow the principles of physics on the
load-bearing capacities of certain materials and the stresses and strains
that follow from particular conjunctions of materials," or, "If you want
to bake a cake like grandma's, then follow her recipe."[38] By contrast,
the categorical imperative is a command that allows no ifs, ands, or
buts: "Do x because that is the right thing to do." Kant claims that
morally sensitive people think and act that way. Acting for any other
reason involves what people recognize as "ulterior motives."[39] Kant
claims that the categorical imperative only formulates the deeper
grounds of common-sense morality. It is common to give as reason
for one's action, "It was the right thing to do," or, "It is what any decent
person in this situation would do," or "It was necessary in order to
correct someone acting without regard for the moral order."

Another aspect of common morality is the recognition that using
people is wrong: it ignores their fundamental dignity. Kant finds the
deeper grounds for such recognition in the character of reason and
its intrinsic *autonomy* or self-(*autos*) legislation (*nomos*). Things act
in accordance with the laws of nature; humans act in terms of a *conception* of law, and ultimately a law that they could give to themselves
as rational agents.[40] Auto-nomy as self-legislation is opposed to *het-*

---

38. Immanuel Kant, *GMM'PP,* 67–69/4:414.
39. Kant, *GMM'PP,* 72–73/4:420–4:421.
40. Kant, *GMM'PP,* 66/4:412.

eronomy, to *nomos* given by another (*heteros*).[41] The Ten Commandments were heteronomous to begin with; but when we were able to
grasp their underlying rationality, that is, their intrinsic suitability for
human flourishing, we became rationally autonomous through them.
I already cited what Lessing said, but I will repeat it: revelation was
given irrationally from without so that it may become rationally comprehended from within. What might have seemed arbitrary imposi-
tions by an overpowering Lawgiver turn out to be the rational expression of divine wisdom discoverable by human reason as the operative
principles for human flourishing.

A conception of law involves the recognition of the universal
as universal. Mind rises above bodily location and the sensory manifestation of the environment; it operates in terms of an inner relation to Space and Time as encompassing wholes that make it possible to see a form that is applicable any time and any place an
instance of that form is found. Further, the mind operates in terms
of Reason as aimed at the Totality.[42] Central to reason is the unrestricted generality of the principle of noncontradiction: the principle applies to everything possible. Though Kant limited responsible
knowing to experiential unities, he maintained that, because of the
principle of noncontradiction, one can *think* beyond that to an All-
Encompassing, but can *know* nothing about It.[43] Whatever It might
be, the principle of noncontradiction would still apply to it. In the
tradition we are attempting to carry forth, this follows from the
notion of Being as applying to absolutely everything, including
God. On this basis, Kant gives a hermeneutic understanding of our

41. Kant, *GMM'PP,* 83/4:443.
42. Emmanuel Levinas has set himself in opposition to the "totalitarianism" of the
notion of Being and argues for an infinite divine beyond Being. *Totality and Infinity,* trans.
A. Lingis (Pittsburgh: Duquesne University Press, 1969), 15, 292–93. He refers to Plato's
designation in the *Republic* of the Good as *epekeina tes ousias,* typically translated as "beyond Being." It should instead be translated as "beyond essence" as correlate to *nous.* Plato
also speaks of the Good as *to tou ontos phanotaton,* the most manifest of being (*to on*).
That is an historical point. The substantive point is that there could *be* nothing beyond
being under penalty of contradiction. To say that something is beyond being is to presuppose a determinate meaning of being that is not all encompassing. Being is, rather, *what
is the case.* The distinction between finite and Infinite Being serves the purpose intended
by Levinas that God is Absolute Mystery.
43. Kant, *Critique of Pure Reason,* A151/B190, p. 222ff; A602/B630, p. 585ff.

relation to God—a reasonable interpretation that will contend with other interpretations.[44]

Reformulating the common-sense moral principles in terms of the autonomy of reason, Kant presented three basic formulations of the categorical imperative. The first consists in the universalizability of the principles chosen for one's action. "Any decent person would do x because it is the right thing to do," becomes, "*Act only in accordance with that maxim through which you can at the same time will that it become a universal law.*"[45]

The rational autonomy underlying that leads to a second formulation: the principle of common moral sensibility. "Don't use people," becomes, "*So act that you treat humanity, whether in your own person or in the person of any other, always as an end, never merely as a means.*"[46] "Humanity" refers to the peculiar quality of humanness, namely, our capacity to choose ends and give ourselves laws, so that respecting humanity in one's own person involves not cultivating one's reason simply to serve one's appetites.

Kant has a third formulation, in effect: *So act that your principles of action could serve to establish a kingdom of ends.*[47] That "kingdom" is the togetherness of rational agents, each as ends in themselves, under rational laws, that is, those which respect the rational dignity of individuals. So for Kant all moral maxims have a *unity* of form: universality; a *plurality* of matter, humanity as end in all persons; and a *totality*, a complete determination in a system, a kingdom of ends.[48]

Adhering to these principles involves duties that can never be completed. With respect to oneself, the imperative is: "Develop your talents"; with respect to others, it is: "Aid others in doing the

44. In Kant's moral teaching, God is the guarantor of the *summum bonum* as the coincidence of happiness and deservedness to be happy. *Critique of Practical Reason*, I, ii: 124–32. In the third critique, He is the apex of a teleological view of nature fashioned by Him as an arena for the development of culture and the achievement of morality. Kant, *Critique of Judgment*, §§84–90/436–66.

45. Kant, *GMM'PP,* 73/4:421.

46. Kant, *GMM'PP,* 80/4:429.

47. Kant, *GMM'PP,* 83–4/4:443–44. He does not formulate the third in the same way as the other two versions, but I have given it a parallel structure.

48. Kant, *GMM'PP,* 85–6/4:436.

same."[49] This leads to the ongoing progress in culture-building within the kingdom of ends: a culture of discipline or self-restraint under law allows one to work at long-range individual and communal projects in the cultivation of skills for the overall benefit of the human community.[50] Here Kant joins Aristotle's observations on virtue and the natural moral law tradition.

Suicide makes one's life into a means rather than an end. Lying to others or taking their property or freedom makes them mere means for our gratification. The end of nature with regard to human beings is to strive for greater perfection—hence the ongoing imperative of developing one's talents. Nature's end is a will giving universal law within a kingdom of ends.[51] Hence the ongoing imperative of benevolence, of aiding others.

In Kant's *Metaphysics of Morals,* he distinguishes "complete" (*vollendeten*) from "incomplete" (*unvollendeten*) duties to oneself and to others. Complete duties are always fulfillable; incomplete duties are ongoing. Complete duties to oneself as rational agent involve self-preservation, not lying, rejecting avarice, and rejecting false humility;[52] incomplete duties involve striving for natural perfection.[53] With regard to others, complete duties involve respect and thus a rejection of arrogance, defiance, and malice (ridicule);[54] incomplete duties are beneficence (and a rejection of envy), gratitude (and a rejection of ingratitude), and sympathy.[55]

Traditional moral teaching can fit under these principles. Kant even says that seeking one's own happiness is a *duty* as a condition for following the moral law, but it cannot be the *motive* of our action.[56]

---

49. The section on the doctrine of the elements of ethics is divided, according to the Table in *GMM'PP*, 602–3/6:492–93, into duties to oneself and to others, and the former into perfect and imperfect duties. "Imperfect" is not a good translation of *unvollendete,* for it does not connote something wrong but something that is not capable of being *completed*. We are never finished developing our talents or helping others.

50. Kant, *Critique of Judgment*, §83/429–34.

51. Kant, *Metaphysics of Morals*, trans. Mary Gregor (New York: Cambridge University Press, 1996), 182–84/6:429–32.

52. This is summarized in *MM'PP*, 174–75/6:419–20; and it is developed in some detail at 176–209/6:421–62.

53. Kant, *MM'PP*, 193–96/6:444–47.

54. Kant, *MM'PP*, 210–13/6:464–68.

55. Kant, *MM'PP*, 200–5/6:451–58.

56. Kant, *MM'PP,* 151–52/6:388.

So he distinguishes the traditional immoral acts and principles from the traditional principles that he considers *amoral*, even though they are useful and necessary for developing human life. The only truly *moral* disposition is one of doing something without ulterior motives—even traditionally moral action—in helping and not simply using others and, in relation to oneself, not subordinating the rational imperatives to other ends. That disposition alone is the only thing that is good without qualification: it is what Kant calls "good will."[57]

Plato was thinking along similar lines when, through the Ring of Gyges exercise, he imaginatively bracketed one's appearance before others (men and gods) and thereby abstracted from the external consequences of one's action.[58] He argued that there is an intrinsic order to the soul, which consists in reason's ruling what is lower in order to look up to what is higher—ultimately to the Good as the Alpha and Omega.[59] He argued negatively that one who is so oriented will not do injustice to one's neighbor.[60] The positive side is exhibited in Socrates' admonishing others first and foremost to care for their souls.[61] But it still seems that the motivation for treating others is the fulfillment of oneself. And that set in motion a concern only for one's own soul and for God as exhibited in Plotinus' desire to be "alone with the Alone."[62]

Aristotle seems to argue along the same lines in promoting the search for happiness proper to a rational being. However, Aristotle concentrates three books upon relations to others: one on justice and two on friendship.[63] Friendship involves doing good to one's friends (that includes family) *for the friend's sake*. In terms of relations to fellow citizens, it involves *harmonia*; and with respect to all human beings, *eunoia* or *good will* is required.[64] So Aristotle seems to have anticipated the second formulation of Kant's imperative. And that imperative seems to ground Christian love of one's neighbor on par with one's love of self.

57. Kant, *GMM'PP*, 49/4:393.
58. Plato, *Republic* II.359d.
59. Plato, *Republic* VI.505a.
60. Plato, *Republic* VI.500c.
61. Plato, *Apology* 29e–30a.
62. Plotinus, *Enneads* 6.9.9.
63. Aristotle, *NE* V, VIII, IX.
64. Aristotle, *NE* IX.1166b30–1167b13. The extension is grounded in the fact that all humans are linguistic-political-rational animals.

The priority of the categorical imperative subordinates individual happiness to the moral order; but the search for happiness is built into our nature. And in this life, moral uprightness might lead one far from happiness and into suffering and death, as it did in the notable cases of Socrates and Jesus. Given this, Kant argues for an afterlife in which happiness will meet with deservedness to be happy due to maintaining the moral disposition. He calls that the *summum bonum*.[65] The condition for that happening is an omnipotent, omniscient, and just Judge who sees into the motivational core of the person and can discern the character of one's underlying disposition.[66]

One cannot but notice here the anthropological reduction of the notion of the *summum bonum*. In the tradition going back to Plato, the highest Good is the Source and End of all things. In the religious tradition, the heart seeks the Face of God as the Fullness of Being and as the Alpha and Omega of all things. In Kant, God is reduced to being the condition for the happiness of human beings. This is odd indeed: where the central principle is to treat persons as ends and not simply means, the supreme Person is reduced to a means for human fulfillment.

ON HAPPINESS

Aristotle famously said that all men desire to be happy. Indeed, it would be foolish to ask someone why they want to be happy: that's just the nature of the human being.[67] However, after underscoring the universality of the desire, Aristotle also noted that one finds a great diversity in what people think happiness consists.[68] Thinkers as different as Hobbes and Kant have noted that happiness is an indeterminate idea of the imagination that varies with different people and changes for any given individual over time, and that we thus cannot possibly build a political or ethical order upon it.[69]

---

65. Kant, *Critique of Practical Reason*, I, ii: 110–113.
66. Kant, *Critique of Practical Reason*, I, ii: 122–132.
67. Aristotle, *NE* I.1097b–1098a20.
68. Aristotle, *NE* I.1098b20.
69. Immanuel Kant, *Critique of Practical Reason*, II: 159; Felicity according to Hobbes is continued success in getting what one desires, which changes from person to person and from age to age: *Leviathan* (New York: Macmillan, 1962), 55.

We are inclined to say that we will be happy when we get what we want, when we attain our hearts' desire. We are inclined to say that when we find something particularly satisfying, we are happy with it. Our early inclination was to identify the satisfying with the sensorily gratifying. However, ordinary sensory gratification eventually becomes rather boring, so one seeks more intense, more exciting forms of sensory gratification. But pursuing these intense forms tends to make everything short of that bland. And when one becomes jaded with one level, one goes in search of more exotic ways of being excited emotionally. By that time, one is probably addicted in some way and finds difficulty in getting out of the trap one is in: sex, drugs, or alcohol. One becomes intensely unhappy.

Max Scheler, in developing criteria for the hierarchy of values,[70] contrasted the increasing depth of satisfaction found in pursuing detached aesthetic, intellectual, and spiritual values, with the increasing emptiness found in the pursuit of hedonistic values. The latter range from gross sensual pleasures to refined taste in food, drink, and even art. In aesthetic values, there is an essential distinction between seeking refined gratification and letting the higher aesthetic values touch and transform oneself.[71] The poet Rainer Maria Rilke said that a great work of art issues the demand: "You must change your life."[72] That goes way beyond cultivated taste.

There is a deeper measure of satisfaction in the achievement of excellence than in sensory gratification, no matter how intense. An athlete might lead a mixed existence by establishing some alternation between dedicating himself to his sport and seeking forms of sensory gratification. Indeed, the money and the notoriety a professional athlete receives afford the opportunity for ongoing gratification; but that might just be what ruins his life.

Intellectual work requires a great deal of self-discipline in order to lead a concentrated existence. The Pythagoreans, who discovered demonstrative geometry, which brought the multiplicity of rules of

70. Scheler, *Formalism*, 345–49.
71. See "Kierkegaard's Critique of the Aesthetic Life" as an appendix to my *Nature, Artforms, and the World*.
72. "On the Ancient Torso of Apollo," see my *Nature, Artforms, and the World*, 91–93.

thumb discovered as useful in the building process into a coherent and ever-developing whole, also discovered the need for discipline to arrive at such understanding. They introduced the first monastic order in the West, which undertook a functional asceticism so that by diminishing biological need, they might learn to turn, in concentrated fashion, *inward and upward* to see the changeless and coherent truths of geometry as an order underlying the surface presented in sensory extroversion. The satisfaction involved in discovering this otherwise hidden level of truth was deemed worth all the renunciation of sensory gratification such pursuit involved.[73] Here, however, the satisfaction is found by seeking the truth rather than seeking satisfaction itself. Likewise, Aristotle wisely remarked that satisfaction is the bloom on activity, that it follows excellence in performance and thus is found where it is not sought.[74]

A less intellectually interested individual might say that he has found happiness when he falls in love and gets married. But when difficult times come, such happiness often disappears. Elizabeth Taylor was married eight times, but she maintained that "it was always for love." Certainly, one cannot expect the exulting emotional state to continue, as apparently Bertrand Russell did when he said of his first wife, "I discovered that I no longer loved Alys."[75] Could one similarly say, "I discovered that I no longer loved my children"?—unless one was a real wretch (which Russell was not). Frank Sinatra sang a song that went, "I can see the thrill is gone. Why let it linger on?" He too was married multiple times.

There is another sort of happiness that looks away from oneself and looks to the success of others. One could be happy with that success, though many would be indifferent or even envious to the point of hatred. The closer these others are, the more their success produces

73. In the *Phaedo* (64a–67d), Socrates addressed his Pythagorean friends on his last day in prison by recalling the Pythagorean teaching that philosophy and geometry involve "gathering the mind from all sides of the flowing distractions of bodily existence."

74. *NE* X.1174b33. This takes some of the wind out of the sails of Kant's critique of eudaimonism: happiness is found as a consequence of a positive response to what deserves a positive response. One does good to one's friend "for the friend's sake" (IX.1066a6), and one appreciates the rabbit for its beauty. For the dog, the rabbit means food.

75. *The Autobiography of Bertrand Russell: 1872—1914* (London: George Allen and Unwin Ltd., 1971), 147.

happiness in the ones who love them. Somewhere Goethe said that the only remedy for the superiority of others is love.[76]

Relevant to our consideration of happiness, the one philosophic insight I found in the television series *Seinfeld* was when Kramer asked George, "Do you yearn?" George thought for a while and then said, "No, I crave." Contrasted with craving, yearning reaches out toward the undefined, toward something that would not make one fulfilled rather than jaded. One yearns for "true love" or for "doing something worthwhile with one's life" or for "seeing the face of God." All three of these objects have a certain terminal character.

Craving operates at a lower level of human endeavor. One craves sensory gratification and can get it, provided one has sufficient funds. One would also speak of money and power as objects of craving. Lust for power is different than sensory craving because it requires competitive excellence. Perhaps the character of craving is that it is insatiable, as Plato noted in his *Republic*. Craving is a leaky vessel: you fill it up and it soon empties out.[77] There is indeed the phenomenon of being unhappy even in the midst of what many people would say is necessary for happiness: money, power, possessions, fame, and multiple opportunities for sensory gratification.[78] There is the opposite phenomenon that one can be happy at a deeper level of one's being, even in the midst of deprivation.

Psychiatrist Viktor Frankl said that "suffering is an invitation to move to a deeper level of existence."[79] He said this after having undergone and survived the unspeakable sufferings of the Nazi death camps. He found *meaning* in the midst of suffering. When the first Christian Apostles were scourged and thrown out of the synagogue, they were *happy* to suffer for the love of Christ; but one could not say that Jesus on the Cross was happy, any more than one could say Frankl was happy in the death camp. It is such noncoincidence of happiness with

76. Cited by Max Scheler in *Ressentiment*, trans. W. Holdheim (New York: Schocken, 1972), 53.

77. Plato, *Gorgias* 494a.

78. See Plato's description of the tyrannical man in *Republic* VII.465dff.

79. *Man's Search for Meaning* (London: Rider, 2004), 118, 120–21. Frankl founded "the Third Vienna School" of *logo-therapy*, which seeks to cure through finding meaning. *Man's Search for Meaning* was earlier called *From the Death Camp to Existentialism*.

deservedness to be happy that for Kant pointed to an afterlife in which that noncoincidence would be overcome.

If we come back to the fundamental orienting framework within which we work, the bipolar character of human awareness, organically grounded reference to the Whole of what-is, pries us loose from any determinate thing and sets in motion a search for the Whole. I would claim that this is the ground of our never being able to be completely satisfied. There's always the question, even at the height of success, "Is this all there is?"[80] So there is a necessary unsettledness, an underlying anxiety that haunts us from our first awakening as rational agents even to our deathbed.[81] It points ahead to the possibility that fulfillment can only happen when we are consciously in the presence of the Fullness of Being. The religious interpretation of this situation is given by Augustine: "You have made us for Yourself, O Lord. And our hearts are restless and shall not rest until they rest in You."[82] In God alone is final rest and complete fulfillment. True happiness is found in God's presence. Indeed, even in this life, living in that Presence, we are led to a detachment from our hopes and fears that leads us from the death of meaning into life. Serenity occurs in the depths, even in the face of frustrations and suffering.

POSTSCRIPT ON ENVIRONMENTAL ETHICS

A recent development in ethical theory is environmental ethics. It was provoked by the unprecedented destruction of the environment by the powers of modern technology in the service of economic power. There is a large strain in Western behavior that views the environment as nothing but means for human development. It was incarnate in Hegel's views on property, which followed in the footsteps of John Locke: human beings have absolute right of disposal over nonhuman things.[83] It was implicit in the command in *Genesis* to "increase and multiply

---

80. See Charles Taylor, *A Secular Age* (Cambridge, Mass.: Belknap Press, 2007), 507.
81. See Heidegger *Being and Time*, I, VI, 44, p. 228, on anxiety as distinguished from fear and being-toward-death. See also II, I, 57, p. 279–311.
82. Augustine, *Confessions*, vol. 1, I.i.1/12.
83. Hegel, *Elements*; John Locke, *Second Treatise on Government*, ed. C. B. Macpherson (Indianapolis: Hackett Publishing Company, 1980), §26, 18–19.

and subdue the earth."[84] There have been attempts to soften that to *tend the earth*; but the Hebrew word *kibshu* means "violent subjugation." The later Hebrew tradition did soften it, and Francis of Assisi established a whole new relation to natural things as brothers and sisters.[85]

We will later propose an evolutionary view of nature, following what we said earlier, which locates the potentiality for life, awareness, and reflective awareness in the original state of our current universe. If ethics develops as the study of ways in which humanness can exist and flourish and entails a respect for human beings as oriented toward the Whole, such respect should then extend down to the earliest phases of our universe and all the things that have emerged from it as our own antecedents.

Emergent from prior stages of the universe, like all living beings we live on the destruction of other beings. Organically living beings transform the elements from which they derive their nourishment; herbivores kill plant life, while carnivores destroy animal beings. We humans are omnivores, consuming plant and animal life; and we stand as prey to larger carnivores. But, projected toward the Whole via the notion of Being, we are not locked into the struggle to survive: we can stand back from the struggle and learn to appreciate both our prey and our predators. We are related to the fullness of Being and thus can appreciate the wholeness of things.

The American Indians hunted the buffalo, which they needed for both food and clothing; but they also addressed the buffalo as a brother and apologized for having to take some of the herd for their own needs. They were horrified at the wanton slaughter practiced by "Christian" men that reduced the buffalo herds from about fifty million to near extinction. It was not only the loss of their livelihood that the Indians bemoaned: it was the needless slaughter of their brothers. It is this surplus act of revering the buffalo that exhibited the Indians' distinctive humanness as a possibility for all humans.

One might move from respect to reverence for all being. It is reverence that unlocks the sense of the mystery of each existent and opens

---

84. Gn 1:28.
85. Edward A. Armstrong, *Saint Francis: Nature Mystic* (Berkeley: University of California Press, 1973), 9.

one to being taken by individual things that step out of indifference and address us. Martin Buber was especially keen on this feature of experience. Known for underscoring the *I-Thou* relation, his first experience of it was not in relation to human beings but in relation to a piece of glittering mica on a mountain path, and later in relation to his horse, to a Doric pillar, and to a poetic or religious text. It was not a matter of an isolated aesthetic experience but more of a vocational experience: an experience of being addressed that calls for a response.[86]

Rainer Maria Rilke was sensitive to that when he concluded his poem, "On the Ancient Torso of Apollo," in an enigmatic way. After claiming that from every spot, the torso looks out at the viewer, he ends with the surprising conclusion: "You must change your life."[87] Buber registers the same type of experience with respect to things of nature as well. But there must be readiness: for Buber it is a matter of a meeting between will and grace.[88] The will aspect involves the dispositions that Dietrich von Hildebrand calls reverence and humility—something that those who slaughtered the buffalo and those who disregard the environment are very far removed from.[89]

Buber thinks that such meetings are the source of the claims about the gods of the brook, the grove, or the mountain: a genuine experience of being addressed that calls for a response of reverence. Buber calls these *moment gods*, and his take on *Genesis* sees the world as divine speech addressed to human beings through all the *moment gods*. The core of biblical revelation is that each such word is spoken by a single Voice.[90] This approach and the dispositions it involves could take us away from the harshness of subduing the earth and could foster reverential tending.

86. See my "Martin Buber's Philosophy of the Word," *Philosophy Today* 30, no. 4 (Winter 1986): n. 12, 322b.

87. See Peter Sloterdijk, *You Must Change Your Life*, trans. Wieland Hoban (Cambridge: Polity Press, 2013), 21–28, in which he presents his interpretation of the poem. See also my interpretation at the end of the chapter on Sculpture, in *Nature, Artforms, and the World*.

88. Buber, *I and Thou*, 62.

89. *The Nature of Love*, trans. J. E. and J. H. Crosby (South Bend, Indiana: St. Augustine's Press, 2009), 77.

90. "Dialogue," in *Between Man and Man*, 15.

Part III
Being and Human Existence

Chapter 8

Being Human and the Question of Being

On the Unitary Ground of Individual and Cultural Pluralism

At this point I want to bring together our central claims by returning to the notion of Being to show that all the distinguishing characteristics of the human follow from the operation of that notion. So that they might be firmly fixed in the reader's awareness, we will refer once more to several features of experience we have laid out above.

Beginning with the revival of Democritian and Epicurean views in the Renaissance, fortified in subsequent centuries by thinkers like Hobbes and Helvetius, and becoming a flood since Darwin, there emerged a view of the place of human beings in the cosmos that rejected the dualistic Platonist, Christian, and Cartesian views that had successively prevailed in the West. As Nietzsche remarked, the view of our descent from primates shut the door on a heavenly origin for human beings.[1] Subsequent biological and especially neuro-physiological research saw the progressive narrowing of the alleged gap between humans and other animals. Awareness has been defocused in favor of its neurological underpinnings, and there is a widespread view that awareness is in principle wholly explicable in terms of neuro-physiological functions.

In recent years, John Searle has chided the Anglo-American Philosophy of Mind community for its neglect—Searle says "terror"—of consciousness.[2] Searle has led the way back to a serious consideration

---

1. Friedrich Nietzsche, *Daybreak*, trans. R. Hollingdale (Cambridge: Cambridge University Press, 1982), §49, p. 47.
2. John Searle, *Rediscovery of Mind,* 55. I suspect that Searle was influenced in this regard by his colleague, Hubert Dreyfus, who works within the Heideggerian orbit.

of consciousness, beginning with his early exploration of speech acts and proceeding to an exposition of the first- and second-person ontologies that support the construction of the social world and its subset in the sciences that operate in terms of third-person ontologies. In particular, he has explored the conscious rationality constitutive of human action.[3] But he himself ends up explaining consciousness as the operation of the brain in a way that is parallel to how the solidity of the surface of a table is explainable in terms of the operation of its subatomic constituents.[4]

In this chapter I will continue the exploration of the field of awareness. I will follow out the direction toward which I gestured several times in this work, namely, a focus upon the notion of Being. I will contend that it is constitutive of the field of distinctively human awareness, providing the grounds for several definitions of humanness—that is, displays of the similarities and differences between animals and humans—that we will examine. In proceeding in this way, I will be following a direction that brings us back to the beginnings of Western philosophy in Parmenides, Plato, and Aristotle, continuing on in the tradition that passes through Aquinas and on to Hegel and also—in a different way—to Heidegger.

* * *

We have several times explored the features we share in common with other animals, placing us under the same genus. As we said, other animals are monopolar; humans are bipolar. In our case, the animal pole plays counterpoint to the pole determined by the notion of Being. As Aquinas would have it, Being is that which first occurs within the mind (*Primum quod cadit in intellectu est ens*); it makes the mind to be a mind.[5] Or, as Aristotle said, "The human soul is, in a way, all things." (*He psyche pos panta estin.*)[6] In what way? By way of *reference* to everything, and to everything about everything: the notion of Being

---

3. Searle, *Intentionality: An Essay in the Philosophy of Mind* (Cambridge: Cambridge University Press, 1983), 90–91.

4. *Intentionality*, 162–72.

5. *Summa theologiae*, I, q. 5, a. 2. "*In intellectu*" is crucial; it is what arises *within* the intellect, unlike *in intellectum*, which is what falls *into* the intellect.

6. *On the Soul* 3.8.431b.21.

includes all; but, to begin with, it includes it emptily.[7] We do not *know* all, but we are *referred* to all in the mode of questioning. As Heidegger would have it, each human being is *Da-Sein*: the place (the *Da*) among beings where the question of Being (*Sein*) emerges, that is, the question about the Whole and the underlying.[8] All humans have attempted to answer or have accepted answers to the questions, "What's it all about? What is the whole scheme of things? And how do we fit within the Whole?" These are questions that necessarily follow from the basic structure of *Da-Sein*. Religions and philosophies emerge as putative answers to these questions. Human awareness is thus fundamentally *ontological*, that is, fixed by the notion of Being (*to on*, genitive *ontos*).[9]

By the distinctive ontological character of our awareness, we stand at an indeterminate distance from the Here-and-Now of our sensory experiences, which are rooted in our organic functioning. As humanly conscious beings, we are by nature abstracted from the Here-and-Now and referred to the Whole, which includes Space and Time as encompassing wholes. But again, as with the notion of Being that grounds it, such inclusion is empty and must be filled with what we concretely discover about occurrences within Space and Time.[10] For hundreds of thousands of years humans thought that, as far as space is concerned, its limit lies in the nocturnally observable dome sprinkled with stars that puncture that dome, allowing the celestial fire to shine through. Who knows? That dome might be farther away than we think—it may be even the distance of a forty days' journey above us! The Copernican revolution radically transformed such a vision by reversing our daily experience and thereby opened our view of space to staggering distances. If the earth moves about the sun in an orbit of some 180 million miles diameter and there is no observable shift in the fix stars when viewed from opposite positions in that orbit, how far away must they

---

7. On the notion of Being, see Bernard Lonergan, *Insight*, 348ff.

8. *Being and Time*, Int., II, 6, p. 21, and I, III, 15, p. 67ff. See above on the peculiar view of Being that Heidegger advances.

9. Heidegger says that "the ontic distinction of *Dasein* consists in its being ontological." *Being and Time*, Int., II, 7, p. 32.

10. Kant proposed that Space and Time are forms of sensibility, basic intuitions that are projected upon appearing things. See *Critique of Pure Reason*, A19/B33–B73, p. 71–104.

be! Later astronomers estimated the distance of the furthest stars at some 13.8 billion light years, with the diameter of the known universe at 91 billion light years: a figure that is truly astonishing.[11]

In the seventeenth century Bishop James Usher, basing himself upon biblical chronology, claimed that the world was created in 4006 B.C.—a long way from the 13.8 billion years of today's estimates. In both cases, the empty a priori forms of Space and Time were filled, but in modern astronomy the observed-inferred filling is beyond even the most sanguine estimations of pre-scientific observers.[12] The impulse to fill these forms comes from our natural reference to Space and Time as encompassing wholes: a reference grounded in the notion of Being that includes the Whole in its reference, and thus also includes emptily the whole of Space and Time.

Empty reference to the whole of Space and Time gives us the basis for the abstraction of eidetic forms, that is, forms applicable any time and any place individual instances of any type of entity or property might be found. From the particular observations of visible things, we abstract from the instances given Here-and-Now the red, blue, yellow, black, and white types and their various mixes, each of which apply to all their instances wherever in space and whenever in time we have met, meet, and will meet them. And we abstract further from these species the notion of color as the generic correlate of the power of seeing. But, whereas red and blue, for example, have sensory correlates, there is no sensory correlate to *color* that abstracts from the peculiarity of each type in order to apply to all. The work we did above in ferreting out the eidetic structures of the sensory fields was made possible by the primordial distance from each Here-and-Now where we are located bodily: the distance afforded by the notion of Being, which refers us to absolutely everything throughout, and possibly beyond,

---

11. See Hawking and Mlodinow, *The Grand Design*. Though highly informative in physics, they exhibit an ignorant contempt for Aristotle, alleging that he based his thought on very limited experience. In fact, Aristotle was a careful empirical investigator of life-forms. Darwin said that "Linnaeus and Cuvier were my gods; but they were as schoolboys compared to Aristotle." Charles Darwin to William Ogle, February 2, 1882.

12. Excluding ancient Indian thinkers who invented the unit called the *kalpa* as a way of thinking about the age of the cosmos. If once a year a bird would pull a silk cloth across the top of a mountain, a kalpa is the time it would take to flatten the mountain. That is only one unit in thinking about the time of the cosmos.

Space and Time. We can abstract because our intellectual operations are themselves abstracted from our bodily location, though necessarily anchored therein. And once we have abstracted, we are able to combine the various forms in judgments and to weave together these judgments into reasoning processes. So the ground of being a *rational animal* lies in our being *ontological*, in having our processes of abstraction, judgment, and reasoning grounded in our a priori reference to Being as a whole.

Furthermore, the notion of Being indeterminately puts us beyond all determinations, giving us over to ourselves and thus condemning us to make choices among the possibilities we understand.[13] We each become an *I* who stands at a distance from Me, from the specific and individual determinants that each of us right now possess. But we have only reached that state after a period of development. We each had our origin in a determinate genetic base that provided and still provides us with our fundamental but limited set of possibilities that differ in various ways from those of others. These remote and fallow possibilities were rendered more proximate by the way we have been inducted into a culture that pre-selected which possibilities are concretely possible.

Regarding both the genetic and the cultural determinants, we had no choice. Our actions up to a certain point in our development were the completely determined resultants of the parallelogram of forces consisting of what Freud called the *Id* and the *Superego*: a bundle of genetically determined impersonal urges and the introjection of the norms and practices taught by others. But at a certain point in our development, we each gained a distance from those determinants, were given over to ourselves as individuals who could weigh options, and came to choose among the concrete possibilities as we understood them. This established another level of determination: the personal-historical level, which constitutes our present habit structure and gives us each our peculiar pre-reflective proclivities to prefer and to act.

We currently have no choice about these three determinants: we are right now what we have come to be through their joint operation.

---

13. Jean-Paul Sartre, "Existentialism is a Humanism," in *Existentialism from Dostoevsky to Sartre*, ed. and trans. W. Kaufmann (New York: Meridian Books, 1956), 295.

They limn the space of current real possibilities for thought and action; they establish felt proclivities whereby we are spontaneously attracted, repelled, or rendered indifferent by what appears in the field of our awareness. We have seen how such spontaneity is centered in *the heart*.[14] We choose among the possibilities afforded in the present insofar as we understand them to be possibilities; but we typically choose in terms of our established proclivities. As Hume remarked, our intellect is and always will be the slave of our passions.[15] That, I think, is true. But I would add that, insofar as we are most deeply determined by the notion of Being, we have sufficient distance from our own deep proclivities to ask, "Where is my heart? Is it where it ought to be? And, where ought it to be?" Intellectual and volitional power, grounded in our reference to the Whole, can serve to re-shape our hearts, little by little, in the direction of what we might come to see as more worthy than our current proclivities indicate; or an over-whelming conversion experience can lead to an immediate re-orientation. In this sense, intellectual and volitional operations are not the end of action; they are directed toward re-shaping our lived sense of things, which is for each of us our deep subjective center, our basic uniquely individual self: our heart. Having been formed by nature and by tradition, we come to take responsibility for our own formation. We are *the individually self-forming* animal or the animal that takes responsibility for its own formation, based upon reaction to prior and enduring genetic and cultural formations.

If we look back at the five eidetic features of sensory objects: that they are each always *individual, actual, immediately present, in observable seamless continuity with antecedent and consequent states,* and typically *contained within their own boundaries,* then we find that the field of distinctively human awareness stands opposite to each trait. The operations that allowed us to grasp the eidetic features yielded objects that are *universal, capable* of being applied to all instances— that is, applying any time and any place their instances are met. Furthermore, even at the sensory level, awareness itself is not confined to

14. See my translation and introduction to Stephan Strasser, *Phenomenology of Feeling: An Essay on the Phenomena of the Heart.*
15. David Hume, *A Treatise of Human Nature,* vol. II, bk. II, §3, pp. 126–27.

one's externally observable outside; that is, the spatial limits of our organic level are transcended by our acts of sensing which bring us *outside our observable inside* to be cognitively *with* the object observed in the two distinctive modes of being that stand opposed to the bodies we can see: the *intentionality* of awareness and the correlative *manifestation* of the object. Contrary to what we are tempted to claim, even if we are sophisticated physiologists—maybe even all the more *because* we are sophisticated physiologists—we find it difficult to resist the claim that what we see is inside our heads.

Modern philosophy had its speculative origin in Descartes' initial confinement of awareness to the interiority of the *cogito*. As we noted above, several generations later Kant said that it was a scandal that we were still not able to get outside the confines of the Cartesian *cogito*. More recently, Heidegger claimed that the scandal is that we ever thought it was a problem. We *begin* our reflective thought by coming back, so to speak, from being *outside* with persons and things. Our awareness is *ec-static* with respect to our observable bodies—in fact, it is triply ec-static: it stands out from the spatial Here in relation to the observable There; but in doing so, awareness also stands out from the immediately given to gather the Past and anticipate the Future. We attend to what is immediately present in function of what we have learned to expect from past experience and in function of what our appetites and projects lead us to expect in our pursuing and coming into contact with the immediately present. Appetite directs us to individual possibilities in the environment beyond the fully present actuality of the sensory features of the thing in question.

Unlike the sensory object, awareness as such—beginning with the sensory field—is not confined within the observable boundaries of the perceiving organism. As we noted before, for Dewey animals live "outside their skin" with the things in the environment.[16] But at the intellectual level, at the abstract level of awareness of the eidetic, we stand not only beyond the inside of our brains and beyond the immediate in function of what we have learned from the past and what we anticipate by reason of our appetites; we stand intellectually in relation

16. Dewey, *Experience and Nature*, 282.

to Space and Time as encompassing wholes because we stand in relation to the Encompassing Whole of what is through the notion of Being. And that relation to the all-encompassing makes us free in relation to past and present determinants and thus freely able to initiate new causal lines: to become responsible for our actions and not simply subject to antecedent conditions. We intervene in the causal network of antecedents and consequents, which appear seamlessly conjoined in the field of sensory observation.

Where seeing *safely leads us pragmatically, visual evidence systematically promotes optomorphism,* that is, viewing everything in visual form, and, more generally, *empirio-morphism,* that is, viewing everything in the form of a sensory object. Awareness, both sensory and intellectual, of sensory objects is radically different in character than any sensory object.

* * *

We have laid out some of the eidetic features of sensory objects and have shown how the peculiarity of our being inwardly referred to the Whole made that apprehension possible. Reference to the Whole includes reference to the whole of Space and Time, abstracting us from the Here-and-Now and allowing us to abstract the universal kind from the individual sensorily presented instances, and to consider the kind in relation to *any time* and *any place* its individual instances may be met.

Now let us reflect upon how, in addition to its inward ground in the notion of Being, the activation of that reference also has an exterior ground: let us reflect upon the *language* in which we have articulated it. We can only think in sensory signs and can think articulately only in and through the system of signs into which we have been inducted by our primary caregivers. If we are essentially rational animals, it is only because we are also *linguistic* animals. That means, first of all, that mental operations require embodiment in sensory signs. The visual pattern at which you are currently looking while you read what I have written is the sensory "outside" for which the "inside" is the set of universal concepts to which the visual signs refer.[17] While the written words are strictly subsidiary, what is focal in your reading are the objects of the

---

17. The standard reference is to Ferdinand de Saussure, *Writings in General Linguistics* (Oxford: Oxford University Press, 2006), 74–75, 197.

movement of thought that continually links those universal concepts together in relation to what they display. One could make the written words focal, noticing their color, the peculiar typeface they exhibit, and the space within and between lines, as well as the white field upon which they have been printed. This is parallel to the physiologist examining the eye's structure and the processes that occur within the nervous system in the patient's act of seeing, without the physiologist's attending to the look of the patient as she or he gazes at the examiner or the physiologist's thinking about his own looking. In the case of the physiologist's explicit focus, he actually looks away from, that is, *abstracts from* the look of the other to attend to the empirical plentitude: in this case, the full actuality of the appearing eyeball. His account of what he is observing is actually an *abstract* account of the sensory actuality of the eyeball whose *concrete* reality is given in its contribution to *expressing* the state of mind of the patient who looks at the physiologist. In a similar way, the words you are seeing are not just empirical objects, but they *express* the meaning for which they stand in.

But it is of the utmost importance to note that they express it, not simply out of the privacy of the writer, but out of and within the common space of meaning shared by those inducted into the language. That is, when in thinking and communicating one necessarily uses language, one is outside of one's own psychic inside, occupying the public space created by the language. That is why for Aristotle the human being is the *zoion logon echon*, not simply the rational animal who uses logical forms, but, antecedent to and grounding that, as the animal that has—or is had by—language. Actually, there is a mutual grounding: only a rational animal can have the fullness of language; but it is only through laying down its tracks in a sensory medium that rationality can develop. And it is only a broader extension of that observation which leads to Aristotle's other definition of the human being as *zoion politikon*, or the political animal, one who lives off of the sedimented words and deeds, language and common practices, along with the institutions that support them, which were formed by those long dead.[18] That is to say, the human animal

18. Aristotle, *Politics* I.125a.2.

uniquely lives out of and within tradition, which gives the rational individual its concrete possibilities in and through linguistic mediation. Another way of saying that is that the human being is *the animal who lives within tradition.*

Now, traditions vary because of the widespread geographical dispersion of populations or the distance between social class levels. The human animal, specified by an open relation to the Whole, must choose ways of acting based on the ways of understanding it has developed. Passed on to others, these become common practices and involve the institutions that sustain these practices. Now understandings and choices are diverse, though they always begin from and remain rooted in the common features of the human being's natural relation to her or his environment, which we are considering here. Human beings are *world-creating animals*; that is, they are fabricators, over the time of linguistically linked generations, of worlds of meaning and modes of behavior that are diverse in separate communities and that each go through processes of development and devolution over time through the way succeeding generations take up, modify, or discard what they have been given. The historical processes led to even more significant alteration as separate groups with their sedimented traditions come into contact with other groups. There is a necessary plurality of worlds in geographically distinct and unrelated areas of the globe, but they all are rafted upon the basic structure of the human being as *ontological animal*, and they all can in principle link up with each other.

One significant feature of the rational, linguistic, political, ontological, world-creating, traditional animal is creative *technology*. Bees make hives, birds build nests, beavers build dams and huts, but with little variation from generation to generation (although animal ethology still needs to explain how species' habits come into being). Chimpanzees learn to use found objects in the environment to reach their food supply and may even subsequently carry an object, such as a stick, to ferret out ants from an anthill or a branch to club the prey they are hunting. In these cases, there is no significant transformation of the found object, nor does the found object serve any speculative interest. Animals seemingly have no interest that does not pertain to their coping with their environment in service to their biological needs. Their intelligence is a purely coping intelligence.[19]

Because we stand at a distance from the Here-and-Now in function of our reference to the Whole, we can abstract regularities, take apart given things to understand their components, and refashion objects in light of the goals we project that include, but also exceed, biological coping. We are thus *technological* animals, or, in an earlier expression, the human being is *homo faber*: man the maker.

And that very same distance that makes the other properties possible allows us to consider objects purely in terms of their *aesthetic* properties—indeed, it allows us to refashion the environmentally given in order to creatively produce objects that have such properties. As Aristotle remarked, contrary to what is possible for humans, dogs love the look of the rabbit, not because they find it beautiful, but because it means food.[20] As we noted above, Kant referred to this distinctive human capacity in the odd expression: a capacity for *disinterested satisfaction*. The *disinterest* refers to an abstraction from biological need and practical projects; and the *satisfaction* refers, not to an inner state that might be replicated today by electrode stimulation, but to what follows from a focus upon the form of the object. It would be perverse to wallow in a state of mind without attention to an object that generates it. Indeed, we can have the state of mind *only* if we respond to the object "for its own sake," as they say. We are thus distinctively *aesthetic* animals.

The factors we have thus far considered—rationality, responsible self-formation, language, tradition, technology, and aesthetics—require, by reason of the ontological ground that makes them possible, an answer to the question about the character of the Whole and of our place within it. The answers are given in terms of the particular religious tradition into which one is inducted in terms of creed, code, and

19. John Searle, in *Rationality In Action* (Cambridge, Mass.: MIT Press, 2001), 2–3, notes five characteristics that differentiate humans from high order primates: action not motivated by organically based desire; concern for one's own death, and thus the ability to plan for the long-term future; a self-conception that is not limited to organic need; the ability to judge in terms of standards that apply to all; and ability to take responsibility within an institutional setting.
20. *Nicomachean Ethics* III.x.1118a21–23.

cult—that is, traditional ways of understanding, acting, and worshiping in relation to the sacred dimension of the cosmos. Indeed, ontological reference is expressly addressed in religious terms. The human being is, most distinctively, a *religious* animal.

A tradition comes to fill the initially empty space of meaning between the Here-and-Now given sensory environment and the permanently deferred completed relation to the Whole with the practices developed in that tradition, providing various subspaces of meaning within the meaning of the Whole that is articulated in religion. The human being, as a world-constructing animal, necessarily contains the factors we have considered. But, since traditions are plural both in terms of geographic separation and in terms of transformation of a given tradition over time, the human being is the *historical* animal, the animal that generates group histories. But in cross-fertilization through contact between differing cultures, and especially through the instantaneous contact between all cultures made possible by modern means of communication, the human race can be considered to have a common history as a species.

But at a certain point in history, new institutions emerge. They grow out of the necessary ingredients of all cultures: institutions of theoretical inquiry, beginning with philosophy as aimed at the Whole not based upon inspiration and proclamation, as in religion and poetry, but based upon rational evidence, and passing on to a division of labor in the various sciences. Philosophy has its root in religion as similarly concerned with the character of the Whole; modern science has its root in the wedding of a purely theoretical interest with technology. The latter makes possible an uncovering through manipulation of what lies hidden beneath the ordinary sensory surface in prescientific life. It was the slave, forced to act against his appetites and at the master's command, who learned to master himself by developing skills that would have lain fallow without different modes of manipulating the environment, and who discovered properties of the surrounding things not available through mere observation. Experimental science goes the way of the slave, only now free from the

21. Kojéve, *Introduction to Reading Hegel*, 51.

master.[21] So the human being is the distinctive *philosophical* and *scientific* animal.

* * *

In conclusion and to summarize, let us review the various features that distinguish the human being from other animals. The human being is the *world-constructing* and thus the *historical* animal, one that lives within the Lifeworlds constructed in different places and at different times. World construction is made possible by our founding reference to the Whole via the notion of Being, for our being pried loose from the animal Here-and-Now allows for abstraction of the universal and free self-disposal. The human being is most fundamentally the *ontological* animal and thus the *rational* and individually *self-disposing* animal.

However, rationality is only possible when essential distinctions are embedded in sensory signs that together constitute a language: we are *linguistic* animals. It is through language that we are able to pass on the interrelation of institutional forms that constitutes the overarching society: we are *political* animals.

Rationality also makes possible creative and accumulative technology, so the rational animal is the *technological* animal. Technology employed in the uncovering of features of the environment beyond the sensory surface becomes experimental science: the human being is thus the *scientific* animal. Further, primordial distance makes possible a desire-independent appreciation of the presentation of things: the ontological animal is the *aesthetic* animal.

All of this is typically held in place by the umbrella of meaning, a view of the Cosmos and our place in it generated by religion: the human being is the *religious* animal. But the development of experimental science and contact between religions served to release the pure, detached, disinterested, and unrestricted desire to know that is speculative philosophy.[22] Philosophy seeks by way of evidence, and not simply inspiration and proclamation, the ground of whatever makes its appearance. Guided by the notion of Being, speculative philosophy, as Plato said, has its eyes fixed on the Whole and the whole

---

22. This felicitous set of adjectives is Bernard Lonergan's. *Insight*, 352.

character of each kind of thing within the Whole.[23] The *philosophic* animal lives in the light of Being, which founds everything distinctively human: we are ontological, by nature emptily directed toward the Totality, and therefore world-constructing, historical, rational, individually self-disposing, linguistic, political, technological, scientific, aesthetic, religious, and philosophic animals. The togetherness of these factors constitutes the various worlds in which we dwell, but it also sets the framework for entering into dialogue between individuals and between cultural worlds.

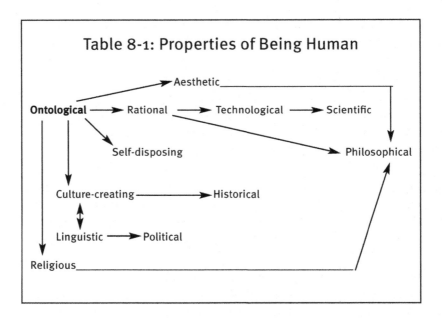

Table 8-1: Properties of Being Human

Chapter 9

Taking the
Universal Point of View
The Articulation of the Notion of Being

n our analyses thus far, we have taken as a starting point attention to all the intelligible strands that are involved in doing what you are now doing: reading a book. We have looked at the various aspects of lived life, the life of the heart. We have explored temporality and the inner life of feeling. I have stressed the bipolarity of the field of human experience and have zeroed in on the way in which the notion of Being grounds all that is distinctively human. We examined the multileveled notion of freedom. I tried to show how the most general principles for moral-political action flow from the immanent structures of human existence and reflected upon happiness. We have attempted to gain fullness of content at the level of description involved.[1]

In a sense, we were following the aforementioned way Hegel began his *Phenomenology of Spirit*, namely, with sensory presence. Now we will follow the beginning of his *Science of Logic* with the

---

1. Aside from this one note and an acknowledgment, this chapter will employ no footnotes. Following Husserl, it claims to attend "to the things themselves." But the historically informed reader will find similar insights in Plato's *Theaetetus* and *Sophist*; in Aristotle's *On the Soul* and *Metaphysics*; in Hegel's *Phenomenology of Spirit* and *Science of Logic* as well as in Husserl's *Ideas: General Introduction to Pure Phenomenology*, vols. I and II (The Hague: M. Nijhoff, 1982); and in Bernard Lonergan's *Insight*—works that have taught us how to attend "to the things themselves." This should also help verify Heidegger's claim that phenomenology is a return to Plato and Aristotle (*Prolegomena to the History of the Concept of Time*, 136). For a different but related approach to the themes developed in this essay, see my *Path into Metaphysics*. For a positioning of these considerations within a cosmological context, see my "Being and Manifestness: Being, Science, and Poetry in an Evolutionary Worldview," *International Philosophical Quarterly* 35, no. 4 (December 1995): 438–47. I will pick up these themes in chapter 10. For the way one can conduct investigations into the history of thought within the framework we have laid out, see my *The Beautiful, the True, and the Good*.

empty notion of Being and will make explicit what is involved in its recognition.[2] Let us attend to the simple, trivial, and seemingly uncontroversial recognition that something *is*, the *estin* that is the object of Parmenides' thought that opened the history of speculative thought.

* * *

Of any entity we consider, the most uncontroversial and yet the least articulated thing we can say about it is that "It is," in the sense that *It exists*. *It is* can be said of an indeterminate number of instances of whatever sort, including the visible marks on this page or the sounds of my voice as I utter "It is" to myself or to my interlocutors or whatever imaginative creatures I am able to conjure up. *It is* is an *eidos*, a universal, a one-over-many, which can be applied to an indeterminate number of instances. Further, *It is* exhibits my recognition that whatever *It* might be, it stands outside of not-being-at-all. ("Why is there something rather than nothing?") But simultaneously we recognize that it is an object of awareness, so that there is an essential distinction and relation between awareness and its objects.

The noun-form related to the *It is* is the term *Being*, which can be said of whatever *It* we might consider, including oneself as considering it. *Being* is an *eidos* or universal, object of reflective awareness; but it is also more than an *eidos*, including as it does all instances of being, eidetic and individual, and everything about them, whether they are aware or not.[3] We see then that there are at least nine *eide*, which show themselves as sharing in being and as involved in the most universal and indeterminate consideration that forms the framework for *any* consideration: the *eide* of (1) *being* and of (2) *nonbeing*, of (3) *instance*, of (4) *object of awareness*, of (5) *awareness* itself and (at another reflective level) of (6) *eidos* itself as (7) *universal*, and of (8) *individual* instances of the *eidos*, and, finally, of (9) *one* and (10) *many*. These forms articulate what is implicit in our beginning with the simple *It is*; they give the first articulation of the notion of Being.

2. See my "Being Human and the Question of Being," *The Modern Schoolman* 87, no. 1 (November, 2009): 53–66; and my "Taking the Universal Viewpoint," *The Review of Metaphysics* 50, no. 4 (June, 1997): 769–81.

3. Spinoza says that philosophers have taken their point of departure from some aspect of the Whole. He begins with the Whole presented in the notion of Being, which includes everything. *Ethics*, trans. T. S. Gregory (London: J. M. Dent and Sons, Ltd., 1910), 143.

An *eidos*, in addition to its distinction from and relation to its instances, involves a distinction between its universal *mode* and its *content*. As *eide*, all *eide* are the *same* in their universal mode but *differ* in content. The instances of *eide* are either other *eide*—as we have shown thus far—or *ultimate particulars*, functioning spatiotemporal unities of which I myself am one. As an *eidos*, each is identical in content in all its individual instances but different in its universal mode. Each *eidos* contains other *eide* within itself, namely, those which define it; some *eide*—several of the ones we are watching unfold here—contain all other *eide* within themselves.

Being is a *one* that contains within itself *many*, a *same* that includes *difference*, an "*is*" that contains an "*is not*." Being is an encompassing one, and each *eidos* is a one over and among many within that oneness. Though all participate in being, each of the *eide* are self-identical, other than the others, and both same and different with respect to their *ultimate particular* instances. Being other, each is *not* any of the others. (Here the "not," as otherness, is distinguished from absolute not-being.) Further, the notions of *sameness* and *difference* are each both the same as themselves and different from each other, so that sameness shares in difference and difference in sameness. Finally, ultimate particulars are defined in terms of *space* and *time*. Our inventory of implicit forms thus also includes (in addition to the *eide* of *being*, of *nonbeing*, of *instance*, of *object of awareness*, of *awareness* itself and—at another reflective level—of *eidos* itself as *universal* and of the *individual*, as well as of *one* and *many*) the *eide* of (11) *content* and (12) *mode*, of (13) *sameness* and (14) *difference*, as well as (15) *the ultimate particular* and (16) *space* along with (17) *time*. So we have now seventeen *eide*.

Now as changing from implicit to explicit, the notion of Being undergoes *development* before the awareness of each of us who are following it. This entails another kind of "not being": not the simple otherness of the various *eide* we have shown thus far to be implicit in the notion of Being, nor the internal otherness in relation to each other of the traits of each *eidos*, but the not-being of antecedent and consequent states, which are chronological in our viewing of them, though a-temporally related among themselves. Furthermore, what is

involved here is not simple succession, but *development*, that is, articulation moving toward completion, from relatively empty to relatively
full vis-à-vis awareness—hence a teleological change. We might recall
that the notion of Being, which contains these *eide* within itself, also
sets itself off from absolute nonbeing, so that, even prior to the development we are following, to be at all is to be other than absolute nonbeing. So we have several senses of nonbeing that are operative: absolute nonbeing, the nonbeing of otherness between and within each
entity, and the nonbeing involved in temporal antecedence and consequence (not-yet-being and no-longer-being).

Consider further that the notion of Being not only presents itself
as unrestricted in extension, but it also presents itself in such a way
that any given being cannot both be and not be at the same time and
in the same respect or, in another variation, that a given attribute cannot both belong and not belong to a given being at the same time and
in the same respect. Not only is this *principle of noncontradiction* the
basis for all logic, but it is also, in its recognizably unrestricted generality, an index of the mind's own scope. *Ho nous pos panta estin*. "The
human mind is, in a way, all things."

We come to awareness of the principle of noncontradiction only
through developed experience. In order to formulate the principle, we
need the sensory appearance of things and the operation of language,
its flow through speech, and its fixity in meaning. But several other
factors are involved, some of which we have already discussed. Recognizing "*a being*" implies its being *one* of *many*. Further, we identify
a being by its endurance over time in displaying the sensory features
as immediately given properties that our sensory system gathers in
phantasms, that is, modes of holistic and multifaceted appearance.
"*Can*" plays in relation to "*is*" as *possibility*; and "*not*" involves a negation that here becomes *impossibility*. "*Property*" involves an aspect of
a being that may be observed in different respects at a given time or
in the same respect at a different time, but only as a dependent aspect
of the thing whose property it is. "*Time*" involves being simultaneous
with, prior to, and after. "*And*" as well as "*both*" involve joining several
separate items: "and" joining one or more, "both" joining two. And
each of the terms involves "*sameness*" in the empirical differences from

which they abstract and a *"difference"* from both the empirical instances and other terms compatible with a generic sameness. *Being, Becoming and Fixity, Sameness and Difference, Unity and Multiplicity, Possibility and Impossibility, Negation and Affirmation, Thing and Property, Joining and Separating, Past-Present-Future, Appearance and Reality,* and *Awareness* in all the aspects that are operative within it— these various concepts are involved in recognizing and being able to formulate the principle of noncontradiction.

Our relation to the Whole also plays out in the givenness of the notion of eternity, exhibited in the fact that any contingent event, once it occurs, is strangely known to be true "forever after." The main issue here is whether eternity is of time itself and thus of the temporal cosmos or if it relates to something beyond time. By such a "beyond" I do not mean the omni-temporality of the *eide* we have been considering, but the possible trans-temporality of a cosmic Source. But let us move to consider actual existence.

* * *

As the first individual instance of *It is*, I will take my own awareness of it. The reader is thereby invited to focus upon the same considerations with respect to her or his *I* as reader. I, as conscious entity Here-and-Now, am an ultimate particular instance of awareness that, like any *it*, is an instance of being (indeed, I am also an instance of the *eide* of *I* and *instance* (6 and 8). *Awareness* (4 and 5) is an eidetic *instance*; I am an ultimate particular *instance* of the *eide being* (1), *awareness, instance, individual* and *I*, which entail *one* and *many* (9 and 10) (my unitary self and my plurality of aspects, mental and physical), *sameness* and *difference* (13 and 14), and development which, in turn, entails temporal antecedence and consequence (*time*—17).

The notion of instance, in itself an *eidos*, is in its content either an ultimate spatiotemporal *particular* (8) or a *universal* (7). *Particular* as an *eidos* here signifies *space-time* (16 and 17) occupancy, which is located within a determinate segment of *space-time*, the same in content but different in *mode* (12) of existence from the *eide* it instantiates, and both *same* and *different* with regard to its own past and future. *Space-time* occupancy entails being *one* of an indefinite plurality (*many*) of like *instances* of *eide, instances* of which are each located in a Here-and-Now. Abstraction from that plurality yields the *eidos*, though abstraction is itself possible because *space-time* as a whole is anticipated in the field of *awareness* that is able to attend to the *eide*, for an *eidos* is what is recognizable as repeatable *any* time and *any* place the proper conditions for its instantiation are met.

Occupants of space and time are both spread out in three dimensions—length, breadth, and depth—and separate from, though in some ways also continuous with, other such objects (since all things are embedded in the space-time-energy matrix and are made up of the elements). Each of the three dimensions in relation to the others yields two opposite directions: for humans they are above and below, in front and in back, to the right and to the left. For other bodies on the earth that do not have the frontal orientation humans have, above and below are present by reason of resting upon the earth and the opposing sides in any two perpendicular horizontal directions are without special orientational names. Each dimension is given as spread indeterminately about a given body. As occupying these dimensions, each individual is composed of a multiplicity containing a mode of otherness that allows that multiplicity both to come together and to come apart. Instantiating the eidetic as a spatiotemporal individual sets each individual within an essentially mutable matrix. Space-time occupants are thus in some way or another always other than they have been and other than they will be—actually in two senses: in an absolute sense as not having been and as aimed toward no longer being the individuals they are; and in a relative sense as no longer being (while they are) what they were, and as not yet being what they will be. Within the latter context, they are nonetheless both in some respect identical and in other respects nonidentical with themselves throughout that span. Within the former context, there are, antecedent and consequent to their origination and end, the elements that will enter or that have entered into their composition. Earlier in this book we have looked at the *eidos time*, linked to the essential transience of spatially extended individuals that exhibit the character of past, present, and future—of the no-longer, the now, and the not-yet. The past and the future are spread indeterminately "backward" and "forward" for our awareness, while the Now moves out of the no-longer into the not-yet—and this before any theory of time such as those offered by Aristotle, Newton, Einstein, Husserl, or Heidegger.

All of this sets the invariant frame for the field of awareness I have been at pains to present throughout this work. I would claim that this field of awareness applies indubitably to all we might consider, including differences of worldview, differences of interpretation, and even the self-contradictory nominalist or deconstructionist efforts to displace the invariant and thus universal. All of this involves further articulations of content as we advance into it. We are able to carry on this articulation by an ongoing reflection upon what we have already seen, both on the side of the object of awareness and on the side of awareness itself, so that the content has not been added from without but unfolded from within and is implicit in any affirmation we might make.

To recapitulate a bit, the notion of Being is, minimally, the notion of Being outside of absolute nonbeing. But there is also a relative sense of nonbeing in the otherness of each of the *eide* thus far considered in their relations to each other and to their instances, and in the otherness, both internal and external as well as both spatial and temporal, involved in operative individuals. The relation between the *eidos* and the individual instance involves an identity of content within a difference of modality: individual in the one case and universal in the other. As all-encompassing, the notion of Being includes both awareness and its objects. It also includes all *eide* and each spatiotemporal individual; and it includes them in such a way as to include everything that may be discovered about each and all of them. It thus sets a fundamental goal of human awareness as a capacity to move toward the horizon of all-encompassing awareness. We are following that direction in articulating what is implicit in our initial focus upon *It is*.

The notion of Being poses a demand that an advance into any entity or eidetic region that circumscribes types of entities be located within the never-fully-disclosed complete Whole of all beings. Such an advance involves showing how the notions of sameness and difference are realized in different instances, eidetic and individual. It also raises the question of the *how* of the relation of awareness to the Whole—a consideration of the utmost importance for human life, as we have seen in a previous chapter. Again, the one encompassing notion of Being shows itself to be intrinsically many without fracturing its own unity.

Now to say all of that is to appeal to a community, to a *we* bound together by the English language. It is to rest upon a tradition available to literate members of that tradition, but also to any human beings, for any normal human being can learn to speak and read that language, and to write and translate what is said into their own native language.

There are several ways we can go from there. One is the path we have already taken: to attend to the fact that *It is* is written, fixed in black patterns appearing on a white background. The fact that there is writing presupposes an eidetic alphabet or an eidetic pictographic, that is, a recognizable indefinite iterability, for each member of the alphabet or pictographic series, of the same letter or pictogram. *It is* can also be spoken, embedded in the sound patterns that succeed one another as they disappear, but which also are instances of an eidetic phonemic. In addition, *It is* can be embossed on a flat surface in Braille with the same implication of eidetic recognition for the elements. In any case, it is the same *It is* that appears in the differences of spatial fixity and temporal disappearance and in differing sensory media.

In the last paragraph I have repeated the same expression *It is* five different times in writing, instantiating it in five different spatial locations by the temporally successive activity of typing. I recognize that the *same* sentence—not a *similar* one—can be instantiated an indeterminate number of times and places in either media, visual or audile or—in the case of Braille—also tactual. Indeed, any visual or audile or tactual pattern is indefinitely repeatable, like dimes from a mint or recordings from a studio. But that involves, as its flip side, an insight into myself: in such recognition I as a reflective observer—though at the same time an organism and a sensory observer immersed in the Here-and-Now—transcend the Here-and-Now of the immediate presence of sights and sounds and tactual sensations. I do so by anticipating—or rather, by my psycho-neural system anticipating the whole of Space and Time as the field for the possible instantiation of the *eide* involved in the situation that come to be represented by the sensible patterns arising by convention in a given ethnic community.

Of course, the meaning of *It is* can be realized also in sentences coming out of different linguistic traditions: Greek *estin*, Latin *id est*, French *il y a*, German *es gibt*, etc. So the meaning transcends not only spatiotemporal instantiation, but also linguistic enculturation, though its apprehension requires both enculturated and spatiotemporally immanent sensory instantiation. And again, as I recognize that, I escape in a certain fashion not only embodiment, but also the enculturation that makes possible my own linguistic articulation of the meaning.

As an instance of awareness, I address you through the medium of writing—In a sense, in addressing you, I in principle also address the eidetic *you*, any *you* able to read English, and, due to the translatability of language, actually any human being. And I have written meaningful English sentences, which, I would claim, you and I can also judge to be *true*, that is, which function to display what is available to any sufficiently attentive and reflective awareness. As we noted previously—but it is worthy of repetition—we have a set of distinctions and relations between the written or embossed or spoken spatiotemporal *instances*, the enculturated *sentence*, the transculturally meaningful *proposition* that is capable of being rendered in a different cultural form, and the *judgment* or truth-claim for which I take responsibility.

But all this is also and essentially object of thought, something manifest to awareness. Object as the manifest is contrasted with the non-manifest—which would either be simply outside of the object in question or hidden within it. Consider as well the implicitly functioning *eide* we have been attempting to make explicit here and the hidden as such. The former is set within the field of awareness but pre-focal; the latter is not within the field of awareness. However, even here we must consider that everything is included in the notion of Being, though not like the implicit we have been unfolding thus far. To reach toward the wholeness of each thing within *the* Whole, we must uncover the hidden from outside the level of co-implicating *eide* constituting the framework of relation between awareness and its objects; we must recur to the other pole of our being and attend to sensorily given regularities.

To repeat: the notion of Being occupies one pole of the bipolar structure of human nature whose other pole gives rise to organically based sensation. The notion of Being is the notion of the encompassing totality; but initially it is an empty notion. We do not begin by *knowing* the Whole; rather, we exist as *the question of Being*. The notion of Being as the notion of the Whole poses the fundamental task of bringing the organically based field of sensory appearance in relation to the full being of things and of ourselves: first by eidetic inventory whereby we locate the individually given *sensum* within the whole of space-time, then by interpretation that attempts to read the regularities on the sensory surface as expressive of ultimate depth, and finally by choices among the options for action made available by such understanding in order to form one's heart. The way the notion of Being is given involves a whole set of eidetic structures that constitutes the enduring framework within which the differences of understanding, choosing, and interacting occur. One who begins to understand that has begun to practice a mode of reflection that catches up with the founding structure of human existence.

The relation to the Whole of what-is calls for the whole of what we are as divinatory of what essentially lies hidden, but which nonetheless essentially concerns us as oriented toward the full being of what is—ourselves included. That full relation is a relation of what a long tradition has called *the heart*; we have explored this relation more fully above. And its divination is not a matter of our cognitive and practical conquests, but a matter of learning appreciative *letting be* through which beings make their claim upon us and through which we are gathered into our fullness as the other to which otherness can appear as such. What we have uncovered provides the enduring framework, not only for further conquests, but also for acting out of the claim of otherness, our own as well as that of others. But that is another story.

The description I have given, I would claim, uncovers the major features of the invariant concrete framework of all our experience. There are two aspects to that framework. First there is the structure of the field of experience as three dimensions of "interiority": sensing, intellection, and presence to Being. But what we have exposed in this chapter is the formal framework within which intellectual activity happens. The awareness of this duality puts us in a position to understand how the major questions in the history of thought came to be and allows us some measure of the adequacy of the proffered answers in terms of how they do justice to those aspects of experience we have uncovered. But our inventory does not provide answers to questions about the origin of that field and indeed of the universe within which it operates. It settles nothing regarding the coming into being of species, the relation between matter and form, life and matter, consciousness and life, or intellect and awareness. It does not even broach the question of the ontological status of the *eidos*. It says nothing directly about possible immortality or the existence and properties of God. It does not settle burning questions concerning what we are to do, which options to select among the myriad possible, or the ground of the authority that might determine those selections. It says nothing of possible revelation, of religious pluralism and authority. It has no direct relation to all the technical problems of how to achieve the various goals given by nature, conditioned by culture, or selected by individuals. But it does make us aware of the common field from which all the above spring and in which they all must operate. And its dispassionate pursuit puts us in the position of some distance from the passions invested in living out these other quests.

"Dispassionate pursuit" here is parallel to Kant's *disinterested satisfaction* involved in the appreciation of beautiful things. *Interest* in Kant involves treating the object as something that serves one's needs. *Disinterest*, on the other hand, involves *unconstrained favoring* or an *interest* of a higher order. Just so, *dispassionate*, qualifying the pursuit we are recommending, involves its own passion, its own mode of "being taken" and being totally involved.[4] But it teaches us to be less partisan and more understanding as regards the various competing claims involved. It creates a clearing in our mutual worlds, open to all humankind. It imposes upon us a dialogical imperative to give witness to our own; to attempt to understand and weigh the various construals offered by others of what lies hidden beneath and beyond the field of awareness as that all-encompassing Totality to which we are all, as humans, essentially directed; and to let ourselves be measured by what emerges from that quest.

---

4. Kant, *Critique of Judgment*, §1–5/203–10.

Chapter 10

A Universe of Creative Empowerment

As a final chapter, we will recapitulate some of the things established above and project them into the framework for an interpretation of evolution and history. In so doing, I will suggest adding *creative empowerment* to the traditional list of the transcendental properties of being, that is, those features that apply analogously to every instance of beings.

To suggest this addition to the transcendentals, I rely upon what I have established in the previous chapters. But we will reiterate that and try to build everything from the bottom up, from the structures given in experience and what we can infer from them, proximately and remotely.[1] That will constitute the first part of this chapter, which has two subsections that we might designate roughly as Nature and History. Regarding Nature, in a basically Aristotelian analysis with Nietzschean overtones, we will look at the notion of potentiality as entailing creativity and relationality in a hierarchy of powers and beings. At the human level, in a basically Hegelian analysis, I will claim that the notion of Being founds History as the accumulation of creative human empowerment through institutionalization. A second major part—which we might call *History of Nature*—will extend the

---

1. This chapter appeared in *The Review of Metaphysics* 59, no. 2 (December 2005): 379–401. Originally it was presented as a tribute to Kenneth Schmitz on his eightieth birthday. The dispositions and directions it exhibits have their roots in his courses in the history of modern and recent thought. His treatment of the history of thought showed his students a model of how to enter sympathetically into the most diverse points of view. His introduction to Husserl showed how to get back, from mere historical exposition, to "the things themselves." The combination of the two dispositions showed his students how to study each thinker sympathetically by focusing through him on "the things themselves." This paper has a special relation to Prof. Schmitz's course on nineteenth century thought: it began as an attempt to appropriate Nietzsche and went on to develop in an Hegelian direction; but it aims directly at "the things themselves."

analysis by appealing to the results of scientific investigation that will
retain but reestablish the previous part. The concluding third part will
then suggest an extension of the transcendentals to include creative
empowerment through relation.

NATURE

Our starting point here involves reflection upon *potentiality*. Potentiality is an inference from actuality. But both notions occupy a very
high level of abstraction from what is always already given. The most
proximate to us are things and persons presented in the Now of sensed
actuality but understood in terms of the powers they exhibit in and
through the patterned sequence of that actuality.[2]

We who make these observations stand in our awareness at the
pinnacle of a hierarchy of structures that are functionally co-present
in ourselves, but we also stand as the term of a developmental process
that reveals the potentialities immanent in the earliest stages of that
development. Our reflections rest upon sensory activity that presupposes an organic base, each level of which emerges serially from each
of our earliest stage as a fertilized ovum. The series of stages exhibits
two critical thresholds: the passage from organic life to sentient awareness and the passage from sentient awareness to reflective awareness.
Observation of the exhibition in sensed actuality of the developing
sequence leads to the inference that the earliest stages contained the
not-yet-exhibited active potentialities for the actualizations that followed. An exhaustive empirical inventory of the observable actuality
of the fertilized ovum by itself yields no insight into the potentialities
it contains. Given its relative incomplexity, its presentation of nothing
remotely approaching its eventual articulation, it is not too difficult
to regard it as being nothing more than what it actually presents itself
to be at that moment to an outside inspection and thus to allow it to

---

2. The following phenomenological descriptions follow the path of Aristotle in his
On the Soul from object to act, to power and essence. However, the description does not
depend upon Aristotle; it illustrates Heidegger's claim that phenomenology is a return to
the practice of Plato and Aristotle (*Prolegomena to the History of the Concept of Time*, 136).
I have tried to illustrate that aspect of Plato and Aristotle in "Phenomenology and the
Perennial Task of Philosophy: A Study of Plato and Aristotle," *Existentia* 12, fasc. 3–4, 2002,
252–63.

be dispensed with when it conflicts with our ends. A more thoughtful relation to the fertilized ovum retains an awareness of the inference to the active powers it contains, still only in the earliest phases of the actualization process.

The sequence of actualization occurs in relation to the environment that corresponds to the active and passive powers of the developing human being. In the environment we find the tri-level phases concurrent in us distributed into three kinds of living beings outside us: plant life, animal life, and the life of other humans. Plant life, together with the corresponding organic level of our own life, continually draws upon the elements in the nonliving environment for its own development and sustenance. That gives us four levels: human, animal, plant, and elemental. Whatever we know of the beings occupying these four levels we know through their being actualized in our own sensory field as sensory objects. But their differing modes of behavior allow us to infer differing underlying, systematically linked potentialities and to sort out functioning wholes of differing types at each of the levels in correlation to our own functioning wholeness.

From the organic types upward, we find a process of what one might call *creative self-transcendence*, involving our second notion: *creativity*. Organic beings set themselves apart from their environment to which they remain essentially tied. They circle back inside themselves and articulate themselves from within: they are the first level of what we call *selves*. They are self-contained processes, being self-formative, self-sustaining, self-repairing, and self-reproducing. Their articulation is a matter of increasing self-empowerment that begins with destroying and transforming those aspects of the environment which are essential to that empowerment, beginning, at the lowest level of life, with the externally available elements. The initial stages of a seed or a fertilized ovum contain the active powers to take in and transform external materials into a progressively more articulated set of organs. The employment of the newly constructed organs allows further powers hitherto latent to be actualized. This self-empowerment involves continual transcendence of the earlier phases. The articulation involved in the growth process culminates in the power of reproduction: the sign of the full maturity of the organism. Here the self-transcendence in progressive self-articulation transcends itself in the production of another of the same type. One might say, with Nietzsche, that living forms exhibit the will to power as self-transcending creativity.[3]

In the case of the animal organism, a much more complicated articulation occurs. In addition to the organs for extracting and processing energy from the environment, new instruments for a completely different function emerge: organs of perception. Embedded also within the causal networks of pre-living processes, animals receive the causal impact of various forms of energy upon the organs of perception, which terminates in the selective manifestation of things astonishingly given *outside* the organism as colored, sounding, smelling, and the like.[4] In the animal case, what emerges at a certain stage of development is a mode of being totally unlike anything lower on the scale: the mode of *manifestation* or *appearance*. We find the exhibition of a mode of inwardness: an incipient, nonreflective self-presence through feeling empirically linked to the integration and complexification of a nervous system. Because it occurs, what is outward is, for the first time, *shown*; it not only exists, but it *appears* as other than the perceiving animal. Incipient self-presence is the condition for the possibility of the appearance of what is other. If we call *material* that which can be visually inspected, then seeing and the self-presence it requires (since seeing transcends itself while being present to itself, as least in the mode of feeling) are traditionally called *immaterial* functions. Here we need a different mode of explanation than we do for the study of the optic nerve and the visual cortex.

However, the appearance of otherness here is in function of the needs of the organism to which it appears.[5] The manifestation of things outside that are involved in awareness is correlated with the

---

3. Nietzsche, *Genealogy of Morals*, §2.12, 79.

4. Though the activity is taken for granted, in order to be aware of its astonishing character one has to see its *toto coelo* difference from the observable nervous system that makes it possible but that it transcends by being "with" the outside. One needs to *meditate* upon this matter to be aware of its astonishing character, for we live spontaneously in sensory exteriority.

5. Aristotle, parallel to the inseparability of act and object, and act and power, maintains the inseparability of sense and appetite in *On the Soul* 3.7.431a.13.

self-experience of the upsurge of desire and serves such desire. Emergent in its own ontogenesis out of the self-enclosing character of organic process, animal self-presence grounds the manifestation of what is outside itself. But with the emergence of the manifestation of the environment comes the emergence of hunger and, in the case of the fully adult organism, of sexual desire as well. In the latter case, another appears as a necessary complement to itself; and from relation to that other, still others emerge as offspring. Thus, central to sensory manifestation is the display and instinctive recognition of appropriate instances of its own kind that is essential for the work of reproduction and nurturing. As in the case of plant forms, one organism is thus in essential continuity with its line: an instance of a type.

The most elemental mode of sensory manifestation involves the sense of touch, which like the organic body, remains the most fundamental presupposition for all higher functions. Unlike other senses, it has no specifically localized organ but, as feeling, it suffuses the body as a functioning whole. I consider this of extreme importance. Touch is the diffuse self-presence of animal being as the expression of the pervasion of the organism by its underlying unifying principle and as the essential condition for the possibility of the manifestation of what is other than itself. It involves an organically pervasive, nonreflective awareness of awareness that gets articulated in further and organically localized modes of sensation. Prior to that self-presence there is causal impact but no manifestation. As John Dewey has it, here causality is turned into participation.[6]

With the addition of other sense powers, manifestation involves another kind of processing of the environment. Through retention of what is received from each of the senses, self-presence involves the integrated operation of the senses to present integrated aspects of integrally functioning wholes outside the perceiver. Because such processive presentation is essentially in function of desire, it is also tied to locomotion and culminates in tactility. It requires retention of the past and anticipation of the future of satisfaction to establish an extensive flowing Now of awareness focused upon the manifest sensory actuality

---

6. Dewey, *Art as Experience*, 3. See also my *Placing Aesthetics*, 239.

of individual bodily beings in the environment. The presentation of individual instances of the types of objects correlative to the desire for nourishment and sexuality moves the animal in the direction of the object that it comes to apprehend tactually and in apprehending consumes or mates with or cares for or attacks. The reproductive capacity of such entities involves the peculiar relationality of sexual union. Even in the case of some plants, the final self-transcendence in reproducing others like itself involves the active functioning of what is other in the pollination process.

As with plant life, for the animal, the power of creative self-transcendence in growth and reproduction involves a preservation of earlier phases and a continued enhancement of power until the animal falls into decline, increasingly unable to mate, care for offspring, and fight its rivals or enemies.[7] But unlike the plant, animal being in its higher levels involves the capacity to learn and thus has a greater empowerment in its command over the environment. It develops habits of response to its manifest environment that make it more flexibly adaptable to the challenges posed by the environment and thus more efficient in reaching its own ends.

At the distinctively human level, manifestation takes a new turn. Our account takes its point of departure primarily from what is available through seeing. Seeing here is a function of a distinctively human interest: a theoretical interest. But that interest arises later in the process of human development. In the early phase of animal-like development, seeing is a function tied to the growth and sustenance of the organism.

Seeing is a cognitive power, that is, a capacity for manifestation. As such it is correlative to the type of object appropriate to it.[8] Though in each case the power of seeing is an individual aspect of an individual animal being, as a power it is open to all the instances of its generic object: the type of aspect we call color. Correlatively, the color of a thing shows its visibility to all who can see. As seeing is a universal openness to all the seeable, color involves a universal openness to all

7. *The Will to Power*, §715, 380.
8. I develop this notion in "Individuals, Universals, and Capacity," 507–28. It is an insight found in Hegel, *Hegel's Philosophy of Mind*, §401, *Zusatz*, 77.

seers on the part of the colored object. But what is manifest through the actualization of the active power of seeing in relation to the passive power of being seen is always only individual and actual. The powers underpinning the actually manifest are available only to reflective awareness that is able to focus upon the sameness and disregard the differences present in the individual sensed actuality.

Initially, one arrives at the notion of power by a reflective inference from observing the types of sensed actuations that are expressive of the power. In reflecting upon the most rudimentary level involved in seeing a yellow bird, one ignores everything but the particular visual quality, and indeed, one even ignores the peculiar suchness of the yellow instance in order to grasp yellowness as common to all its instances. One moves further up the logical line to the notion of color as the generic correlate to seeing. Cutting through the peculiarities of instances, intellectual power here grasps in an immediate *Wesenschau* the horizon of a given organic power in its generic object. One retains the sameness and ignores the differences between the yellow of the canary, the yellow of the tie, and the yellow of the cab to grasp the species *yellowness*; and one retains the sameness and ignores the differences between the species red, blue, yellow, black, white, and their combinations to grasp the generic object, *color*. The latter is indifferent in itself to the color-species. Though the species of color have peculiar images associated with them, the generic color has no such associated image. There is no existent color that is not specific. Because of his own peculiar presuppositions, Berkeley found that a problem.[9] However, that lack of direct imagery involved in the grasp of the notion of color is parallel to the cognitive activity correlative to color, namely, seeing: neither the activity of seeing nor color as its generic object are seeable, but they are intellectually apprehensible. And one can also move inferentially at the same time to the see-ability of the seen and the power to see in the seer that are likewise not available to vision. Visibility and visual power are universal orientations toward their mutual activation in the peculiar manifest relation between individual instances

9. George Berkeley, introduction to *A Treatise Concerning the Principles of Human Knowledge* (Philadelphia: J. B. Lippincott and Co., 1874), §8.

of the types that can be seen and the types that can see in individual instances of color. Sense reveals the individual and actual instance. It operates in terms of the universality of its own orientation, but it never by itself shows the universality of the power or the correlative universal type of its object; it only shows the individual and actual sensory objects.

The sensing animal is identical with itself as an organic process and unreflectively present to itself as a functioning whole in its wakeful life. But though the sensory agent is necessarily present to itself in its act, it cannot reflect upon itself. The capacity to grasp the specific and generic universality of the types involved as well as the concrete universality of the powers is a capacity activated, not by individuals as such, but by the modes of universality peculiar to understanding the situation that is focally apprehended. This power, activated by the universal as such, is what we have come to call *intellect* as the power of reflective self-presence.[10] Intellect is, we might say, the self-presence of the awareness of types as abstract universals and of the powers. It is abstractly and concretely universal, immanent in nature, and its locus of manifestation is sensorily grounded intellect. But that is because it is present to itself as the concrete universal that, through the notion of Being, includes all potentialities for instantiation in the individuals that exhibit them.

What I want to do at this point is to show a necessary linkage between the levels of the universe outside ourselves, which are correlative to our own powers. Return, then, to the initial and enduring nontheoretical function of seeing. It identifies opportunities and threats to the organic wellbeing of the seer. As such it is essentially tied to eating. Now, eating is not oriented, as is seeing, to *phenomenal aspects* of environmentally given things, but to those kinds of *things* that are correlative to the appetite. One might think of seeing as in a phenomenal sense and thus as a kind of illusion. Nietzsche said that the senses lie.[11] Seeing presents to us solid and stable objects that are separated from us by empty space. However, the space is anything

10. See Aristotle: "The soul is, in a way, all things—all things sensible by sense, all things intelligible by intellect." *On the Soul* 3.8.431b22.
11. *Daybreak*, §117, p. 73.

but empty and the objects are ultimately processes composed of processes. But appetite does not simply require the appearance of objects but the *reality* of objects: those that, as natural prey, can really sustain the organism. *Phenomenal* food might satisfy the eye, but the appetite requires *real* food; and the test of its reality is the actual nourishing of the organism that eats it. As a variation on a Feuerbachian theme—itself a variation on what I think is a Stoic theme—we might say, *Primum edere deinde philosophari*, "First eat, then philosophize."[12] But I might add that eating ought to be a primary object of philosophic reflection that moves us reflectively beyond phenomenalism because we have already been carried beyond it by eating.[13] Both individual sense powers and the appetitive powers they serve are concrete universal orientations requiring specific kinds of aspects and things in the environment.

Such things, through their active and passive powers, are essentially interrelated hierarchically in the food chain. Carnivores have their appetitive powers oriented toward herbivores, and herbivores toward plants; the powers of plants in turn are oriented toward the kinds of elemental forms that nourish them. All of this has one of the conditions for its possibility in the earth's location in the solar system, for that location provides the heat range within which organic forms can grow and makes possible the photosynthesis requisite for plant life near the bottom of the food chain. And these factors can appear only because light is reflected upon bodily surfaces from the same source of heat and photosynthesis.

The first point here is that *things are the locus of powers, active and passive, that are systematically integrated, both within living and conscious things and in the systems that they necessarily presuppose.* One might *imagine* a separate and self-contained entity, but any *real* entity is oriented, via its active and passive powers, toward the things that

---

12. See Ludwig Feuerbach, *Principles of the Philosophy of the Future*, trans. M. Vogel (Indianapolis: Hackett, 1986), §52–53.

13. The Kantian distinction of noumena and phenomena is significant, involving as it does the setting off of a discursive and receptive intellect from a hypothetically intuitive and creative one. It is the severance of the two that I think reflection upon eating overcomes. See Leon Kass, *The Hungry Soul: Eating and the Perfecting of Our Nature* (New York: Free Press, 1994).

sustain and threaten it. And each of those things, in their turn, are oriented toward still others to constitute the ecosystem, the solar system, and, indeed, the cosmic system.[14]

The second point is that all these powers, though individual aspects of individual things, are nonetheless *concretely universal orientations* requiring the *kinds* of aspects and things in the environment that are correlative to them. Each power anticipates all the instances of its correlative objects, wherever and whenever they might appear. If there are powers, there are not simply sensed individuals but *kinds* of correlative objects.

Let me add a third point: the kinds of things that can see and eat are necessarily the *results of a reproductive process* and are in principle capable of reproducing offspring. They thus necessarily belong to a species, that is, to a natural kind. This means that the specific powers found in the individual are also in the genetic line, so that seeing, for example, is not simply *my* power, but a *type* of power found diachronically in my genetic line. And one also finds the same types of functions distributed synchronically in other species and thus in their genetic lines.

The conclusion is that these observations give the lie to nominalism. Cognitive and appetitive powers are necessarily oriented toward *kinds* of aspects and things and can only exist because the things that have them necessarily belong to a *species*. Kinds or species are universal notions. A relation between intelligible and sensible, between universals and particulars, functions in any natural power and not simply in intellectual beings. Powers are relations to the whole of space and time as the possible locus of their activation under the specific conditions of their operation. Not only are cognitive powers "in a way, all things," but each power of any being is, in a way, all those things correlative to it that can act upon it and upon which it can act. That way is the way of a priori reference. The problem of induction is solved at the level of natural cognitive and appetitive powers, for the generic features of their objects are always verified and not subjected to falsifiability as the verifiers themselves are oriented toward types of aspects and things, and

14. The "enemy" here is Hume's notion of sensations as "loose and separate" in *Enquiry Concerning Human Understanding*, VII, 49.

necessarily come in biological kinds.[15] This cuts through the problem of universals by showing what the *fundamentum in re* is: native power. Intellect is the capacity to recognize *types* of powers as powers in their active and passive forms and their correlative *types* of objects.

These observations give grounds for Plato's claim in the *Sophist* that the definition of being is the *dynamis* of acting and being acted upon.[16] *To be anything at all is to be the locus of powers, both active and passive, each systematically interrelated with everything else within their system.*[17] This raises us to the level of intellectual apprehension that corresponds to the native object of intellect: being as such. And this brings us to the second subsection (the *secunda primae*): human history.

HISTORY

Once more, let us consider more closely the notion of Being.[18] It is, I claimed, that which grounds the distinctively human as the being that creates history. In our own ontogenesis, the notion of Being emerges at a certain stage to turn the monopolar animal, which is fixated on the individuals presented sensorily as objects of desire, into a bipolar human being distinguished by its orientation toward the Whole.[19] Though *bipolarity* is obviously intended here in the non-dysfunctional sense, I would say that the emptiness of the notion of Being blows the lid off the reliability of animal appetite and makes the human being the potentially chaotic animal.[20] Though initially empty, the notion of

15. Karl Popper, *The Logic of Scientific Discovery* (New York: Basic Books, 1959), 40–42.

16. Plato, *Sophist* 247e.

17. This is a point Leibniz made with his notion of compossibility. Each thing that is must be compossible with the system within which it exists. The difference here is that Leibniz was not simply talking (as we are) about compossibility of *powers* but with compossibility of every concrete *act*. See *Monadology*, trans. R. Latta (London: Oxford University Press, 1951), §§56–57. There remains the question whether this describes all beings, thus whether there is something "beyond finite beings" as their ground.

18. I am much indebted to the analysis of the notion of Being in Bernard Lonergan's *Insight*, 348–74.

19. See my *Path into Metaphysics*, chap. 1, for a further development of the structure of the field of experience in relation to matters aesthetic.

20. For Nietzsche man is the chaotic animal, and the task of life involves the practice of natural asceticism to "compel the chaos within to take on form." *The Will to Power*, §868.465, §915.483.

Being includes everything by way of reference, because outside being there is nothing. The initial emptiness of the notion makes us the locus of the question of Being as the question about the Whole: the Whole of all beings and the wholeness of each being within that Whole.[21] "What's it all about? How do we fit within the whole scheme of things? What is the whole scheme of things?" These are the perennial questions built into human existence. But what we know of the Whole must be constructed through sensation, abstraction, reflection, and inference along the lines explored above. Things rise up to meet us in the actuated sensory field, but they fall back into the mystery of their own being, which draws on inquiry.

The notion of Being pries us loose from the environmentally given, allows us to consider it apart from our needs, and condemns us to choose among the possibilities revealed by what we come to understand of it and of ourselves. The understandings and choices sediment into habits. Passed on to others, they constitute the institutions in which succeeding generations are raised. Together they form a cultural world, a predetermined and interlinked set of ways of thinking, acting, and feeling that comprises the accumulated power of a given culture. Institutions are related in various forms of complementarity and tension, both internally and externally, that propel a culture beyond itself at any given time. Into such a complex each of us is thrown. Having the bipolar structure of organically grounded empty reference to the Whole, an individual human being comes into possession of itself through the mediations of others. Reference to the Whole places each individual at a distance from its own embodiment, and, indeed, from all finitude, and condemns it to choose. What it must choose from are determined by three antecedent structures.

First is its genetic endowment that sets the basic possibilities of each individual. Second is the cultural stamp that has already identified possibilities immanent in the human gene pool and has focused them and honed them through the creation of institutions. Those who raise the individual mediate the culture within their own more or less limited understanding. Through the emergence of the reflective *I*, the

21. See Heidegger, *Being and Time*, Int., II.
22. Hegel, *Hegel's Philosophy of Mind*, §413, *Zusatz*, 153–54.

individual's own likewise limited understanding and consequent choices give further focus. Any adult human has already made her or his own choices from the genetic and cultural possibilities in the limited way she or he has become aware of them. Through the reflective *I*, she or he develops her or his own set of habits as a third level of determinants specifying her or his current concrete possibilities. These three levels—genetic, cultural, and personal-historical—constitute the Me, that is, what can in principle be objectified about myself as my real determinants, setting the scope of my real possibilities at any given moment in my own history. They sediment into *the heart* as the locus of spontaneous tendencies to behave correlated with the appearance of significant presences. But by reason of its reference to the Whole of Being, the *I* that objectifies and chooses stands at an infinite distance from the determinate Me.[22] Reference to the Whole establishes a desire beneath all particular desires: a passion for the Whole.[23] On its basis I have to ask myself a second set of questions: "Where is my heart? Is it where it ought to be? Where ought it to be?" On that basis, too, the individual becomes not simply the recipient of the culture; the individual can also be its cutting edge by her or his ability to create new possibilities of understanding and action that can be added to the cultural repertoire, just as she or he can be the locus of the degeneration of the culture. What is crucial is that such understandings and skills are accumulated by passing them on to others. It is by reason of such systematic interrelations that individuals are empowered. As individuals take their places within these systematically functioning cross-generational wholes, both the individuals and the wholes may be further empowered.

We have already considered the institution of language as the primary institution that mediates between members of a linguistic community and enables the passing on of the practices of that community into the indefinite future. Let us focus upon just one other institution: music. It has developed along three institutional lines: the technology of instruments, the proliferation of musical genres and repertoire, and the techniques of performance. Music requires, to begin with, the iso-

23. See my "The Heart in/of Augustine's *Confessions*," in *The Beautiful, the True, and the Good*, 154–79.

lation of the Harmonic Series from the cacophony of sounds that appear within the environment. It developed through the invention of different more or less complex genres. It developed through the invention of musical notation, which supported the invention of increasingly complex genres. It developed through the invention of increasingly complex instruments until it reached the complexity of the modern piano and pipe organ. It developed through learning increasingly complex performance techniques. All of this is sustained by the development of the musical conservatory.

Born within such a tradition, one is able to identify and hone to perfection whatever performance possibilities lie within. Without these traditions, talents would lie hidden within the gene pool. How many classical pianists were there seven thousand years ago? How many are there today among the inhabitants of the rain forests?

History is the process of a cumulative unlocking, not only of the hidden potentialities of nature outside us, but especially of those human potentialities of operation hitherto undiscovered. In working over nature, we discover what we could not discover by mere description, but at the same time we develop the correlative skills to work it over as well as new ways of employing both the knowledge and the skills.[24] In our working for the community, knowledge of the powers of nature, and of skills in discovering and employing them, lead over time to the increasing self-empowerment of the human community as such.

Let me add that the ability to stand back from the environment, sensorily given in function of need, allows one not only to know and use, but also to identify appreciatively with any given other. It allows one to exhibit the kind of love that creatively empowers the other as well as oneself. Indeed, self-empowerment in all the legitimate ways in which that can happen is a way of being able to empower others ever more effectively.

* * *

---

24. This insight lies at the center of Hegel's discussion of the master-slave relation in his *Phenomenology of Spirit*, §178–96, p. 111–19. It is the center of Alexandre Kojéve's brilliantly one-sided interpretation of Hegel's work in *Introduction to Reading Hegel*, 26–27.

At this point I want to extend the field of application of the notion of creative empowerment through relational systems until we arrive at their transcendental extension. And we will attempt to do so by moving from a view based on the enduring givens of our experience to one based upon extensive specialized empirical investigation.

EVOLVING NATURE

Patient empirical inquiry accumulated over generations lifted the scientific community beyond the limitation of an Aristotelian cosmos of the eternal repetition of forms—even the forms of history[25]—and pointed to a series of species that appear sequentially over time, an evolving rather than a static set of forms, systems on the move rather than eternally repetitive systems. Empedocles had inferred as much in a very general way from examining the geological strata in the quarries at Syracuse, which showed less complex fossils at the lowest levels and more complex forms at the higher levels. He postulated mutations through random combinations.[26] Aristotle dismissed all this with the observation that cows produce cows produce cows, and tomatoes produce tomatoes produce tomatoes, leaping from this observation to *et sic ad infinitum*. He also noted that deviations from normality in each species die out rather than persist as new species.[27]

I take it that the sequence of forms is well established by the fossil record. The problem is explanation of that sequence as the serial appearance of the three distinctively different kinds of things—living things, things with sensory awareness, and things with reflective awareness—operating within and drawing upon the environment of nonliving things that preceded them. The Aristotelian view is based upon the irreducibility of the properties belonging to each of the levels. Each level beyond the elemental one requires soul as integrating

---

25. In his *Politics* (7.9.1329b.25) Aristotle said that the arts and sciences are lost and found again and again, and that philosophy rises from and declines again into mythology as the polis supporting the arts and sciences develops and declines again and again for all eternity. Even the fine arts have their "natural form," as it appears for tragedy in Sophocles. *Poetics* 4.1229a.10.

26. Empedocles, "Empedocles of Acragas," in *The Presocratic Philosophers*, 281–84n336–40.

27. Aristotle, *Physics* 2.8.198b30.

principle of each living whole, and each requires a different kind of soul than the others, though the higher presuppose and subsume the lower.[28] "Mere bodies" remain as the elemental basis drawn upon by organisms produced by the offspring of adult organisms and as the residue of living forms.[29]

Now, given the three critical thresholds, it is not unintelligent to first infer, as did Aristotle, that each is independently immanent in the universe—until the accumulation of data through modern scientific investigation showed the chronological sequence in their appearance within the known universe. What emerged was the awareness of the limited temporality of at least the phase of the universe since the Big Bang and the factual temporal sequence of forms from incomplex to complex, passing the critical thresholds in turn. But it is also not unintelligent to infer that, if we grant the temporal succession of threshold types, then some "higher power" is needed to introduce each newly appearing level—self-replicating systems, sensory awareness, and reflective intelligence—in an evolving universe.[30] However, the scientific inclination—probably aesthetically grounded in a sense of elegance—is to employ Occam's Razor and attempt explanation with the fewest principles possible.

We would here suggest that the same argument that projects all the powers of the fully adult human back into the fertilized ovum could also be used to do the same for the earliest stages of the universe—in fact, I see nothing to necessarily preclude that. What is required is to preserve attention to the differences at each level. But we can never claim to know enough about the lower to preclude the impossibility of the higher emerging from it. Like the case of the fer-

28. Aristotle, *On the Soul* 2.4.415a; 3.7.431a15.
29. Robert Sokolowski notes that the notion of organic matter as residue of living forms reestablishes Aristotle's distinction between earthly and heavenly matter on a new basis. "Modern Science and Material and Formal Causality," *Recovery of Form, Proceedings of the American Catholic Philosophical Association* 69 (1995): 61.
30. In the Catholic tradition, Pope Pius XII allowed that forms up to the level of the rational could emerge evolutionarily but claimed that the emergence of the distinctively human soul required "special creation" by God. Encyclical Letter *Humani generis* (August 12, 1950), 36. But as God is operative in sustaining the processes of nature and history, He is also operative in the emergence of humanness from its natural basis in primate forms. See Karl Rahner, *Hominisation* (New York: Herder and Herder, 1965), 93–94, 100–1.

tilized ovum, no empirical inspection of the earliest stratum in scientific inquiry yields by itself the potentialities it contains. On the Newtonian model, one would not have expected, from an empirically based imaginative model of the atom, that real atoms contained the possibility of combination that would release hitherto-unheard-of power in atomic fission or fusion. This involves the transformation of the notion of matter composed of bits of extension moved from without to a notion that involves the interchangeability of mass and energy.

An inference, parallel to that from reflective adult to the active powers of the fertilized ovum, would transform the notion of the elements or "mere matter" into the locus of creative powers, which, under specific combinations, would exhibit the levels that have factually succeeded one another. What is crucial to observe, however, is that the potentialities would not lie in isolated individual particles—as if a subatomic particle, an atom, or a stone could be aware. The power would lie in their systematic *relations*. Joining with others unlocks the potentialities for the emergence of form that would otherwise remain fallow in the initial system. Here we would have, at the lowest level of the universe, the creative empowerment through relationality that we have observed, along with the development from organic to sentient to rational existence at the human level.[31]

Living forms gathering power to transcend themselves in growth and reproduction would themselves have come into being through the self-transcendence of elements initially functioning outside the combinations that unlocked the powers for life, for awareness, and for reflective awareness in the cosmic system. This is the first stage of the form-giving powers at the base of the system. And the repetition of the same in each species would transcend itself in the progressive emergence of more complex forms, increasingly more integrated until they emerge as beings that are self-present through being in touch with their own functional totality. Here their own incipient self-presence makes possible a self-transcendence through the manifestation of what is other than themselves.

---

31. For the scientific basis for such a view, see Errol Harris, *The Foundations of Metaphysics in Science* (New York: University Press of America, 1983), summarized in *Cosmos and Anthropos* (New York: Humanities Press, 1991).

Finally, the highest modality of self-transcendence occurs through reflective awareness set at an infinite distance from its determinate self by being referred to the Whole that it presupposes. This makes the human the locus of manifestation of the underlying powers of the empirically given universe. Human awareness is the manifestation of the evolutionary cosmos itself as our own presupposition, but at the same time it is also the self-present center of creative empowerment. Such manifestation and creativity are only possible through the development of centuries-long institutions of inquiry and practice.[32]

One of the consequences of such a view is the defeat of the notion that the embodied human spirit lives in an alien place.[33] Whatever belongs to embodiment is not temporary but belongs to the essence of humanness. And its relation to the physical environment is a relation to its home rather than to its prison. Nietzsche's *fidelity to the earth* expresses an essential imperative of the human condition.

As has natural science generally, evolutionary theory has been dogged by a basic but utterly unnecessary materialism. Our initial notion of matter is what appears to an empirical inspection: extended, moving, colored, sounding, actual individuals, presented (at least in the living and in most manufactured things) as contained within their own boundaries and in seamless observable connection with their antecedents and consequents. What we come to know about the most elemental level was modeled upon such objectivity. Awareness came to be considered as some intracerebral occurrence that was either identical with or epiphenomenal to brain processes. Evolution was a matter of more and more complex, externally observable mechanisms.

---

32. Minus the evolutionary view for which he thought evidence during his time was still insufficient, the view is basically that found in Hegel, *Hegel's Philosophy of Mind*. See Errol Harris, *Nature, Mind, and Modern Science* (London: George Allen and Unwin, 1954), 255. See also my "Five Bodies and a Sixth: On the Place of Awareness in an Evolutionary Universe," *American Catholic Philosophical Quarterly* 93, no. 1 (Winter 2009): 95–105. As we have noted, more recently Thomas Nagel has presented a similar view in *Mind and Cosmos*, 49–53.

33. Paul the Apostle said in *Romans* that we are strangers on the earth. That has had disastrous effects on the way Christians have viewed the material world and the work involved in shaping a humanized world. It has to be counterbalanced by emphasis upon the essentially incarnate character of the human being and of Christianity itself, which proclaims the resurrection of the body as the final act of history and the Incarnation as the central event.

But such a view gives a distorted framework for understanding the Whole. It exhibits what I call *the empiriomorphic fallacy*, which is considering all things in the form of the sensorily given, or, more narrowly, *the optomorphic fallacy*, which is considering all things in the form of visual objects.[34]

But there is another way of looking at nature that is equally compatible with the externally observed phenomena, but especially attentive to the inner conditions for observation and inference we have presented in our first section and throughout the text. Over against the dominant empiriomorphism, this view reestablishes anthropomorphism on a more sophisticated basis. One of the first to advance it was Schelling, who viewed matter as "frozen mind."[35] He was foreshadowed by Leibniz's idea that "perception and appetition" constituted the "inward" nature of all things,[36] and followed by twentieth-century thinkers like Alfred North Whitehead and theological popularizers like Teilhard de Chardin.[37] The position is known as *emergent evolutionism*, according to which the most basic explanation is from higher to lower, that is, from the later, more complex forms to the earlier and simpler forms. It is actually Aristotelian in form: the simpler and earlier are *potentially* what the later, more complex forms are *actually*. And since the later possess the inwardness of perception and desire and, more deeply, of thought and choice, the earlier must possess the same potentially—though only remotely. An immensely long and complex intervening set of stages must be traversed, but that is statistically well-nigh impossible under the assumption of chance and the denial of teleology.[38]

In such a view, our notions of both matter and mind would undergo transformation. *Matter*, not as "stuff" but as a principle, would still remain a principle of passive potency with all the work that

34. I introduced this expression in my *Path into Metaphysics*, 36.
35. F. W. J. Schelling, *Ideas for a Philosophy of Nature*, trans. E. Harris and P. Heath (Cambridge: Cambridge University Press, 1988), 181.
36. Leibniz, *Monadology*, §§14–15.
37. Whitehead, *Science and the Modern World* (New York: Free Press, 1967), 39–55, 100ff; de Chardin, *The Phenomenon of Man*.
38. See Lonergan, *Insight*, 259–61, on the idea that the universe of our experience exhibits the general form of "emergent probability," which presents to us "systems on the move" rather than a universe of statically repeated forms.

was assignable to such a principle in the past (change, individuation, spatiotemporal location, passivity, exteriority, assunderness, and self-opaqueness).[39] But matter in the sense of the elements would have the active potencies inferable from what emerges from them. Such *matter* is neither a region absolutely other than *mind* nor the ultimate explanation of *mind*; it is *mind* in an early phase of its development, *mind* still immersed in the principle of exteriority, assunderness, and darkness. Though matter in observed exteriority furnishes the factual conditions for the emergence of the higher levels, the explanation for the lower lies teleologically in the higher as act explains potency.

This leads us to our concluding section. To briefly recapitulate our path: a reading of the hierarchy of experienced beings from living beings upward yields the notion of the active power of creative self-transcendence through relation manifest to the kind of being that can grasp the essential structure of that hierarchy and creatively empower itself through inventive individuals to develop in history through the relational systems it creates. Natural scientific inquiry as one such system or set of systems suggests an extension of the notion of creative empowerment through relationality down below the threshold of organic process to the level of the elemental. This now puts us in a position to suggest that relational creative empowerment is a transcendental property. And here we will have to be even more sketchy than we have been thus far.

TRANSCENDENTAL EXTENSION

The traditional notion of the transcendentals goes back to the ancient Greeks. In Plato we find all things participating in the Good, the Beautiful, and the One, functioning together as the ground of Truth and as the term of the human ascent, with each thing participating in them in its own way.[40] In Aquinas' list of the transcendentals in *De veritate* we find an expansion of the list to include thinghood (*res*) and other-

39. This is an agglomeration of insights in Aristotle, Aquinas, Schopenhauer, and Hegel. On Aristotle, see my *Path into Metaphysics*, 165–66; on Aquinas, see *Path into Metaphysics*, 180; on Schopenhauer, see my *Placing Aesthetics*, 188; on Hegel, see his *Hegel's Philosophy of Mind*, §381.9.

40. Plato, *Republic* VI.508Cff; *Symposium* 210Eff.

ness (*aliquid*) as modes of articulating that formality under which the mind operates, namely, the notion of Being as *esse habens* as that which possesses the act of existing.[41]

Each transcendental property is coterminous with being. Each is realized according to the degree to which any given being participates in the self-subsistent act of being, *esse subsistens* or God. Each thing that is, *insofar as it is*, is thingly, unitary, other, intelligible, good, and—some have added—beautiful. *Insofar as it is* means insofar as it fulfills its essence and stands at a higher or lower level of types in the hierarchy of being determined by degrees of "remotion from matter." Each higher level is less restricted in its realization of being by what it is essentially in itself. But the hierarchy in which things operate was conceived of as essentially static. As Aristotle saw it, the cosmos involves the eternal repetition of the same types imitating the eternally same Unmoved Mover Who functioned as Exemplar for all the rest.[42] Elsewhere Aquinas points out that not only notions like being and unity, but also notions like act and potency extend beyond the sensorily given things from which we take our point of departure and apply to all things.[43] I underscore *act and potency* here, where potency has to mean *active* potency since it applies to God as well. We might then suggest that the *esse* that each *ens habet* is itself creative act, since it derives its act from the original creative act of the *esse subsistens*, God Himself.

The act of existence is not only a standing outside of nothing. Each thing that is ex-ists as standing outside of its earlier phases by contributing to the self-transcendence involved in the universe we inhabit. Material elements transcend themselves by joining to unlock the power of self-replication. Self-replication leads to progressively higher, that is, more complex and centralized, forms of self-development. The hierarchy of being involves the mutual creative empowerment of individuals and relational systems. One might also suggest that relationality as the basis for creative self-transcendence mirrors an all-powerful creative Divinity whose own being is relational.

---

41. Aquinas, *Quaestiones*, 1.1. See also my *The Beautiful, the True, and the Good*, 170–90.

42. Aristotle, *Metaphysics* XII.vi.1071b3 and the following, and *On the Soul* 2.4.415b.

43. Aquinas, *Summa theologiae*, I, q. 84, ad 1.

If we follow the direction of the notion of Being and are faced with any putative limit—like the Big Bang and the expanding universe, which some cosmologists suggest is the locus of all meaningful questioning[44]—then we can always ask what lies beyond the limit. This direction of the excess of the question beyond any limit may be linked to questioning the ground of finitude itself.[45] If the horizon of the questioning of beings is unlimited, then how can being be limited in the things that are? And as Aquinas noted, essence, as limiting the mode of being of each thing, is indifferent to being either in the existential mode in individuals or in the intellectual mode as universal. That any finite being has gotten beyond that indifference can only be due to One whose Essence is To-Be. The only adequate explanation of finitude would be absolute Infinitude. This would not only transcend the finitude of an Aristotelian divinity, but also its lack of awareness of, concern for, or effective power over things beneath it in the hierarchy. Absolute Infinity is absolute Creative power, giving being to all finitude.[46]

But we might also suggest that the existence of what is other than divine Infinity requires a principle of otherness within God that pre-contains all the ways in which what is other than God can be. And the notion of persons as grounded in and contributing to ongoing community suggests inner personal relatedness within God Himself.[47] God is the One (Father) and the Other (*Logos*) linked by Love (Holy Spirit). Creation is the overflow of Divine Power by reason of the generosity of Divine Love through the Otherness within God as the *Logos*.

If the unity, goodness, intelligibility, beauty, and otherness of creatures are their ways of imitating God, then might one not say the same

---

44. See Stephen Hawking, interview by Neil deGrasse Tyson, *StarTalk*, National Geographic, March 14, 2018.

45. Karl Rahner takes this direction in *Spirit in the World*, trans. W. Dyche (New York: Herder and Herder, 1968), 57ff, 179ff.

46. Christianity says that that Principle, as *Logos*, entered into the otherness of creation through becoming man, a finite being open to the Infinite. Human being and the *Logos* are the dual bases for the Incarnation.

47. This is related to the notion of *imago dei* advanced by Richard of St. Victor in his *Liber Exceptionum*, Pars Prima, 1.1, which follows Genesis 1:27: "In his image he made him, male and female he made him." Etienne Gilson remarks that Richard "made no original contribution to metaphysical speculation." *History of Christian Philosophy in the Middle Ages* (New York: Random House, 1955), 171. I would say Richard was ahead of his time concerning the *imago dei*.

for creative power? God's power is omnipotence by which, as community of Persons, He is Creator of heaven and earth. Creatures imitate Him by transcending themselves, gathering power to create beyond where they are at any given moment, and, in the human case, passing on the results of their creativity to subsequent generations. In the static view of the hierarchy, the elements do not have the power of creative self-transcendence; in an emergent evolutionist view, they do. Following Whitehead, we could then claim that everything finite is in the grip of a primordial creativity.[48]

This view re-situates the observations made in the first part of this chapter and involves a transformation of our understanding of the nature of *theoria* and its relation to creative activity. Empirical inquiry linked to active manipulation through creative technology uncovers hidden properties not available to simple contemplation. But inquiry is also linked to creative theorizing, producing the successive paradigms that expand our theoretical and practical hold on things. The primacy of *theoria* in Aristotle was linked to a notion of what we might call a narcissistic divinity who could not care for, nor do anything to those beneath it. In Plotinus it involves the ultimate aspiration to be "alone with the Alone."[49] In a view in which God is the power of being as a Community of Love, creativity under the aegis of love carries the community forward as *imitatio dei*. It is a way of being together with the Together, imitating the togetherness of the divine Trinity. Love transcends the self into the community that continues on after the death of the individual. Love is ever creative of fresh ways of showing itself in all the small things in life as well as in the greater.[50]

But the community of love is not only the human community: it is that community enriched by the humans' appreciative relation to all that stands along the hierarchy leading up to it. Emergentism has as a significant consequent that the respect due to human being must be extended downward to our antecedents, even to the bottom of the

48. Alfred North Whitehead, *Process and Reality*, pt. I, chap. 1, §1, 11.

49. *Enneads* 5.1.6, 6.7.34, 6.9.11.

50. See Marcel's notion of *creative fidelity* in his book by the same title, *Creative Fidelity*, trans. R. Rosthal (New York: Noonday Press, 1964).

chain of being.[51] Respect for the integrity of natural things follows. But this also entails a set of priorities, with the lower yielding to the higher as instrumental, exhibited quite clearly in the need to eat. The resultant is a *respectful* instrumentalism, not wanton imposition. Such appreciation would not only let nature be, it would also gather it up into formative activity.[52] And this can occur not only in art but also in technology itself when the aesthetic properties learned from nature are brought over into technological transformations. Further, a form of government that respects the free self-disposition of every human being unleashes the creative potential of the whole community, giving as free a reign as possible to creative enterprise in all its forms.[53]

A merely theoretical approach to things—such as the one we have given—is not necessarily a superior mode of life, as the philosophical and theological traditions since Plato held. In a universe of emergent creativity, active service through creative empowerment across the height and breadth of human activities stands at least at as high a level. And "being alone with the Alone" might even be inferior to being together with the Together, assimilating the past to create a future of greater human empowerment as *imitatio dei*. Such a view would be able to respond to Nietzsche's charges: it would be "faithful to the earth"[54] and to a Divinity Who, having created the crocodile as well as the deer, saw it all as good.

51. For a splendidly argued development of this theme, see Holmes Ralston III, *Environmental Ethics: Duties to and Values in the Natural World* (Philadelphia: Temple University Press, 1988), 1, 302, 337.

52. Though one might find vegans odd, their overall, surprisingly well-documented basis in better health (diminishment of cancer, diabetes, and coronary disease) links up with a respect for animal life. See Lee Fulkerson's film, *Forks over Knives* (Monica Beach Media, 2011); the title refers to eating properly over the knives of the surgeon.

53. See Michael Novak, *The Spirit of Democratic Capitalism* (Lanham, Md.: Madison Books, 1982), 357. This remarkable book, combined with my youngest sons' development of a landscape design and installation company, removed the blinders from my eyes regarding business and engineering. In my own seminary and liberal arts background, there was at least an implicit looking down upon such "worldly" or "base and mechanical" things in favor of "the contemplative life" or the life of *theoria*.

54. "Fidelity to the earth" is Zarathustra's basic charge to his disciples against at least one strong strand in Christianity, exemplified by Dostoevsky's Fr. Ferapont in *The Brothers Karamazov*, trans. Andrew R. MacAndrew (New York: Bantam Books, 1970), 404–6. See my "Monasticism, Eternity, and the Heart: Hegel, Nietzsche, and Dostoevsky," *Philosophy and Theology* 13, no. 1 (Winter 2001): 193–211.

Bibliography

Abbott, Edwin. *Flatland: A Romance of Many Dimensions*. New York: Dover, 1992. First published 1884 by Seeley & Co., Ltd. (London).

Aquinas, Thomas. *Quaestiones disputatae de veritate*. Vol. 2, *Questions X–XX*, translated by James V. McGlynn. Chicago: Henry Regnery Company, 1953.

———. *Summa contra gentiles: Book II: Creation*. Translated by James F. Anderson. Notre Dame: University of Notre Dame Press, 1956.

———. *On Being and Essence*. Translated by Armand Maurer. Toronto: The Pontificate Institute of Medieval Studies, 1968.

———. *Commentary on Dionysius's Divine Names*, I.3.83–4. Translated by Brian Davies. In Brian Davies. *Aquinas*. New York: Continuum, 2002.

———. *Summa theologiae*. Translated by Laurence Shapcote, OP. Edited by John Mortensen and Enrique Alarcón. Lander, Wyo.: The Aquinas Institute for the Study of Sacred Doctrine, 2012.

Armstrong, Edward A. *Saint Francis: Nature Mystic*. Berkeley: University of California Press, 1973.

Aristotle. *Poetics*. Translated by W. Fyfe. Cambridge, Mass.: Harvard University Press, 1973.

Augustine. *Confessions*. Translated by W. Watts. 2 vols. Cambridge, Mass.: Harvard University Press, 1974.

Barfield, Owen. *Saving the Appearances: An Essay in Idolatry*. New York: Harcourt, Brace, and World, 1957.

Berkeley, George. *A Treatise Concerning the Principles of Human Knowledge*. Philadelphia: J. B. Lippincott and Co., 1874.

Buber, Martin. *Between Man and Man*. Translated by R. G. Smith. Boston: Beacon, 1961.

———. "Dialogue." In *Between Man and Man*, 1–39.

———. *The Knowledge of Man*. Translated by M. Friedman. New York: Harper, 1965.

———. *Daniel: Dialogues on Realization*. Translated by M. Friedman. New York: McGraw-Hill, 1969.

———. *I and Thou*. Translated by W. Kaufmann. New York: Scribners, 1970.

———. *Moses: The Revelation and the Covenant*. New York: Harper and Brothers, 1958.

Carlson, Allen. "Appreciation and the Natural Environment." In *The Aesthetics of Natural Environments*, edited by Allen Carlson and Arnold Berleant, 63–75. Toronto: Broadview Press, 2004.

Carnegie, Andrew. *Gospel of Wealth*. New York: Applewood Books, 1998.

Cicero. *Academics*. In *On the Nature of the Gods, Academics*, translated by H. Rackham, 410–64. Loeb Classical Library 268. Cambridge, Mass.: Harvard University Press, 1933.

Crick, Francis. *The Astonishing Hypothesis: The Scientific Search for the Soul*. New York: Charles Scribner's Sons, 1994.

Darwin, Charles. Charles Darwin to William Ogle, February 22, 1882.

de Chardin, Pierre Teilhard. *The Phenomenon of Man*. Translated by B. Wall. New York: Harper, 1959.

———. "On Seeing." Foreword to *The Phenomenon of Man*, 31–36.

———. *The Divine Milieu*. New York: Harper and Row Publishers, 1960.

Derrida, Jacques. *Of Grammatology*. Translated by G. Spivak. Baltimore: Johns Hopkins University Press, 1976.

de Saussure, Ferdinand. *Writings in General Linguistics*. Oxford: Oxford University Press, 2006.

Descartes, René. *Meditations on First Philosophy*. In *Discourse on Method and Mediations on First Philosophy*, translated by Donald A. Cress, 59–103. Indianapolis: Hackett, 1998.

———. *Rules for the Direction of the Mind, Philosophical Works of Descartes*. Translated by E. Haldane and G. Ross. New York: Dover, 1931.

Dewey, John. *Experience and Nature*. London: Allen and Unwin, 1929.

———. *Art as Experience*. New York: Capricorn, 1934.

Dostoevsky, Fyodor. *The Brothers Karamazov*. Translated by Andrew R. MacAndrew. New York: Bantam Books, 1970.

Engelland, Chad. *On Ostension*. Boston: MIT Press, 2014.

Empedocles. "Empedocles of Acragas." In *The Presocratic Philosophers*, edited by C. S. Kirk and J. E. Raven, 280–321. London: Cambridge University Press, 1966.

Epictetus. *The Stoic and Epicurean Philosophers*. Edited by W. Oates. New York: Modern Library, 1957.

Feuerbach, Ludwig. *Principles of the Philosophy of the Future*. Translated by M. Vogel. Indianapolis: Hackett, 1986.

Focillon, Henri. *The Life of Forms in Art*. Translated by C. Hogan and G. Kubler. New York: Zone Books, 1989.

Frankl, Victor. *Man's Search for Meaning*. London: Rider, 2004.

Fromm, Eric. *Sane Society*. New York: Holt, 1990.

Fulkerson, Lee, dir. *Forks over Knives*. Monica Beach Media, 2011.

Gadamer, Hans-Georg. *Truth and Method*. New York: Crossroad, 1982.

Gilson, Etienne. *History of Christian Philosophy in the Middle Ages*. New York: Random House, 1955.

Habermas, Jürgen. *Knowledge and Human Interests*. Translated by J. Shapiro. Boston: Beacon Press, 1971.

Harris, Errol. *Nature, Mind, and Modern Science*. London: George Allen and Unwin, 1954.

———. *The Foundations of Metaphysics in Science*. New York: University Press of America, 1983.

———. *Cosmos and Anthropos*. New York: Humanities Press, 1991.

Hawking, Stephen. Interview by Neil deGrasse Tyson. *StarTalk*. National Geographic. March 14, 2018.

Hawking, Stephen and Leonard Mlodinow. *The Grand Design*. New York: Bantam Books, 2010.

Hawking, Stephen and Roger Penrose. *The Nature of Space and Time*. Princeton, N.J.: Princeton University Press, 1996.

Hegel, G. W. F. *Lectures on the Philosophy of Religion*. Translated by E. Spiers and J. Sanderson. London: Kegan Paul, Trench, and Truebners, 1895.

———. *Reason in History*. Translated by R. Hartmann. New York: Macmillan, 1953.

———. *Lectures on the Philosophy of History*. Translated by J. Sibree. New York: Dover, 1956.

———. *Hegel's Philosophy of Mind*. Translated by W. Wallace and A. Miller. Oxford: Clarendon Press, 1973.

———. *Hegel's Science of Logic*. Translated by A. Miller. New York: Humanities Press, 1976.

———. *Phenomenology of Spirit*. Translated by A. Miller. Oxford: Oxford University Press, 1981.

———. *Hegel's Elements of the Philosophy of Right*. Translated by R. Nisbet. New York: Cambridge University Press, 1991.

———. *Hegel's Introduction to the System*. Translated by Robert E. Wood. Toronto: University of Toronto Press, 2014.

Heidegger, Martin. "Memorial Address." In *Discourse on Thinking*, translated by J. Anders and E. Freund, 42–57. New York: Harper, 1966.

———. *What Is Called Thinking?* Translated by F. Wieck and J. Glenn Grey. New York: Harper, 1968.

———. *Identity and Difference*. Translated by J. Stambaugh. New York: Harper and Row, 1969.

———. "The Onto-theo-logical Constitution of Metaphysics," in *Identity and Difference*, 42–74.

———. "A Dialogue on Language." In *On the Way to Language*, translated by P. Hertz, 1–56. San Francisco: Harper and Row, 1971.

———. *The End of Philosophy*. Translated by J. Stambaugh. New York: Harper and Row, 1973.

———. "Phenomenology and Theology." In *The Piety of Thinking*, translated by J. Hart and J. Maraldo, 5–21. Bloomington: Indiana University Press, 1976.

———. "On the Essence of Truth." In *Basic Writings*, edited and translated by D. Krell, 111–38. New York: Harper and Row, 1977.

———. *The Question Concerning Technology and Other Essays*. Translated by W. Lovitt. New York: Harper and Row, 1977.

———. *Prolegomena to the History of the Concept of Time*. Translated by T. Kisiel. Bloomington: Indiana University Press, 1992.

———. *Being and Time*. Translated by J. Stambaugh. Albany: State University of New York Press, 1996.

———. "Introduction to 'What is Metaphysics?' (1949)." In *Pathmarks*, translated by William McNeil, 277–90. Cambridge: Cambridge University Press, 1998.

———. "Letter on Humanism." In *Pathmarks*, translated by William McNeil, 239–76. Cambridge: Cambridge University Press, 1998.

———. *Introduction to Metaphysics*. Translated by G. Fried and R. Polt. New Haven, Conn.: Yale University Press, 2000.

———. *What Is Philosophy?* Translated by J. Wilde and W. Kluback. Lanham: Rowan and Littlefield, 2003.

———. *Origin of the Work of Art*. Translated by Roger Berkowitz and Phillipe Nonet. Unpublished manuscript, revised by P. Nonet, December 2006.

Heraclitus. "Heraclitus of Ephesus." In *The Presocratic Philosophers*, edited by C. S. Kirk and J. E. Raven, 181–213. London: Cambridge University Press, 1966.

Hildebrand, Dietrich von. *The Heart*. South Bend: St. Augustine's Press, 2007.

———. *The Nature of Love*. Translated by J. E. and J. H. Crosby. South Bend, Indiana: St. Augustine's Press, 2009.

Hobbes, Thomas. *Leviathan*. New York: Macmillan, 1962.

Hume, David. *A Treatise of Human Nature*. 3 vols. London: J. M. Dent and Sons, 1911.

———. *An Enquiry Concerning Human Understanding*. Edited by E. Steinberg. Indianapolis: Hackett, 1977.

Husserl, Edmund. *Crisis in European Philosophy and Transcendental Phenomenology*. Translated by D. Carr. Evanston: Northwestern University Press, 1970.

———. *Logical Investigations*. Translated by J. N. Findlay. Vol. 1. Oxford: Routledge and Kegan, 1970.

———. *Ideas Pertaining to a Pure Phenomenology and to a Phenomenological Philosophy, Third Book: Phenomenology and the Foundations of the Sciences*. Translated by T. E. Klein and W. E. Pohl. Dordrecht: Kluwer: 1980.

———. *Ideas: General Introduction to Pure Phenomenology*. Vols. I and II. The Hague: M. Nijhoff, 1982.

———. *Ideas Pertaining to a Pure Phenomenology and to a Phenomenological Philosophy, Second Book: Studies in the Phenomenology of Constitution*. Translated by R. Rojcewicz and A. Schuwer. Dordrecht: Kluwer, 1989.

———. *Ideas for a Pure Phenomenology and Phenomenological Philosophy, First Book, General Introduction to Phenomenological Philosophy*, translated by D. Dahlstrom. Indianapolis: Hackett, 2014.

James, William. *The Principles of Psychology*. Vol. 1. New York: Henry Holt, 1890.

Jaspers, Karl. *Philosophy*. 3 vols. Translated by E. Ashton. Chicago: University of Chicago Press, 1970.

Jaworski, William. *Philosophy of Mind: A Comprehensive Introduction*. Hoboken, N.J.: Wiley Blackwell, 2011.

John Paul II. *Fides et ratio*. Encyclical Letter. September 14, 1998.

Kant, Immanuel. *Critique of Practical Reason*. Translated by L. W. Beck. Indianapolis: Bobbs-Merrill, 1956.

———. *Critique of Pure Reason: Unified Edition*. Translated by Werner S. Pluhar. Indianapolis: Hackett, 1996.

———. *Critique of Judgment*. Translated by W. Pluhar. Indianapolis: Hackett, 1987.

———. *Metaphysics of Morals*. Translated by Mary Gregor. New York: Cambridge University Press, 1996.

———. *Groundwork of the Metaphysics of Morals*. Translated by M. Gregor. Cambridge: Cambridge University Press, 1998.

Kass, Leon. *The Hungry Soul: Eating and the Perfecting of Our Nature*. New York: Free Press, 1994.

Kirk, G. S. *Homer and the Oral Tradition*. Cambridge: Cambridge University Press, 1976.

Kierkegaard, Søren. *The Concept of Dread*. Translated by W. Lowrie. Princeton: Princeton University Press, 1957.

———. *Concluding Unscientific Postscript to Philosophical Fragments*. Translated by A. Hannay. Cambridge: Cambridge University Press, 2009.

Klein, Jacob. *Plato's Trilogy*. Chicago: University of Chicago Press, 1977.

Kojéve, Alexandre. *Introduction to the Reading of Hegel*. Translated by J. Nichols. Ithaca: Cornell University Press, 1969.

Leibniz, Gottfried Wilhelm. *Monadology*. Translated by R. Latta. London: Oxford University Press, 1951.

Leroy, Pierre. "Teilhard de Chardin: The Man." Introduction to *The Divine Milieu*, by Pierre Teilhard de Chardin, 13–42. New York: Harper and Row Publishers, 1960.

Lessing, Gotthold Ephraim. *The Education of the Human Race*. London: Kegan Paul, Trench, and Co., 1883.

Levinas, Immanuel. *Totality and Infinity*. Translated by A. Lingis. Pittsburgh: Duquesne University Press, 1969.

Lewis, C. S. *The Four Loves*. New York: Harcourt, Brace, and World, 1960.

Locke, John. *Second Treatise on Government*. Edited by C. B. Macpherson. Indianapolis: Hackett Publishing Company, 1980.

———. *Essay Concerning Human Understanding*. Baltimore: Penguin, 1998.

London, Jack. *The Sea-Wolf*. New York: Grosset and Dunlap, 1904.

Lonergan, Bernard. *Insight: A Study of Human Understanding*. London: Longmans Green, 1957.

———. "The Notion of Being." In *Insight*.

———. *Method in Theology*. New York: Herder and Herder, 1972.

Marcel, Gabriel. *The Mystery of Being*. Translated by G. Fraser. Chicago: Regnery, 1960.

———. "The Ontological Mystery." In *The Philosophy of Existentialism*, translated by M. Harari. New York: Citadel, 1961.

———. *Creative Fidelity*. Translated by R. Rosthal. New York: Noonday Press, 1964.

McLuhan, Marshall. *The Guttenberg Galaxy: The Making of Typographic Man*. Toronto: University of Toronto Press, 1962.

Merleau-Ponty, Maurice. *Phenomenology of Perception*. Translated by C. Smith. London: Routledge and Kegan Paul, 1962.

———. *The Structure of Behavior*. Translated by A. Fisher. Boston: Beacon Press, 1967.

Milton, John. *Paradise Lost*. Edited by M. Kelley. New York: Walter J. Black, 1943.

Nagel, Thomas. *Mind and Cosmos*. Oxford: Oxford University Press, 2012.

Nietzsche, Friedrich. "On Truth and Lie in an Extra-Moral Sense." In *Portable Nietzsche*, edited and translated by W. Kaufmann, 42–46. New York: Viking, 1954.

———. *The Birth of Tragedy*. Translated by W. Kaufmann. New York: Vintage, 1967.

———. *The Will to Power*. Translated by W. Kaufmann and R. J. Hollingdale. New York: Random House, 1967.

———. *Twilight of the Idols*. In *Twilight of the Idols and The Anti-Christ*, translated by R. Hollingdale. Baltimore: Penguin, 1968.

———. *Genealogy of Morals*. Translated by W. Kaufmann. New York: Vintage, 1969.

———. *The Gay Science*. Translated by W. Kaufmann. New York: Random House, 1974.

———. *Daybreak*. Translated by R. Hollingdale. Cambridge: Cambridge University Press, 1982.

Novak, Michael. *The Spirit of Democratic Capitalism*. Lanham, Md.: Madison Books, 1982.

Nygren, Anders. *Agape and Eros*. Translated by Philip S. Watson. Philadelphia: Westminster Press, 1953.

O'Connor, David. *Hume on Religion*. London and New York: Routledge, 2001.

Otto, Rudolph. *The Idea of the Holy*. Translated by J. Harvey. New York: Oxford University Press, 1964.

Peirce, C. S. "The Scientific Attitude and Fallibilism." In *Philosophical Writings of Peirce*, edited by J. Buchler, 42–59. New York: Dover, 1955.

Pinkard, Terry. *Hegel's Naturalism: Mind, Nature, and the Final Ends of Life*. London: Oxford, 2012.

Pippin, Robert. *After the Beautiful: Hegel on the Philosophy of Pictorial Modernism.* Chicago: University of Chicago Press, 2014.

Pirsig, Robert. *Zen and the Art of Motorcycle Maintenance.* New York: William Morrow and Company, 1974.

Pius XII. *Humani generis.* Encyclical Letter. August 12, 1950.

Plato. *Complete Works.* Edited by John Cooper. Indianapolis: Hackett, 1997.

———. *Apology.* Translated by G. M. A. Grube. In *Complete Works*, 18–36.

———. *Cratylus.* Translated by C. D. C. Reeve. In *Complete Works*, 102–56.

———. *Meno.* Translated by G. M. A. Grube. In *Complete Works*, 871–97.

———. *Parmenides.* Translated by Mary Louise Gill and Paul Ryan. In *Complete Works*, 340–97.

———. *Phaedo.* Translated by G. M. A. Grube. In *Complete Works*, 50–100.

———. *Phaedrus.* Translated by Alexander Nehamas and Paul Woodruff. In *Complete Works*, 507–56.

———. *Republic.* Translated by G. M. A. Grube. Revised by C. D. C. Reeve. In Cooper, *Complete Works*, 972–1223.

———. *Sophist.* Translated by Nicholas P. White. In *Complete Works*, 236–93.

———. *Statesman.* Translated by C. J. Rowe. In *Complete Works*, 295–358.

———. *Symposium.* Translated by Alexander Nehamas and Paul Woodruff. In *Complete Works*, 458–505.

———. *Theaetetus.* Translated by M. J. Levett. Revised by Miles Burnyeat. In *Complete Works*, 158–234.

Poe, Edgar Allen. "The Philosophy of Composition." In *Selected Prose and Poetry of Edgar Allen Poe*, edited by T. Mabbott, 363–73. New York: Modern Library, 1951.

Polanyi, Michael. *The Study of Man.* Chicago: University of Chicago Press, 1959.

———. *Personal Knowledge: Towards a Post-Critical Philosophy.* New York: Harper, 1964.

———. *The Tacit Dimension.* Garden City: Doubleday, 1966.

Popper, Karl. *The Logic of Scientific Discovery.* New York: Basic Books, 1959.

———. *Conjectures and Refutations: The Growth of Scientific Knowledge.* Vol. 2. New York: Harper, 1963.

Rahner, Karl. *Hominisation.* New York: Herder and Herder, 1965.

——. "Some Theses for a Theology of Devotion to the Sacred Heart." In *Theological Investigations*. Vol. 3, *The Theology of the Spiritual Life*, translated by Karl-H. Kruger and Boniface Kruger, 331–54. Baltimore: Helicon Press, 1967.

——. *Spirit in the World*. Translated by W. Dyche. New York: Herder and Herder, 1968.

Ralston, Holmes, III. *Environmental Ethics: Duties to and Values in the Natural World*. Philadelphia: Temple University Press, 1988.

Ricoeur, Paul. *Freedom and Nature: The Voluntary and the Involuntary*. Translated by E. Kohak. Evanston: Northwestern University Press, 1966.

Russell, Bertrand. *Mysticism and Logic*. Totowa, N.J.: Barnes and Noble Books, 1951.

——. *The Autobiography of Bertrand Russell: 1872–1914*. London: George Allen and Unwin Ltd., 1971.

Sartre, Jean-Paul. "Existentialism is a Humanism." In *Existentialism from Dostoevsky to Sartre*, edited and translated by W. Kaufmann, 287–311. New York: Meridian Books, 1956.

——. *Being and Nothingness*. Translated by H. Barnes. New York: Harper, 1965.

——. *No Exit and Three Other Plays*. Translated by S. Gilbert. New York: Vintage, 1989.

Scheler, Max. *On the Eternal in Man*. Translated by B. Noble. London: SCM Press, 1960.

——. *Formalism in Ethics and Material Ethics of Value*. Translated by M. Frings. Evanston, Ill.: Northwestern University Press, 1972.

——. *Ressentiment*. Translated by W. Holdheim. New York: Schocken, 1972.

——. *The Nature of Sympathy*. Translated by P. Heath. New York: The Shoe String Press, 1973.

Schelling, F. W. J. *Ideas for a Philosophy of Nature*. Translated by E. Harris and P. Heath. Cambridge: Cambridge University Press, 1988.

Schleiermacher, Friedrich. *On Religion: Speeches to Its Cultured Despisers*. Translated by John Oman. London: Kegan Paul, Trench, Trübner, and Co., 1893.

Schopenhauer, Arthur. *The World as Will and Representation*. Vol. 1. New York: Dover, 1966.

Searle, John. *Intentionality: An Essay in the Philosophy of Mind*. Cambridge: Cambridge University Press, 1983.

——. *The Construction of Social Reality*. New York: Free Press, 1995.

——. *The Mystery of Consciousness*. New York: New York Review Books, 1997.

———. *The Rediscovery of the Mind*. Cambridge, Mass.: MIT Press, 1992.

———. *Mind, Language and Society: Philosophy in the Real World*. New York: Basic Books, 1998.

———. *Rationality In Action*. Cambridge, Mass.: MIT Press, 2001.

Shakespeare, William. *Hamlet*. Edited by Sylvan Barnet. New York: Signet Classics, 1998.

Sloterdijk, Peter. *You Must Change Your Life*. Translated by Wieland Hoban. Cambridge: Polity Press, 2013.

Spinoza, Baruch. *Ethics*. Translated by T. S. Gregory. London: J. M. Dent and Sons, Ltd., 1910.

———. *On the Improvement of the Understanding, The Ethics, Correspondence*. Translated by R. Elwes. New York: Dover, n.d.

Stein, Edith. *Finite and Eternal Being: An Attempt at an Ascent to the Meaning of Being*. Translated by K. Reinhardt. Washington, D.C.: ICS Publications, 2002.

———. "The Being of the Ego and Eternal Being." In *Finite and Eternal Being*, 55–60.

Strasser, Stephen. *Phenomenology of Feeling: An Essay on the Phenomena of the Heart*. Translated by Robert E. Wood. Pittsburgh: Duquesne University Press, 1977.

Sokolowski, Robert. *Eucharistic Presence: A Study in the Theology of Disclosure*. Washington, D.C.: The Catholic University of America Press, 1993.

———. "Modern Science and Material and Formal Causality." In *Recovery of Form, Proceedings of the American Catholic Philosophical Association* 69 (1995): 57–67.

Tillich, Paul. *The Courage to Be*. New Haven: Yale University Press, 1952.

Taylor, Charles. *A Secular Age*. Cambridge, Mass.: Belknap Press, 2007.

Vonnegut, Kurt. *Slaughterhouse Five or The Children's Crusade: A Duty-Dance with Death*. New York: Dial Press, 1969.

Weiss, Peter. *Marat/Sade*. New York: Pocketbooks, 1963.

Whitehead, Alfred North. *Adventures of Ideas*. New York: Macmillan, 1933.

———. *Process and Reality: An Essay in Cosmology*. New York: Harper, 1957.

———. *Science and the Modern World*. New York: Free Press, 1967.

Wood, Robert. *Martin Buber's Ontology*. Evanston, Ill.: Northwestern University Press, 1969.

———. "Martin Buber's Philosophy of the Word." *Philosophy Today* 30, no. 4 (Winter 1986): 317–24.

———. "Image, Structure, and Content: A Remark on a Passage in Plato's *Republic*." *The Review of Metaphysics* 40, no. 3 (March 1987): 495–514.

———. "Aspects of Freedom." *Philosophy Today* 35, no. 1 (Spring 1991): 106–15.

———. *A Path into Metaphysics: Phenomenological, Hermeneutic, and Dialogical Studies*. Albany: State University of New York Press, 1991.

———. "Being and Manifestness: Being, Science, and Poetry in an Evolutionary Worldview." *International Philosophical Quarterly* 35, no. 4 (December 1995): 438–47.

———. "Taking the Universal Viewpoint." *The Review of Metaphysics* 50, no. 4 (June 1997): 769–81.

———. *Placing Aesthetics: Reflections on the Philosophic Tradition*. Athens: Ohio University Press, 1999.

———. "On Touch: A Phenomenological Inquiry." *Southwestern Philosophy Review* 17, no. 1 (January 2000): 19–26.

———. "Hegel on the Heart." *International Philosophical Quarterly* 41, no. 2 (June 2001): 131–44.

———. "Individuals, Universals, and Capacity." *The Review of Metaphysics* 54, no. 3 (March 2001): 507–28.

———. "Monasticism, Eternity, and the Heart: Hegel, Nietzsche, and Dostoevsky." *Philosophy and Theology* 13, no. 1 (Winter 2001): 193–211.

———. "Phenomenology and the Perennial Task of Philosophy: A Study of Plato and Aristotle." *Existentia* 12, fasc. 3–4 (2002): 252–63.

———. "Phenomenology of the Mailbox." *Philosophy Today* 47, no. 2 (Summer 2003): 147–59.

———. "Potentiality, Creativity, and Relationality: Creative Power as a 'New' Transcendental?" *The Review of Metaphysics* 59, no. 2 (December 2005): 379–401.

———. "*Doxa* and *Eros*, Speech and Writing, with Special Attention to Plato's *Symposium*." *Existentia* 18, fasc. 3–4 (2008): 247–61.

———. "Being Human and the Question of Being: The Unitary Ground of Individual and Cultural Pluralism." *The Modern Schoolman* 87, no. 1 (November 2009): 53–66.

———. "Five Bodies and a Sixth: On the Place of Awareness in an Evolutionary Universe." *American Catholic Philosophical Quarterly* 93, no. 1 (Winter 2009): 95–105.

———. "The Heart: An Analysis of Human and Divine Affectivity." *American Catholic Philosophical Quarterly* 83, no. 2 (Spring 2009): 303–9.

———. "Dietrich von Hildebrand on the Heart." *Quaestiones disputatae* 3, no. 2 (Spring 2013): 107–19.

———. "Virtues, Values, and the Heart: The Phenomenology of Max Scheler and Dietrich von Hildebrand." In *Phenomenology and the Virtue Ethics*, edited by P. Gyllenhammer and L. Hemberg, New York: 132–46. London: Bloomberg, 2013.

———. "First Things First: On the Primacy of the Notion of Being." *The Review of Metaphysics* 67, no. 4 (June 2014): 719–41.

———. *The Beautiful, the True, and the Good: Studies in the History of Thought*. Washington, D.C.: The Catholic University of America Press, 2015.

———. "Five Bodies and a Sixth: On the Place of Awareness in an Evolutionary World." In *The Beautiful, the True, and the Good*, 312–23.

———. "Nature, Culture, and the Dialogical Imperative." In *The Beautiful, the True, and the Good*, xix–xxxii.

———. "Phenomenology and the Perennial Task of Philosophy: A Study of Plato and Aristotle." In *The Beautiful, the True, and the Good*, 42–61.

———. "Plato's Line Revisited." In *The Beautiful, the True, and the Good*, 21–41.

———. "The Heart in/of Augustine's Confessions." In *The Beautiful, the True, and the Good*, 154–69.

———. "The Heart in Heidegger's Thought." *Continental Philosophy Review* 48 (2015): 445–62.

———. "True and False in Nietzsche's Truth and Lies." *Existentia* 25, fasc. 3–4 (2015): 201–213.

———. *Nature, Artforms, and the World around Us*. Cham, Switzerland: Palgrave-Macmillan, 2017.

———. *Being and the Cosmos*. Washington, D.C.: The Catholic University of America Press, 2018.

———. "The Cosmos Has an Inside." In *Being and the Cosmos*, 81–104.

———. "First Things First: On the Priority of the Notion of Being." In *Being and the Cosmos*, 33–62.

———. "What Is Seeing? A Phenomenological Approach to Neuropsychology." In *Being and the Cosmos*, 9–32.

———. *Ratio et Fides: A Preliminary Intro-duction to Philosophy for Theology*. Eugene, Ore.: Pickwick Publications, 2018.

Wooldridge, Dean. *Mechanical Man: The Physical Basis of Intelligent Life*. New York: McGraw-Hill, 1972.

Author Index

Abbott, Edwin, 15n50, 21–25, 62–63, 108

Aquinas, Thomas: on Being (with capital "B," as reference to the Whole of beings and to the Whole itself, 5n21), 40–42, 200–201; on contingent events, 44n37; on the Decalogue containing secondary principles, 181; on distinction between *medium quod* and *medium quo*, 28–29; on distinction between *ratio* and *intellectus*, 14n47; and feelings, 93–94; and freedom-from the partial and necessary directedness toward the totality, 156; on human beings and boundary between time and eternity, 72; as important influence for this book, 200; on overall conceptual frame, 12n43; and religious tradition, 62; and the single absolute, infinite fullness of Being, 179; on transcendentals and Being, 244–46; on virtue, 169, 174–75

Aristotle: on anger, 59, 87; and Aquinas, 62; and attending "to the things themselves," 213n1; on Being (with capital "B," as reference to the Whole of beings and to the Whole itself, 5n21), 39, 41, 65; on cardinal virtues, 175–76; on common life, 153–54; on definition of man, 112, 175; on Democritus, 46n40; and divinity, 246–47; on dogs, 209; and emergent evolution, 243; and evolution, 239–40; and extensive properties, 33; on friendship, 95n17; on happiness, 188–89; and Kant, 184, 187–88; on language, 138–39, 207; on literature, 142–45; as major influence for this

book, 2, 15; and matter, 244n39; on music and felt disposition, 102; on *phantasmata*, 34; and phenomenology, 15n48, 68, 213n1; on pleasure, 90, 191; and potentiality and Nietzsche, 225; on practical wisdom, 162n22; on pride, 99; on principle of noncontradiction, 42–44; and psycho-physical holism, 15; as scientist, 202n11; on the senses, 37n19; on the soul, 41n32, 54n50, 173, 200, 226n2, 228n5, 232n10; and time, 219; and tradition, 207–8; and types, 245; on virtue in general, 100–101, 106, 169; and Western philosophy, 200

Armstrong, Edward A., 194n85

Augustine, Aurelius, 27, 60, 62, 69, 70n2, 91, 93, 105, 129–30, 179, 193

Barfield, Owen, 6n23, 39

Berkeley, George, 231–32

Berleant, Arnold, 4n15, 103n35

Buber, Martin, 8, 14–15, 61–62, 66, 104n43, 134–35, 163n27, 172, 179n32, 194–95

Carlson, Allen, 4, 103n35, 148n50

Carnegie, Andrew, 170

Cicero, 143–45

Cleanthes, 101

Crick, Francis, 45n39

Darwin, Charles, 202n11

de Chardin, Pierre Teilhard, 8, 129n21, 147–48, 243

Derrida, Jacques, 1–2, 28n2

de Saussure, Ferdinand, 206n17

Descartes, Rene, 12n43, 14–15, 33n11, 35, 50n45, 61, 63–64, 87, 205

Subject Index

abstraction, 1, 7, 17; and color, 37–38; and God, 41–42; individual mode of, 41–42; and second reflection, 7; universal mode of, 41–42, 59, 87, 115, 129, 135, 138, 202–3, 209, 211, 218, 226, 236

actuality, 62–63, 103, 174, 181, 205, 207, 226, 229, 231

adoration, 104

admiration, 100

aesthetic(s): as appreciated in the natural environment, 4; as considered by major philosophers, 2n5; and definition of man, 208, 211–12; as distinctively human attribute, 17; and evolutionary history, 148; experience of, in contrast to vocational experience, 195; and field of experience, 235n19; as form in relation to content, 145; of Kant, 101n29; and ontology, 9n32, 211–12; and properties, 208; of properties brought over into technological transformation, 248; and scientific inclination to employ Occam's Razor, 240; and *spiritual feelings*, 88, 102–6; and values of hedonism, 190; of visual presentation, 145; and the Whole, 209–10

afterlife, 189, 192–93

agape, 96

analogy, 136

analysis, 3, 43, 70, 74n9, 84n2, 91, 94n16, 115, 135, 147, 176n20, 213, 225–26, 235n18

analytic, 1–2

anger, 59, 87, 91, 98–100

anthropology, 1–2, 106, 189

anthropomorphism, 243

anxiety, 90–93, 157, 193

apathia, 101

appetite, 56, 176, 233–35, 243

appreciation, 4, 61–62, 103, 117, 149, 180, 211, 223, 248

a priori, 11, 37n20, 81, 178–79, 202–3, 234–35

arrogance, 98, 100, 187

art, 9n32, 16, 35, 76–77, 97, 102, 139, 143, 145, 159, 190, 248

ataraxia, 101

autonomy, 153–54, 162–63, 184–86

authentic, 60, 76

awareness: as always *of* or *about* something, 10; as analogous to the hierarchy of the book, 114; in animals, 13, 50, 67; and appearance of otherness, 89, 228–31; as appreciative, 149; and Being (with capital "B," as reference to the Whole of beings and to the Whole itself, 5n21), 135–36, 200–201, 214–16, 219–20; and being (with lowercase "b," reference to things that are, 5n21), 41, 135–36, 216; and Braille, 109; bipolar character of, 193; coming into being of, 222–23; and *dashboard knowing*, 6; of Descartes' *cogito*, 33n11, 204; on distinction between sensory and intellectual awareness, 69, 85–86, 107–8, 239–40; and *eros*, 95; exhibited by triple "ecstasy" of past, present and future, 48; and existence, 217–18; and feelings, 73, 88–90; and felt proclivities, 203–4; and freedom and choice, 107–8, 154, 157–58; and the heart, 85, 87; and intellect, 65, 232; and *intellectual* feelings, 102;

45, 248; as *imitatio dei*, 248; self-, 227–28, 238

environment: ability to stand back from the, 238; and aesthetic form, 145; and animals, 45, 53, 84, 205, 208–9, 228, 230; and appetite, 205, 233; and artefacts, 120–21; of awareness, 48, 67; built, 4, 9, 114–15, 117, 148–49; challenges of, 89; and culture, 158; destruction of the, 193; and ecosystem, 4; and ethics, 193–94; as given, 209–10, 232, 236; Heidegger on, 33n11; human relation to, 208, 227, 242; and institutions, 164; and logic, 174n13; manifestation of the, 228–30; and master-slave dialectic, 210–11; and meaning, 109; and meditation, 149; and mind, 185; and music, 237–38; natural, 4, 9, 149, 170, 242; of one's bodily location, 37; and ontology and history, 9; of organic beings, 227; and plants, 227, 230; and power, 233–34; and relation of self and other, 88–89, 228–29; and self-empowerment, 227; and the senses, 52, 64, 147–48, 210, 233; and sensory field, 6; and sensory objects, 51; and technology, 211; and things, 48, 116, 147, 233, 239; of this book, 147; von Hildebrand on, 195

envy, 96, 98, 100, 187, 191–92

epic, 139, 143–44

epiphenomena, 63–64, 242–43

eros, 4–6, 57, 161n21, 171; as linked to the Whole, 59–60, 171; and *Thanatos*, 95–96, 174

esse, 182, 244–45

essence, 41–42, 136, 226n2, 246; and "beyond Being," 185n42; and embodied human spirit, 242; eternal, 42, 245–46; and Heidegger, 116n11

ethics: in Aristotle, 95n17, 184, 189–90; and awareness, 242; environmental, 193–94; and Kant, 101, 183–84, 187n49

evolution, 102, 247; and Big Bang, 173–74; and Carlson, 4n15; *emergent*, 243; and Hegel, 242n32; and history, 4n15, 9, 148, 225; and materialism, 242; and Pius XII, 240n30; and view of nature, 194; and the Whole, 242–43

experience, 36, 68, 72, 85, 199, 239; and the absolutely unrestricted, 43; aesthetic, 195; of anger, 99; and appearance, 56; and arguments, 5; and articulations, 41; aspects of, 47; and awareness, 1, 43, 50, 69, 102, 107, 224–25; and awe, 171; and Being, 3–4, 178; of beings, 244; bipolar character of, 10, 213; and contemporary philosophical scholarship, 1; conversion, 204; of cultures, 56–57; of desirability, 155; and eidetic features, 27, 36–39; and *eros*, 171; and existence, 102; and feelings, 96–97, 99, 171; field of, 1–5, 11, 13, 18, 21, 29–31, 56–57, 61, 68, 114, 142–43, 147, 153, 162, 213, 222, 235n19; in Flatland, 22–23, 62–63; framework of all our, 222; and freedom, 154, 158; of God, 104; and the heart, 59, 83–84, 86–87, 96–97, 106, 204; at the heart of human, 83–84; and Institutions, 166; and intellectual activity, 222–23; "internal horizon" of things presented in, 11; Kant on, 49n44; Lonergan on, 243n38; and Meaning-Center, 163; of motion, 64; and mystery of existence, 194–95; and nature, 195; and "orientation," 8; of the Other, 162, 171; Otto on, 104; and our judgments, 54; and phenomenology, 10–11, 13; Plato on, 39; and principle of noncontradiction, 43, 216; rational pattern of, 161–63, 165–66, 168; regions of, 147; and religion, 161–63; of the sacred, 171; and science, 31, 56–57; self-, 224–25; sensory, 24, 29, 32–34, 36–37, 47, 52, 63–65, 89–90, 107, 114, 201; seven-dimensional view of, 15; sexual, 89–90, 171; and Space and Time, 24, 37, 107, 178; stream of, 73; structures given in, 225; of *techne* and *phusis*, 13; and time, 64–65, 67, 71, 73, 205; of this book, 29–30, 34, 147; and three a priori forms, 178; of unities, 185; vocational, 195; Weiss on, 35n16; what is given in, 68; and the Whole, 56–57, 148

expression, 83, 88, 113, 163–64, 209, 229; and awareness, 88; "dashboard knowledge" as, 38–39; and divine wisdom, 184–85; and empathy, 97; *empiriomorphic fallacy* as, 242–43; heart muscle as, 59; "*It is*" as, 220; in language, 53, 125, 132, 138–39; as revealing what underlies sensory presentation, 67; sexual desire as, 95; "tumbling along contents in streaming of consciousness" as, 73

feeling(s), 94; and aesthetics, 88, 102–6; of aggression, 90; of anger, 99; Aquinas on, 93–94; Aristotle on, 106; and awareness, 73, 88–90, 102; of awe, 4–5, 171; and the body, 89–90; of boredom, 92; and the brain, 33; conflicting, 101; and cultural world, 236; and *curiosity*, 102; and "depression," 92; of *empathy* and *sympathy*, 97; and *eros*, 95–96; and experience, 96–97, 99, 171; of freedom, 160; of great emptiness, 93; and the heart, 16, 88,

93, 106, 108; hierarchy of, 88; *intellectual*, 102; intensifications of, 33–34; intentionally directed, 88; and language, 109; -lessness, 101; multiform life of, 101; and music, 102; negative, 96–97; neutral state of, 93; as nonreflective self-presence, 33, 88–89; and the numinous, 105; organically grounded pole and, 90–91; and the other, 33; and pain, 90; and phenomenon of "falling in love," 95; pleasurable, 89; *religious*, 104–6; and seeing, 228; sensory, 89–90, 229; and *Seven Capital Sins*, 98; sexual, 59, 89–90; and *sloth*, 98–99; and space of meaning, 86; *spiritual*, 88, 93–94, 101–6; and *temperaments*, 91–92; in terms of attraction and repulsion, 93–94; and time, 89, 213; of touch, 229; -types, 93–97

finite, the: and Being, 12, 41–42; and Christ, 246n46; and God (Infinite Being), 42, 178, 185n42, 246–47; and infinite, 178–79, 185n42; Leibniz on, 235n17, 246n46; and mystery, 42, 185n42; and primordial creativity, 246–47; and totality of being, 178–79; as type, 41; and the Whole, 236–37

form(s), 202–3, 223; abstraction of eidetic, 202; of any here-and-now, 37; in Aristotelian cosmos, 239; and creative empowerment, 241; as *eide*, 215–17; and *emergent evolutionism*, 243–44; and general flux of physical things, 120; giving-powers, 241; hierarchies of, 3, 41, 239; human, 95, 120, 168; in Husserl (*eidos*), 31; in Kant, 186–87, 209; living, 55, 95, 168, 202n11, 227–29, 233, 240–41; logical, 207; Nietzsche on, 164, 170, 235n20; ontological status of, 223;